LEXICOGRAPHY
IN THE ELECTRONIC AGE

organised by

The Commission of the European Communities
Directorate General
Information Market and Innovation

Symposium coordination:
R. RAPPARINI

Publication arrangements:
P. P. ROTONDÓ

LEXICOGRAPHY
IN THE ELECTRONIC AGE

Proceedings of a Symposium held in
Luxembourg, 7-9 July, 1981

edited by

J. GOETSCHALCKX and L. ROLLING
Commission of the European Communities

1982

NORTH-HOLLAND PUBLISHING COMPANY – AMSTERDAM · NEW YORK · OXFORD

ISBN: 0 444 86404 0

Published by
NORTH-HOLLAND PUBLISHING COMPANY
AMSTERDAM · NEW YORK · OXFORD

Sole distributors for the U.S.A. and Canada:
ELSEVIER SCIENCE PUBLISHING COMPANY, INC.
52 VANDERBILT AVENUE
NEW YORK, N.Y. 10017

for
The Commission of the European Communities
Directorate General
Information Market and Innovation
Luxembourg

EUR 7526

LEGAL NOTICE
Neither the Commission of the European Communities nor any person acting on behalf of the Commission is responsible for the use which might be made of the following information.

Library of Congress Cataloging in Publication Data
Main entry under title:

Lexicography in the electronic age.

    1. Lexicography--Data processing--Congresses.
2. Terms and phrases--Data processing--Congresses.
I. Goetschalckx, J., 1925-   . II. Rolling, L.
P327.L433   413'.028   82-6341
ISBN 0-444-86404-0 (U.S.)   AACR2

PRINTED IN THE NETHERLANDS

CONTENTS

Panel Discussion on Publishing and the Future Use of Lexicons

LEXICOGRAPHY IN THE ELECTRONIC AGE
J. Goetschalckx and L. Rolling (editors)
North-Holland Publishing Company
© ECSC, EEC, EAEC, 1982

INTRODUCTION

by

J. Goetschalckx

Adviser
Medium and long term Translation service
Commission of the European Communities

Everyone nowadays is wondering what effect such things as informatics,
telematics, office automation, computers and microprocessors are likely to
have on his work, his private life and on society as a whole.
Small wonder, then, that lexicographers are likewise explorating what
effects these innovations are likely to have on their particular trade.

A little over fifteen years ago, a variation on classical lexicography, in
the form of terminology data banks, first saw the light of day, and
lexicographers have come to value the many benefits of the enormous storage
capacity and ultra-fast sorting and search facilities of computers.

Generally speaking, though, those of us who keep reasonably in touch with
developments in the field of computers and microprocessors are convinced
that tomorrow's generation of computers - not to mention the present
generation - could be made to do a lot more.

The advent of cable and satellite communications and the interpretation
of various technologies, of economic sectors and of national and multi-
national companies call for increased exchanges, standardization and an
interdisciplinary approach. Ivory towers have become prisons and "splendid
isolation" is no more than a sweet illusion.

With all this going on, it is interesting and important to keep in touch
with developments in this field throughout the world.
Special attention has been focused on solutions to the problem of non
-Latin alphabets- in particular Chinese, Japanese, Greek and Russian.

Some mentioned the desirability and feasibility of digitalizing graphic
displays, while others addressed themselves to data acquisition on a phonetic
basis, given that we are living in a world in which oral information is
becoming increasingly dominant.

If we are to find a way out of the impasse caused by the compartmenta-
tization of information, we must have recourse to existing structures
(e.g. Infodok and Infoterm) for the collection of relevant data.

The same goes for the problem of standardization, which is a <u>sine qua non</u>
as regards modularity. Here again, the structures exist, and the ISO's
technical committees have long been wrestling with the problem.
TC 37 is concerned with the principles and rules of terminology, TC 46
covers documentation and even the terminology of documentation, TC 97's
field of study is data processing.

However, any discussion of exchange, particularly the exchange of intellectual property, automatically involves copyright.
One is bound to say that, in the humanities, the concept of intellectual
property rights is a woolly one. Unesco and the WIPO have addressed
themselves to the problem, but there is still quite a degree of divergence
in the attitudes adopted by the various countries concerned. Nonetheless,
the presence of an expert has resulted in an in-depth look at this question
as well, and there are grounds for believing that, given a genuine
cooperative effort, the problems in this field could be alleviated.

It seems not inconceivable, in any case, that terminology data banks might
make use of the computerized material used in the publication of dictionaries
and glossaries. On the other side of the coin, it is not unreasonable to
think that the publishers of dictionaries might draw on one or more
terminology data banks the production of a new work or the updating of an
existing one. Such things are already going on, but could become more
widespread.
The Luxembourg conference was the first to tackle this whole problem on a
major scale. It was a highly instructive and significant explorations
exercise, and clearly, many people returned home to reflect on the prospects
for collaboration between publishers and the operators of terminology data
banks, between data processing experts and lexicographers or terminologists.

Let us hope that the fruits of this exercise will be new developments which will come about more quickly and under more favourable conditions thanks to the Luxembourg conference on lexicography in the electronic age, AD 1981.

SESSION I
CREATION OF LEXICONS

The Natural Computer

or

Paradigm Lost

M. Boot / H. Koppelaar

Introduction

For many hundreds of years people are trying to understand human thinking and reasoning. A part of this effort has been into understanding our natural language. In the last three decades it is felt that there is considerable progress made, as far as three aspects of this understanding natural language are concerned. In the realm of theoretical linguistics the theory of Transformational Grammar was considered to be a revolution. In the realm of psychology models for understanding human language processes were developed. These models were strongly influenced by the TG-revolution. The third aspect concerns computer algorithms for under-standing natural language. Here also the impact of TG-theory was over-whelming in the beginnings.

To-day we percieve a decisive conceptual change as far as the view on the problem of computer simulation of language processes is concerned. In the present state of the art computational linguistics (CL) using the lingui-stic theory of transformational of logical grammar reached her bound-aries. With the current knowledge of TG theory the problem turns out to be unsolvable. On the other hand, we see the promising developments emerging from the artificial intelligent (AI)- approach. From this view, a new attack upon the problem of simulating human language behaviour becomes possible in our opinion.

Kuhnian theory of Science marks the distinction between traditional science and conceptual revolutions by certain rare events called para-digm shifts. A paradigm shift happens if a current level of knowledge is exhausted up to its boundaries, that is when a problem turns out to be insoluble with current knowledge. A paradigm shift then means a concep-tual change in problem view, such that a new attack upon the problem becomes possible.

In this paper we will characterize the paradigm shift as the Pattern Recognition Model (PRM). The final goal for this paradigm shift is to build a natural computer. That is a computer capable of understanding and producing human natural language texts.

1. NETWORKS and SENTENCES

Theoretical linguists have properly concentrated on describing and analysing what natural language is. In their work details of how language is actually processed need not to be relevant, and indeed should probably not be allowed to obscure language definition. Because of that, however, there is a large gap between the work of theoretical linguists and philosophers, such as N.Chomsky and R. Montague and the work of those, such as R. Schank and W. Woods, concerned with engeneering practical language systems. This gap was not always clearly discovered by the researchers concerned with engeneering problems. This is quite understandable if one remembers the enormous impact the Chomsky-paradigm had in the linguistic world. But there is also a reason inherent in the TG-Theory itself. One of the basic assumptions of Chomky's theory is that human languages are recursive sets. A recursive set is a set of strings such that there exists a program that can effectively determine if a given string is in the set or not. Generally, it's assumed that people posses just such a program with respect to their native language. People are assumed to classify linguistic signals into well defined sets: sentences and non-sentences.

One of the main reasons, why many researchers such as W. Woods didn't recognize that Chomskyan theory was not a model of language processing, is the fact that this theory suggests that it has something to do with mental processes. For that reason, it was quite incomprehensible to many linguists that Chomsky so vehemently protested against the opinion that his work grew out of computer work. In this respect the Chomsky-paradigm leads to misunderstandings provoked by Chomsky himself, because he suggested that human language users had "programs" for scanning grammatical structures.

The Chomskyan paradigm emerged from automata theory and in a way linguistic competence is considered to be a kind of automaton for recognizing grammatical sentences. One of the major disadvantaged of this theory, as far as the natural computer is concerned, is the fact that nearly all efforts of linguistic theory were devoted to sentences and not to texts. Another disadvantage is the fact that TG theory led to a strict dichotomy between syntax and semantics. The postulated syntactical structure of sentences is underpinned by a so-called Recursive Transition Network (RTN).

A RTN is a diagram showing various paths which can be followed to accomplish a task. Each path consists of a number of nodes or little boxes with words in them, joined by arcs, or lines with arrows. The first and last nodes have the words 'begin' and 'end' in them. All the other nodes contain either very short directions to perform, or else names of other RTN's.

It was quite natural that computational linguists were attracted by his kind of formalism for natural language, and that they tried to transform it into a formalism for natural language processing.

For natural language processing one wants a procedure which will act variably according to context. Such a procedure either applies what is stored in memory and selects its actions accordingly, or it uses parameters which guide its choice of what actions to take. In RTN terminology, choosing the sequence of actions to carry out amounts to choosing which pathway to follow. A RTN which has been augmented with information that control the choice of pathways inside it is called an Augmented Transition Network (ATN). The extra information would allow for example the insertion of various semantic constraints. W. Woods, the inventor of the ATN's for natural language processing, claimed that this mechanism could be considered as the implementation of TG grammar. In fact, ATN is not really different from a RTN: ATN is also based on abstract automata theory.

According to the extra information the ATN model provides a means for solving syntactic problems on the word level and on the phrase level.

Example 1: The word level.
The <u>old train</u> was in the station / the <u>old train</u> the young.

Example 2: The phrase level (conjunction)
Old women <u>and</u> men were on the beach.

To solve these ambiguities the ATN model tries all possible strings and matches them against the strings allowed in the grammar. There is no possibility of avoiding nonsence sequences. They all have to be matched against the grammar rewrite rules. Here the abstract basis of the model is evident. This feat of the ATN model is called 'the combinatorial explosion', based on back tracking.

At the time W. Woods developed his language engeneering system, it was not fully clear that the TG model was not a process model, nor was it clear how the theoretical formalism could be used as a basis for practical engeneering systems to actually carry out language analysis. One of the major differences between the ATN formalism and the TG formalism is the use of the assigment operator, a concept virtually unknown outside computing, and one which doesn't naturally enter into the description of natural languages.

Nets in Psychology

In psychology, the modelling of human language processing was also heavily influenced and inspired by transformational theory. Various experiments were performed to assess the feasability of this model. Also experiments were performed to prove the psychological reality of the ATN model for human language processing. One of those experiments were performed by R. Kaplan and E..Wanner/M. Maratsos. Open to debate, however, are the following usual features of ATN's:

1) The role of the segmentation of sentences into clauses for language comprehension and production.

2) The role of back tracking in human information processing.

Back tracking refers to the fact that all possible word sequences have to be matched against the grammar rewrite rules.

E. Wanner/Maratsos discuss two sentences:

1) The witch whom sorcerers despised frightened little children.

2) The witch who despised sorcerers frightened little children.

It's evident that the first sentence is more difficult to understand than the second one. Thus, the first sentence needs more processing time. The hypothesis of E. Wanner/Maratsos was that the noun phrase 'the witch' in both sentences has to be remembered in different ways. In the first sentences humans should remember the word 'witch' till the word 'frightened', while in the second sentence the function of the witch is clear after the appearance of the word 'despised'.

For this remembering function Wanner/Maratsos propose an ATN memory mechanism called the HOLD LIST. Their general prediction was that keeping information on this HOLD list produces a performance decrement. The experiments gave the predicted results, i.e. the performance decrement. However, no reason could be given, why only in this case keeping information should cause difficulty. Actually, holding information of partial results is vital to the ATN formalism. Apart from that, as soon as the words, 'the' and 'which' are removed from the HOLD LIST they must be stored somewhere else. Thus, in ATN the amount of information to be stored doesn't change, only the location of storage, as J. Anderson quite rightly remarks. Thus, the Wanner/Maratsos hypothesis raises more open questions than that it comes to explanations.

There might be a more sensible explanation of the fact that the second sentence is processed faster than the first one. The reason of this might be that in the second sentence there is less information processing to do. This smaller effort could be explained from the fact that the second sentence is more conform to the expectations of the native speaker. Processing from left to right, the hearer expects sentences like:

The witch who despised sorcerers,
because these structures are more frequent than
The witch whom sorcerers despised.

PATTERNS : The PRM MODEL

From this hypothesis based on expectancies a different model of language processing emerges as far as the native speaker is concerned. This model is not to the same extent hierarchic in the syntactic level. On the contrary, it is more based on left to right pattern recognition. The most vital premise of the model is that a competent native speaker tries to match complete syntactic patterns, not merely words, against his expectations. This pattern recognition model (PRM) would provide an elegant explanation to the fact that language processing doesn't take much time to the native speaker and that it is mostly unconscious. Therefore, the role of back tracking, as it stands now, as a function in human language processing is unrealistic. This implies that it is also unrealistic for a computer simulating human behavior, i.e. for a natural computer. As a plausible alternative we advocate a pattern recognition model (PRM). This PRM concieves language learning as acquiring a repertoire of linear structures, not of hierarchic structuring. Once the repertoire is acquired, language processing regains its normal properties, i.e. to a large extent unconscious and extremely fast.

The PRM hypothesis has further advantages. It would explain syntactic processing in terms applicable to other types of information processing. So called semantic processing could be as a process based on the same principle of expectancy. Or simply stated, it would give an explanation to the fact that it's easier to understand a subject one is accustomed to than new subjects. The same basic principle would underlie processing of what is called pragmatic information. The more is known about the emotional reactions one is expected to have, the faster one would find the proper reaction.

APPLICATIONS OF THE PRM MODEL

In the field of CL and AI several computer programs were developed on the basis of a PRM model. We could refer to the work of R. Schank and his school at Yale for applications in the field of text understanding, but also to M. Boot at Utrecht for the field of categorial grammar and the design of a reading machine for the blind. As a concrete demonstration of what is meant by 'natural computer' as well as the PRM model, however, we would like to concentrate on the work of J.R. Meehan on writing simple stories by computer.

The work of Meehan grew out of the school of R. Schank. Meehan wrote a computer program called TALE SPIN that is able to write Aesop like fables. To begin with we quote an example of a story generated by TALE SPIN. The program produced the story using the Conceptual Dependency (cd) representation for meaning. This CD output is rendered to another part of the program which expresses it in English. This program gives an adequate rendering, but it lacks style, so we take the translation Meehan gave for easy of reading. All the events in the story were produced by TALE SPIN, only the English is Meehan's:

'The Fox and the Crow
Once upon a time, there was a dishonest fox named Henry who lived in a cave, and a vain and trusting crow named Joe who lived in an elm tree. Joe had gotten a piece of cheese and was holding it in his mouth. One day, Henry walked from his cave, across the meadow to the elm tree. He saw Joe Crow and the cheese and became hungry. He decided that he might get the cheese if Joe Crow spoke, so he told Joe that he liked his singing very much and wanted to hear him sing. Joe was very pleased with Henry and began to sing. The cheese fell out of his mouth, down to the ground. Henry picked up the cheese and told Joe Crow that he was stupid. Joe was angry, and didn't trust Henry anymore. Henry returned to his cave.'

To produce this kind of stories the program TALE SPIN needs a model of the physical world and a model of the world of human behavior. It simulates characters who have motives, emotions and relationships with other characters. The motive of the Fox is his want of food. His knowledge of the character of the crow is used to get this food by flattering the crow.

But also the program has to know about stories, what's interestings, what's coherent.
The overall structure of TALE SPIN is a simulation of rational behavior by the characters in the model. The simulator has three active components. There is a problem solver which given a goal produces other goals (subgoals) and actual events.
There is an assertion mechanism which takes an event and adds it to the world model.

Finally, there is an inference maker which, given an event, produces a set of consequent events.

The world model in its present state (after updating etc.) is held in a memory.

As a demonstration of what is actually different from previous computer programs for simulating intelligent behavior, we will now focus on two vital parts of TALE SPIN, the problem solver and the inference mechanism.

PROBLEM SOLVING in the NATURAL COMPUTER

Problem solving is a topic is AI. A. Newell and H. Simon proposed a vary famous technique, called means-end analysis. In their General Problem Solver (GPS) problem solving is viewed as the task of reducing the difference between the current state of the world and the disired state of the world by applying successive transformations which are known to be useful. To determine whether something is true in a given world, resolution theorem-proving is used. The states are represented in predicate calculus. This technique of problem solving tries to translate all problems into one single problem domain, i.e. the domain of logical operations.

This quite unnatural, because it implies the premise that humans solve all questions by predicate calculus. Let's give some example sentences to prove this:

1) Luxembourg is the capital of Luxembourg
2) Five is the square root of twentyfive
3) D is the dominant of A.

These sentences are superficially very similar, when we assume that those are all simple facts. Now Meehan claims that people don't think of them in the same way. Because all those sentences refer to different problem domains, different techniques inherent to those domains are used to represent the knowledge.

In our words (PRM): different patterns are matched and used in processing the knowledge contained in these sentences.

Because of this difference in human knowledge representation computer representations for them don't need to look alike. Certainly, you can present them all with semantic triples ("X is the Y of Z"), but that doesn't help. It hurts, another type of combinatorial explosion is produced. This becomes unmanegeable with a large body of knowledge. This is undoubtely the reason why Question Answering (QA) systems based on predicate calculus only work in very restricted domains. Memory retrieval techniques in humans must vary from one domain to the next. To put it the other way round: one cann't imagine that in searching for the answer for what is the dominant of A, we come across the idea that five is the square root of twenty five.

To summarize, as far as problem solving is concerned, the natural computer should recognize and make use of the fact that there are seperate problem domains, areas of knowledge with their own representations (or patterns) and problem solving procedures.

Here again we find the fact we discovered in our discussion about linguistic problem solving. There are problems which can be solved without doing any cognitive problem solving. These solutions are simply assumed and expected. Talking another domain as an example, we could refer to walking for an adult person. It comes to a domain where the primitives are related to coordinating muscles and inner-ear balance mechanisms. An adult, however, doesn't worry about that any more, he simply walks. So he doesn't have to solve the problems all the way down the hierarchy of domains: "now I have to move my right leg; now I have to leave it where it is ...etc."

INFERENCES

Inferences are the links in causal chains. It's commonly known that in natural texts, much information isn't stated explicitly because it's evident for human beings. If we read the statements:

> "John went to New York by bus. On the bus he talked to an old
> lady."

It's evident that John had to go to a bus stop; that he waited at it a few minutes; that the bus came down; that she stopped; that John entered the bus; that the driver got the ticket from John; that he went to a seat and that he sat down on it. A causal chain of events, all necessary but self-evident for human beings, for John to be able to talk to the old

ladv. These self-evident events don't appear in the natural text. They
are know as inferences to be made.

Inferences normally are thought of as consequences, but our understanding
of the term is greatly expanded by the work of C. Rieger from the Schank
group in his thesis on memory. He described sixteen kinds of inferences
used in understanding text and wrote a program to handle examples of all
sixteen types.

The role of inference making in a language understanding system, however,
is different than in a text producing system like TALE SPIN. TALE SPIN
uses inferences primarily to define the consequences of actions that come
from plans. Also often the inference mechanism in TALE SPIN is used
"backwards", i.e. inferences are not made before they are needed. If e.g.
Henry Fox figures out using the enablement of inferences that he can get
the cheese Tom Crow is holding, if Tom drops it, he needs to figure out
motivational inferences: What could cause Tom to drop the cheese. TALE
SPIN is not constructed in the way SAM is made, that is making all
possible inferences at once. TALE SPIN is more natural because it only
makes inferences if it's motivated to make them, not as a kind of con-
ditioned reflex.

From this it can be concluded that inferences heavily rely on memory.
Some even require information which, if not in memory, must be asked of
the reader. TALE SPIN provides this facility.

Some inferences are "context free" that is, they are always true. This
kind of inferences is shown in our initial example about John and the bus
to New York. Here again we observe that inference mechanisms relying on
purely logical operations like predicate calculus, are a very poor
instrument for the development of a natural computer.

HOW FAR OFF IS PARADISE?

So far, our discussion of the natural computer might give the impression
that to-day we already have this type of computer at our disposal.
Therefore, it might be good to give some examples of stories that went
wrong during the development of TALE SPIN.

"One day Joe Bear was hungry. He asked his friend Irving Bird where some
honey was. Irving told him there was a beehive in the oak tree. Joe
threatened to hit Irving if he didn't tell him where some honey was."

'Joe Bear was hungry. He asked Irving Bird where some honey was. Irving refused to tell him, so Joe offered to bring him a worm if he'd tell him where some honey was. Irving agreed. But Joe didn't know where any worms were, so he asked Irving, who refused to say. So Joe offered to bring him a worm if he'd tell him where a worm was. Irving agreed. But Joe didn't know where any worms were, so he asked Irving, who refused to say. So Joe offered to bring him a worm if he'd tell him where a worm was....'

'One day Joe Bear was hungry. He asked his friend Irving Bird where some honey was. Irving told him there was a beehive in the oak tree. Joe walked to the oak tree. He ate the beehive.'

As can be concluded from the examples, it was often the inferencing mechanism that produced the mistakes. Meehan had to face e.g. the problem that also in answers some inferencing has to be done (a beehive contains honey). Also the actual goals should be very well kept account of in natural communication.

CONCLUSION

A language understander is guided by what he wants to know. This enables him to not see all the ambiguities, triple meanings, myriad implications and other problems with what he hears. This enablement comes from the fact that he uses special techniques for memory retrieval in specific domains. A natural language understander doesn't attempt to parse everything he reads or hears. He determines what's most interesting and concentrates on that ignoring the rest. Human-like understanding and language producing systems must be integrated to the extent that they can be guided by their inherent interests, delving into what they fancy and skipping what they don't. This could be the true meaning of variable depth of processing. This variable depth of processing is based on the extensive use of patterns learned in the past and it leads to natural speed of processing and a lack of fragility in human beings. We should give our machines the same knowledge of those patterns on all levels of communications and have them guided by this knowledge. First experiments have been carried out and it seems to be that then our machines indeed have the same advantages as human beings have in language processing. This is a reason why CL is a challenging field of scientific endeavour.

REFERENCES

J. Anderson   : Language, Memory and Thought, 1976
M. Bates   : "The theory and practice of augmented transition network
                   grammars" in: L. Bolc: Natural Language Communication with
                   Computers, 1978
D. Bobrow/   :
A Collins   Representation and understanding, 1975
M. Boot   : Homographie. Ein Beitrag zur automatischen Wortklassenzu-
                   weisung in der Computerlinguistik., 1979
M. Boot   : A computer model for automated phonemization, 1980
E. Charniak/
Y. Wilks   : Computational Semantics, 1976
N. Chomsky   : Syntactic Structures, 1976
R. Kaplan   : "On process models for sentence analysis" in: D. Norman/
                   D. Rummelhart: Explorations in Cognition, 1975
T. Kuhn   : The Structure of Scientific Revolution, 1970
J. Meehan   : The Metanovel: Writing Stories by Computer, 1980
A. Newell/
H. Simon   : Human Problem Solving, 1972
C. Rieger   : Conceptual Memory: A theory and Computer Program for
                   Processing the Meaning Content of Natural Language
                   Utterances, 1974
R. Schank   : Conceptual Information Processing, 1975
R. Schank and
the Yale AI
Project SAM   : A story understander, 1975
R. Schank/
R. Abelson   : Scripts, Plans, Goals: The Elements of Understanding,
                   1977
R. Thomason   : Formal Phylosophy, Selected papers of Richard Montague,
                   1974
E. Wanner/
M. Maratsos   : Augmented transition network model of relative clause
                   comprehension, 1975
Y. Wilks   : Grammar, Meaning and the Machine Analysis of Language,
                   1972
R. Schank/
C. Colby   : Computer Models of Thought and Language, 1973
W. Woods/
R. Kaplan/
B. Nash-Weber   : The Lunar Sciences Natural Language Information System:
                   final report, 1972
W. Woods   : Cascaded Grammar, 1981
N. Chomsky   : Introduction to the Logical Structure of Linguistic
                   Theory, 1974

LEXICOGRAPHY IN THE ELECTRONIC AGE
J. Goetschalckx and L. Rolling (editors)
North-Holland Publishing Company
© ECSC, EEC, EAEC, 1982

THE DEVELOPMENT OF INFORMATION DESIGN RESEARCH
1960-1980: CURRENT TRENDS AND FUTURE PROSPECTS

M ENNIS

Elsevier International Bulletins
Oxford, England

(formerly of Primary Communications Research Centre,
University of Leicester, Leicester, England)

Summary

Recent trends in research on the design and presentation of printed
information are reviewed. Particular attention is paid to the way in
which legibility research has expanded in the last ten years from the
study of the printed word to encompass a much wider area, including the
presentation and use of illustrative material, and factors affecting the
comprehension of text. While their approaches differ, modern researchers
are especially concerned to involve information producers in arriving at
an agreed consensus of views. The development of this new research
perspective is traced from a historical viewpoint, and it is suggested
that a unified discipline - information design research - has resulted
from the recent broad-based approach to the different factors involved in
the presentation of information.

A brief concluding section takes a look at the role of national and
international standards in the presentation and dissemination of
information, and the presence of documentation standards within national
standards organisations throughout the world. Some ideas for improving
standards are put forward, and the relationship between research work and
standards is briefly discussed.

The aim of this paper is to provide a review of recent research on factors
affecting the design and presentation of printed information, highlighting
current research trends and possible aims and directions for the future.
The focus of the discussion will be on the applicability of different
research methodologies to the study of scholarly journal presentation, the
latter being one of the principal areas studied in a research project
conducted in the Primary Communications Research Centre (PCRC) of the
University of Leicester, between October 1978 and April 1981. (1) It must
be emphasised from the outset that this paper is aiming to do little more
than set the scene for the symposium, as it is not directly concerned with
the problems involved in the dissemination of lexicographical
information. Nevertheless, the following review of research work in the
field of information design will be of interest to those involved in the
compilation of lexicographical material, as the format and presentation of
dictionaries, glossaries and associated materials should always be easy to
comprehend, otherwise assimilation of the required information by the user
will be impaired.

In terms of overcoming language difficulties in a multingual society,
increasingly committed to the rapid, worldwide dissemination of scientific
and technical information, the journal article plays an important –
possibly the most important – role in the dissemination process. Perhaps
more than any other type of printed information, the producers of
scholarly journals must strive for optimal presentation so that articles
are geared for effective reading by an international audience. The impact
of new technological developments on journal publishing over the last two
decades makes it necessary to consider other methods of presentation apart
from the conventional print medium. However, the aim of the PCRC project
was to arrive at some conclusions re: the effectiveness of the various
methods of presenting print on paper, and the research reviewed here will
therefore be primarily concerned with the print medium, although some
account will be taken of the effect of transferring printed materials onto
microforms. Research into electronic publishing techniques is currently
on the increase as the feasibility of such operations are being tested.
Unfortunately, the limitations on time, and the scope of my work, preclude
more than passing reference to this important area of research.

DEFINITIONS AND DIVISIONS

It is possible to divide up work on information design issues that may be
relevant to conventional (i.e. printed) journal presentation into six
subject areas - three of major importance, and a further three of more
peripheral interest in the present context. The most important three
areas are as follows:

(1) Typographic research, studying the legibility of the printed word
    through analysis of factors connected with the physical attributes of
    text - e.g. type face, type style, type size, line length etc. and the
    total design of the printed text in relation to the ease with which it
    can be both seen and read.

(2) Research dealing with the presentation of graphical and alphanumeric
    material principally through measuring the effect of various
    categories of material (e.g. illustrations, graphs, maps, numerical
    tables) on the cognitive processes in different types of experimental
    subject.

(3) The readability of verbal material concerned with the link between
    language usage and comprehensibility, and the means of assessing or
    predicting the extent to which readers from different disciplines, and
    different educational levels, are capable of understanding texts
    written in different styles.

The above three areas of research are most central to journal
presentation, and will be referred to as 'legibility research', 'graphics
research', and 'readability research' respectively.

Three further research areas will be mentioned as they have some bearing
on journal presentation. Firstly, the different theories of comprehension
and their associated methodologies should be considered, as they form a
nexus betwen legibility/graphics research and readability research, with
some form of comprehension testing exercise usually incorporated into the
methodological framework through which legibility, readability and
graphics are evaluated. Secondly, the various methods which are used to
study the reading processes of different types of readers need to be taken

into account; in particular the link between reading purpose and reading strategies. Finally, one cannot ignore work which has been done on the reading habits and the information needs of users.

Having divided research in the information design field into these six 'compartments', it should be noted that the division is intended primarily for convenience of discussion and elucidation, as in many respects the six types of research work are interrelated rather than discrete. Indeed, the major premise postulated in this paper is that a unification process is currently taking place, with many researchers - aware above all else of the necessity to direct their work towards the requirements of practitioners (e.g. publishers, printers, graphic designers) - adopting a broad-based approach in which, for example, matters such as the selection of a type size, and how best to present a histogram, are taken as constituent parts of the total design process, rather than as two unrelated issues. More will be said on this subject presently, but the whole basis of the argument here is that the 'molecular' approach of earlier researchers which saw design issues examined in isolation or "simplified and divorced from their real-life context," (2) is now redundant. The way forward is with a unified approach which enables us to talk of 'information design research' as a coherent body of knowledge encompassing the six 'compartments' listed above.

THE DEVELOPMENT OF LEGIBILITY RESEARCH

During the last fifteen to twenty years, legibility research has undergone a theoretical redefinition to encompass a much wider area than in the past. A significant body of research has been developing in England recently, which goes beyond the confines of legibility research, graphics research and readability research in considering the symbolic form in which a message is produced as an agent of the communication's effectiveness, in addition to the physical structure and the style in which information is presented. We will return to this work later, but first, in order to understand why this new approach emerged, it is necessary to briefly examine the history of legibility research. The greater part of the discussion will be on new developments in legibility research, for this may be more central to the needs of lexicographers than graphics and readability research, which will of necessity receive less attention.

Earlier studies concentrated solely on the legibility of the printed word, and consisted of both survey and experimental work, although the latter was by far the most popular approach. Survey work often involved a detailed analysis of printing methods, an example being the report by Tinker (1963) on a publishers' survey of 1500 American books, magazines and journals of varying kinds, to discover differences which existed in the presentation of the physical features of text such as type size, type face, number of columns, margin size, proportion of text to white space on a page etc. Part of the PCRC project, mentioned earlier, was a comparative survey of 100 U.K. scholarly journal issues published in 1975 with the 1980 issues of the same journals, aiming to highlight differences in presentation over time. However, the scope of this survey extended beyond legibility research's boundaries by examining the presentation of graphical material, and adherence to the relevant British Standard on journal presentation (3).

Work has also been conducted to elicit readers' opinions and judgements on the legibility of text, often in conjunction (or as an afterthought!) with experimental work (see, for example, Tinker and Paterson, 1942); while readers' opinions on the aesthetic aspects or "judged pleasingness" of different typographic arrangements were collected by, amongst others, Zachrisson (1965). However, the laboratory experiment was the most common form of early legibility research. Work on single symbols which attempted to establish threshold measures of pure visual function in relation to different kinds of print are not very useful, either in terms of journal presentation, or for lexicographical material; the results have more bearing for display purposes such as traffic signs or labels.

The most relevant of the early studies to journal presentation were experiments with connected prose which generally aimed to determine the relative efficiency of different typographical arrangements using quantitative measures. This is not the place to give a full review of the work carried out - Katzen (1977) provides an excellent overview for those wishing to investigate further - the main point to note here is that this

kind of research, apart from focusing exclusively on prose material,
ignored comprehension as a variable. Legibility was measured through: (i)
visual fatigue (i.e. ease of seeing), for example, Luckiesh and Moss'
(1940) reflex blink rate; (ii) reading speed, taken as a criterion of
legibility with the aim of discovering the range within which optimal
legibiity could be maintained in relation to physical features of text;
(iii) eye movement patterns, as used by Tinker (1963) to supplement his
work on reading speeds.

The work of Poulton (1957, 1960), who introduced comprehension as a
variable into his reading speed experiments, started the move towards a
wider approach in which the effect of different formats on different types
of readers were taken into account. Poulton (1967) also introduced the
concept of 'scanning' into his tests, referring to a method of rapidly
skimming through text to simulate the natural reading situation when
glancing through a journal.

THE STRUCTURAL APPROACH TO LEGIBILITY

Recent studies on typographical issues have come to realise that the
interrelationship of the various factors in a particular typographical
arrangement is highly complex, and that a new theoretical framework is
needed to replace misguided empiricism, and to direct research work
towards: (i) an awareness of the importance of the structural
characteristics of printed matter; and (ii) the importance of taking into
account economic considerations, and the needs of practitioners.

Hartley (1978) considers that the new framework should be especially
concerned with the overall structure of text, and the utilization of space
on a standardised page. Although he is interested in all aspects of
information design, Hartley's work is ruled by the principle that larger
structural factors (e.g. page size) constrain smaller ones, such as type
size or column width. In his 1978 study 'Space and Structure in
Instructional Text,' Hartley argues that both comprehension and retrieval
from printed text are affected most by "the use that is made of the space
on a page-size of known dimensions - rather than the print."

Over the past ten years, Hartley has published a considerable number of studies on the design of textbooks, journals, college prospectuses, questionnaires etc., in addition to work on specific aspects of journal design, such as the lay-out of contents pages, indexes and references. Particularly useful is the book 'Designing Instructional Text' (1978), in which Hartley's ideas are applied to a wide variety of informational material, with empirical studies produced to support his findings. This work is a new approach to legibility research, concentrating on space and structure, and insisting that, before assessing specific typographic issues, factors such as page size must be determined. Further empirical work is needed to see if the conclusions reached are fully justified, but Hartley has evidently made a major contribution to widening the scope of recent legibility research. All varieties of material, not just continuous prose, are examined; and throughout his work runs an awareness of the importance of economic factors as a constraining influence on information design.

The Graphic Information Research Unit (GIRU) has produced a large number of studies concerned with various typographic issues. Spencer (1974) makes it clear that the GIRU are also fully aware of the need to produce research with the potential for practical application: 'properly conducted, objective research can provide the designer, the printer and the publisher with much valuable information about those factors in design which may affect the functional efficiency of what is produced.' (4)

The GIRU are working within a narrower interpretation of the term 'legibility' than Hartley: Spencer (1978) suggests that it might be used when referring to studies ranging from the visibility of individual characters and words, to the ease and speed of reading of continuous text, which is much nearer to the theoretical position of earlier legibility research. This in no way detracts from the value of the GIRU's work, however, for they have examined a large number of typographic issues both in terms of legibility for the reader, and economics for the designer and publisher. Other important contributions from the GIRU include a study of the relative legibility of alternative letter shapes (1973); the effect of background 'noise' and lack of contrast on legibility; and a study focusing on how the legibility of printed text and numerals is affected by image degradation (1975).

A great deal of valuable work has been carried out by Hartley and the GIRU on specific issues within the area of scholarly journal presentation. Hartley's work on the design of journal contents pages and journal references – with spatial layout being cited as more important than typographic cueing – being of particular interest. (For a full treatment of research dealing with journal presentation, see my article "The Design and Presentation of Informational Material" in J. Res. Comm. Studies 2, 1979/80, pp 67-81).

Macdonald Ross and Waller (1975) stress the need for researchers to be aware of the practical implications of their work, with attention directed towards the requirements of those actively involved in the production of information of different types. They suggest that the 'tacit knowledge' possessed by typographers, designers and others can be an important aid to researchers. Instead of relying on experimental testing, wrongly based on the empiricist paradigm of the physical sciences we should value the personal skills of typographers and designers, and take them as the starting point for more fruitful typographic research. A 'modern consensus' between researchers and practioners is needed, according to Macdonald Ross and Waller, but this can only be achieved if research is given a more practical orientation. To this end, they have used a method in their own research called "criticism of alternatives." Sections of Open University text material were given to final year undergraduates of the BA in Typography at Reading University, who were asked to criticise them and to provide constructive alternatives. The "one variable model of research" is rejected in favour of "the testing of one coherent alternative against another." (5)

THE UNIFICATION PROCESS

Earlier work on the presentation of graphical material was almost entirely experimental, usually involving the testing of people's ability to recognise and discriminate between elements in different types of graphical and alphanumeric material. The subjects used in these tests were often stratified by such variables as age, sex, aptitude, IQ and prior knowledge of the material. Miller (1938) testing childrens' ability to recognise the main items in pictures; and Feliciano et al (1963) with experiments on students' abilities to extract information from different types of graphs, are two examples of the experimental approach. The latter study used comprehension as a variable in the testing procedure by asking the subjects both a retrieval question, and an inspection question which involved using more than one item on the graph.

Modern researchers have criticised the treatment of graphical and alphanumeric material in isolation, and studies have emerged (6) which compare algorithms, tables, charts etc. with one another; and with prose presentations, in the wider context of the relative appropriateness of different formats in different situations. Thus, the style in which the information is being presented is considered in addition to physical characteristics. Another recent innovation is the construction of theoretical classification systems, such as that devised by Foster (1973) in which every piece of legibility research should fit, including work exclusively concerned with the presentation of illustrative material. In a similar manner to Foster,   Twyman (1976) stresses how important it is to take account of the illustrative material found in various types of informational text, and provides a scheme to cover all the forms of what he calls 'graphic language'. His work does not prescribe which particular form to use in a specific situation. He is more concerned with drawing attention to two important questions which must be asked when deciding on the form of graphic presentation to be used. These are: (i) what form should 'the mode of symbolisation' take? and (ii) what form should 'the method of configuration' take?

Twyman produces a 28 cell matrix, one axis of which consists of the 'methods of configuration'. These concern the way in which the graphic organisation, or structure, of a message might affect, or even determine, the different reading strategies of the information receiver. The other axis represents 'the mode of symbolisation' - that is the different forms in which the 'graphic language' appears. Twyman's paper is aimed at helping those involved in practical decision making. An attempt is made to see which of the 28 cells are most commonly used; and a brief survey is undertaken to discover which empirical studies can be 'fitted' into the various cells.

Twyman appears to favour an approach which postulates a strong
relationship between legibility research, readability research, and the
presentation of illustrative material, corresponding to the current
widening scope in research on information design.

THE IMPORTANCE OF READABILITY

There is also a move to integrate the vast field of readability research
with typographic research. This is a much more difficult task, but it is
essential to have an appreciation of the context in which information is
going to be used, and a degree of sensitivity to the requirements of
different kinds of reader, as well as an awareness of typographic
factors. Readability research is concerned with the effectiveness of a
text's language for different readers, and readability formulae - such as
the Flesch Reading Ease Formula (1948) and Gunning's Fog Index (1968) -
have been produced in order to try and predict the probable level of
difficulty of a text for its readers. It is impossible in this brief
paper to attempt an evaluation of the vast amount of work completed on
readability and comprehension, but Klare (1975) and Katzen (1977) provide
excellent reviews of the literature.

Studies such as that by Wright (1977) in which comprehension is taken as
an important variable in the presentation of technical information are
further evidence of the move towards as 'across the board' package in
which legibility research would be linked with research on reading
strategies, reading purposes and the type of audience who will be
receiving the information. Wright argues that one method of presentation,
or form of expression, may be appropriate for one purpose, but
inappropriate for another.

PRESENTATION FOR DIFFERENT MEDIA

Some important work on the presentation of material in formats other than
the conventional print medium has been conducted by the Graphic
Information Research Unit recently (7). These include the presentation of
bibliographic information for Prestel; the problems facing the designers

of teletext and viewdata; and a study examining the visual presentation of COM library catalogues. As new technological developments have an increasing effect on the form in which information is presented, this type of work is very significant. Another area in need of research is in the presentation of the information produced through electronic publishing techniques – a topic extremely relevant to lexicographic information which is being increasingly presented in this form. At present, there is little work on the presentation in this media, as the current focus is understandably on the economic viability of such projects which are still very much in the early stages of development.

A WORD ON STANDARDS

Another part of the PCRC project mentioned earlier was an examination of the role played by national and international standards in the presentation and dissemination of research information. Particular attention was paid to standards on (1) journal presentation; and (2) presentation of 'grey literature' – e.g. research and development reports, theses, conference proceedings and other material not published through the usual commercial channels. Although the detailed results emerging from this project may not be directly relevant to the demands of the symposium, some of the general principles raised a number of interesting questions which are relevant to those involved in the production and dissemination of all types of information. For example, why are standards on documentation held in such low esteem by editors and publishers? Is there any way in which research can help improve the content of standards? And more generally, what is the current situation throughout the world in terms of standards work on documentation and related topics?

To answer the last of these three questions first, a survey of the 67 member bodies (taken from 1979 listing) of the International Organisation for Standardisation (ISO) was conducted to discover the extent to which national standards organisations produced their own standards on documentation. Out of the 59 countries who responded to the questionnaire sent to them, 38 had at least one standard on a documentation subject, and 19 had a standard specifically on the presentation of serial publications. All of the 38 countries with a section responsible for

documentation standards had begun work in this area after 1950, 27 after
1960. All of the European countries who replied had a set of
documentation standards, excepting 4, and some countries, such as Belgium
with 36 seperate standards on documentation subjects, clearly considered
the communication and presentation of information to be of growing
importance. Unfortunately, no detailed information was collected on the
existence of lexicographic standards in the 67 countries, although it is
reasonable to suggest on the data available that lexicography is one area
in which an easily identifiable gap in national standards work is apparent.

On the more complex issue of whether the producers of information actually
conform to the recommendations laid down in standards, a study of the
implementation of 4 British Standards in 100 science, social science and
humanities journals was carried out, the main objective being an analysis
of changing patterns of adherence to standards over a five year period.
Hence, journal issues from 1975 and 1980 were compared. The results of
the survey showed that some recommendations (e.g. presence of abstracts,
positioning of contents list) were widely implemented, whereas other
recommendations, notably on the presentation of bibliographic references,
were largely ignored. Furthermore, interviews conducted with editors,
publishers and printers suggested that standards were generally seen as
too expensive, difficult to obtain, and too rigid in laying down one
method of presentation, rather than providing a range of alternatives.
Editors appeared to pay more attention to research work on legibility,
readability, and the presentation of graphical material, and if a standard
on a certain topic did not reflect the latest research findings, then it
was discarded.

There have been some successes in recent standards, such as the widespread
adoption of the Anglo-American Cataloguing Rules (AACR), and the use of
standard formats for sharing bibliographic data on magnetic media (MARC);
but an obvious failure to take research findings into account, was in
standards on the legibility required from microforms which are now being
seriously questioned as a viable alternative to print. Standards on
documentation cannot be mandatory in the same way as standards on safety
issues, and therefore face much greater implementation problems. In spite
of this fact, the advent of new technology has increased the importance of
the role documentation standards have to play in the dissemination of

information if: (a) attention is paid to research work, and a range of
flexible alternatives is supplied for each standard; (b) the drafting time
for standards is greatly speeded up - some ISO standards can take up to
four years before publication, and run the danger of being out of date
before they are even available for implementation. At the present time,
it seems highly debatable whether standards are meeting the needs of those
involved in the production, design and presentation of information.

CONCLUSION:

If this paper has demonstrated how research into the design of printed
information has changed over the last two decades to examine the different
issues in legibility, readability and the presentation of graphical
material as part of the same subject, then it will have succeeded in its
principal aim. Recent work has made it possible to talk of information
design research as an emerging discipline examining design issues within a
broad perspective, and in their proper context. A lot more work needs to
be done, especially in the area of 'marrying' research findings with the
needs of those involved in the production of information. The first steps
have been taken, however, in moving research on to a more practical
basis. If there can also be a marked improvement in the nature of
standards work on documentation, the problems involved in disseminating
information to an increasingly information-conscious society may well
diminish during the next few years, especially if more research on the
presentation of information in the new media is quickly and efficiently
carried out.

REFERENCES

For a full bibliography covering all sources referred to in this paper see Ennis, M., 1980. The design and presentation of informational material: a review of U.K. research trends. J. Res. Comm. Stud., 2, 1979–80: 67–81. A copy of this article can be supplied on request.

(1) The full title of this project is "The Role of National and International Standards in the Communication of Research Information."

(2) Hartley, J. and Burnhill, P. (1977) Understanding instructional text: typography, layout and design. In: Idowe, MJA, Adult Learning, London: Wiley, 1977.

(3) B.S. 2509 'The presentation of serial publications including periodicals. 1970.

(4) Spencer, H. (1974). Typography: art, craft or science? Professional Printer, vol 18, no 5.

(5) Macdonald-Ross, M. and Waller R. (1975). Criticism, alternatives and tests: A conceptual framework for improving typography. Programmed Learning, March 1975, pp 75–83.

(6) See for example: Wright, P. and Ried, F. (1973) Written information: some alternatives to prose for expressing the outcomes of complex contingencies. J. of App. Psychology, vol 57, no 2, pp 160–6.

(7) See for example: Reynolds, L. (1979) Teletext and viewdata a new challenge for the designer Information Design Journal, vol 1, no 1, pp 2–14.

Reynolds, L. (1980) The presentation of bibliographical information on Prestel. London: Graphic Information Research Unit, Royal College of Art.

LEXICOGRAPHY IN THE ELECTRONIC AGE
J. Goetschalckx and L. Rolling (editors)
North-Holland Publishing Company
© ECSC, EEC, EAEC, 1982

THE BONNLEX LEXICON SYSTEM

J. BRUSTKERN and K.D. HESS

Institut für Kommunikationsforschung und Phonetik,

University of Bonn

Summary

The Institut für Kommunikationsforschung und Phonetik at the University of Bonn is developing a cumulative and integrated word data bank designed to provide lexical information for users involved in linguistic data-processing work.

This project is based on the investigations into the size, contents and structure of existing computerized lexica carried out as part of the project entitled "Comparative Analysis of machine-readable German lexica", the aim is to incorporate the results of these investigations - both at the formal level and, as far as possible, as regards content - into one word data bank so as to avoid duplication of effort when producing dictionaries. In addition to this review of existing computer lexica, a methodology has been worked out for machine-readable dictionarieswhich is to be presented at the colloquium as a structure for the ideal comprehensive dictionary. At the same time, suggestions are made for ways of extracting sub-items of information from the machine-readable lexica examined. The outlines of a lexicon system for implementing the word data bank are also presented; here particular attention is paid to the lexicographical requirements to be met by a system of this kind. Finally, a user profile is given for the word data bank.

1. AN ANALYSIS OF MACHINE-READABLE GERMAN LEXICA

The research project 'Comparative analysis of machine-readable German
lexica' is financed by the Gesellschaft für Information und Dokumentation
(GID) and the Federal Ministry for Research and Technology (BMFT) and is
being carried out by the Institut für Kommunikationsforschung und Phonetik,
Bonn. It is scheduled to last from 1 September to 31 December 81.

This project has so far concentrated on a comparative study of existing
machine-readable German lexica, the aim being to relate the various terminologies, lexical data and grammatical models to one another and develop
ideas for a practical, integrated and cumulative lexicon for use in linguistic data-processing applications (e.g. question/answer systems, automatic indexing or machine translation).

The lexicon systems examined are listed in Table 1.

These lexica were chosen, inter alia, on the following criteria :
- machine readability, i.e. lexica transferred to data media by machine
  processing;
- use in a linguistic data-processing system (see above);
- adequate size, usability and level of development.

The main features investigated were as follows :
- role of the lexicon in the total system;
- size;
- data chosen and principles governing this choice (function words/content
  words, overall vocabulary/specialized vocabulary);
- lexeme types (full or inflected forms, basic forms, stems);
- macro- and microstructure;
- linguistic theory;
- terminology.

After information on the lexicon projects had been gathered and classified
in this way, specific aspects of the contents of the dictionaries were
compared, namely word-type classification, morphosyntactic information,
semantic descriptions and information on valency.

Table 1

PROJECT/DURATION/RESEARCH BODY	SHORT TITLE	AIM
Institut für deutsche Sprache, work started 1972, sponsored by BMFT, pilot study in Stuttgart, tests version ready at the end of 1979; now completed.	PLIDIS	Information system on monitoring industrial effluent. Question/answer system taking into account syntactic, semantic and pragmatic aspects.
Institut für angewandte Informatik, TU (University of Technology) Berlin, 1975–31.7.81 : 'Computerized generation of semantic networks'.	BACON	Question/answer system for generating semantic networks from texts.
Germanistisches Seminar Hamburg, since 1975; sponsored by the DFG (German Research Association) until 1981.	HAM-RPM	Dialogue simulation ('partner-oriented speech strategy') of linguistic, communicative and cognitive skills.
SIEMENS, Munich; viable versions available since August 1976.	PASSAT	Set of programs for automatic selection of key-words from text (indexing), to be used in an IR system.
SIEMENS, Munich, since 1972, sponsored by BMFT, Version 1 at test stage, Version 2 at development stage.	CONDOR	Analysis and indexing of natural-language documents (creating data banks).
Kandler (Sprachwissenschaftliches Institut), Bünting (IKP), Bonn.	MACKENSEN	Segmentation of the word-stock into 'sense elements' ($\triangleq$ morpheme).
Systran Institute, Munich, ready for use, now being tested.	SYSTRAN	Machine translation of specialized texts : development of a universal language-independent basic software system.
Research project 'Linguistics and computerized language processing', 1965–76, Bonn.	LIMAS	Giving concrete form to A. Hoppe's communicative grammar.
Mainz University project, led by Wahrig, 1974–78.	WAHRIG	Studies on the structure of natural languages ('semantic universals').
SFB 100 (Saarbrücken University).	SATAN SUSY	Development of dictionaries for computerized text analysis and machine translation.
Regensburg University	JUDO	Processing legal documents.

There was also some discussion of the problem of standardizing individual
lexica in accordance with DIN draft standard No. 2341 (magnetic tape exchange format).

All the results of these investigations and a draft methodology for
machine-readable dictionaries are now contained in a research report
('Comparative Study') at the IKP in Bonn.

2. CONSTRUCTION OF A WORD DATA BANK (PHASE 2)

The aim of the second phase, based on the 'Comparative Study', is to produce an integrated, cumulative word data bank which includes lexical material from the dictionaries examined and thus avoids duplication of effort
in the production of dictionaries.

The word data bank being developed in Bonn is intended to provide users
with lexical information. It consists of an integrated and cumulative lexicon and is operated by a lexicon system (computer-assisted processing system). For this, a suitable lexicon structure (2.1) and a pilot system for
operating the lexicon (2.2) have first to be devised.

2.1 Lexicon structure

As a result of work done so far, the rough outlines of a structure for the
ideal comprehensive dictionary can now be presented.

In formal terms, a dictionary can be represented as a set of lexical
entries LE_i :

$$W = LE_1, \quad LE_2, \quad \ldots \quad LE_m$$

This is the macrostructure. Each lexical entry, in turn, consists of an
n-tuple of information units.

$$LE_i = (I_{i,1}, \; I_{i,2}, \; I_{i,3}, \; \ldots \; I_{i,n}); \; I_{i,j} \in K_j$$

These information units, $I_{i,j}$, come from lexicologically-determined information classes, K_j, which can be listed as follows :

K_1 : spelling (graphemics) WG

   of the lexeme entered in the lexicon

K_2 : phonology P

   the phonetic transcription, with information on syllabification
   and stress

K_3 : lemma L

   information on the basic form found in each form of an inflectional paradigm

K_4 : word class WK

   classification of word types defined in syntactic, morphological
   or semantic terms

K_5 : information on the morphology of inflections F

   details on the declension of substantive elements, such as case,
   number, gender and degree of comparison, on the conjugation of
   verbal elements, such as person, number, mood, tense and voice
   (active/passive), and on ways of forming the compound past

K_6 : derivation data D

   details on the word formation process using derivational morphemes

K_7 : syntactic environment OS

   surface structure, valency, rection, surface case

K_8 : deep case TS

   the required deep-case frame

K_9 : semantic information SEM

   (see below)

In an entry of this kind, which consists of the tuple

   $LE_i = (WG_i, P_i, L_i, WK_i, F_i, O_i, OS_i, TS_i, SEM_i)$

individual informations units can be broken down still further.

Thus, the semantic part of the lexicon (SEM) might itself consist of a
6-tuple :

   SEM = (DEF, SEMKON, ANW, SEREL, PRIM, FG)

where

DEF	=	semantic definition, explanation of meaning
SEMKON	=	semantically relevant context, semantic environment
ANW	=	examples of use
SEREL	=	semantic relationships
PRIM	=	semantic primitives
FG	=	marking of specialized field

For each of the information units mentioned, suggestions will be made in the presentation as to which of the existing machine-readable lexica can be used to provide data for constructing the ideal comprehensive word data bank which could be of value to the interested user.

2.2 The lexicon systems

The dictionaries examined during the project 'Comparative analysis of machine-readable German lexica' and the resulting proposed structure for an integrated, cumulative lexicon are fundamental elements in the design of a word data bank. The cumulative lexicon in the form of a word data bank represents a readily-available, uniform lexical basis for widely-differing development projects in the field of informational linguistics.

At the same time, efforts are being made to ensure a coordinated continuation of lexical work on a machine-readable German lexicon. In order to be able to implement a word data bank of this kind using an EDP installation, it is necessary to have a set of programs with which all the essential functions of lexicon creation, maintenance and search can be performed. The need to continue the various lexica creates particular problems here, since these lexica have been designed for use in different fields and, as a result, use different codes.

The machine-readable lexica examined in the abovementioned project, which are to serve as a basis for a cumulative lexicon, will hereafter be termed 'base lexica'. The cumulative lexicon and the set of programs constitute a lexicon system for operating a dynamic word data bank. This system must meet certain requirements if it is to perform lexicographical tasks.

The most important of these can be classified as follows :
- requirements relating to the lexicon :
  these requirements stem from the nature of the lexical data to be processed. The structures of the base lexica and of the cumulative lexicon,
  as well as the coding of the lexical items, will therefore be of particular importance here.
- requirements relating to the data bank :
  this includes the basic requirements to be met by a data bank system in
  respect of updating, retrieval and user-friendly man/machine communication.

For the time being, technical and economic requirements are being given
less priority. The lexicon-related requirements to be met by the lexicon
system, which arise from the generation and operation of a dynamic word
data bank, can be summarized as follows :

- transfer of structural components from one lexicon to another; this involves a computer-assisted comparison of lexica and an automatic coding
  algorithm;

- the ability to reconstitute parts of the base lexica which have been
  transferred to the cumulative lexicon, to enable the lexicon to be used
  for as many purposes as possible without information loss;

- computer-aided processing of data on relationships between lexical
  elements;

- computerized generation of lexical elements wherever possible,e.g. trac-
  ing a word form back to its basic form (computerized lemmatization);

- computerized extension of the lexicon by
  a) comparing the lexicon with texts,
  b) comparing the lexicon with external lexica;

- computer-aided extension of the lexicon by means of simple text analyses,
  e.g. concordance, vertical text generation, etc.

The lexicon system should meet the following data bank-related require
ments :
- the system must be designed so that the user does not require any knowledge of file formats, algorithms employed in the program or the internal
  structure of the data in order to be able to operate the system;
- user-friendly design of the data bank's basic functions of updating and
  retrieval;
- capacity for monitoring the use of data and guaranteeing copyright;
- provision of parametrized external programs for the points of acces,
  avoiding the need for involvement with the EDP installation's operating
  system;
- on- and off-line operation of the system with presentation of data on
  screens or printouts.

The Institut für Kommunikationsforschung und Phonetik at Bonn University
is developing a pilot system based on the requirements listed above.

3. USER PROFILE

The information needs of the user of an information system can be identified by means of a user profile questionnaire. A questionnaire of this
kind, to be completed by users in the lexicographical field, has been
devised for the projected word data bank.

The questionnaire, which will be presented at the colloquium, is primarily
intended to investigate users' ideas as to nature and scope of the information which should be available in a lexicon system.

LEXICOGRAPHY IN THE ELECTRONIC AGE
J. Goetschalckx and L. Rolling (editors)
North-Holland Publishing Company
© ECSC, EEC, EAEC, 1982

REPORT ON THE DISCUSSION OF SESSION 1

by

J. M. FROIDCOEUR

In the absence of Mr Boot the first address was given, as originally
programmed by Mr Tombeur, who reported on the colloquium held in Pisa
in May 1981.

This colloquium had been called by the European Science Foundation, and
had brought together representatives of various national research
foundations with a view to coordinating ideas and work on the subject of
the "limits and possibilities for the use of computers in dictionary-
making". A number of projects had been described, giving a broad view of
the current state of lexicography in scientific terms.

The report by Mr Quemada had provided the historical background to this
picture ; lexicography had been born of printing and remained dependent
on this one means of communication ; now that computers were taking over
print, it would be quite natural for lexicography adapt to the new
technology even to the extent of revolutioninzing methods which had become
inadequate on the road to a new science of computer-based dictionaries.
In this context Mr Bratley's report has stressed that such changes would
necessarily bring difficulties at the user stage, but he considered that
the specific abilities of the computer which were far more extensive than
was generally realized were still underused.

The fact was that semantic threshold was not precise, and the questions
raised by Mr Lyons' report as regards principles were an explanation of
the disparity between practice and theory, that is between words and
what they mean.

This disparity was also a reflection of the state of lexicography itself;

41

the confusion which has been demonstrated by this colloquium being all
the more dangerous since the trend was towards further diversification of
dictionaries.

The colloquium proposed that the Foundation should put a stop to incoherence
and waste by no longer subsidizing the publication of texts which were not
recorded for data processing ; that the Foundation should draw up a standart
for the recording of such texts, and finally that the Foundation insist
that researchers be as precise as possible in the description of their
work.

Mr Ennis introduced his address with a threefold question : in the current
economic and scientific context was the development of new publication
formats using advanced technology possible, useful or standardizable ?

The University of Leicester had attempted to discover how to benefit from
progress in this field by studying trends over the last 20 years,
distinguishing between those aspects of the problem which related to the
material itself, those relating to the alpha numeric data and those relating to printed typography, of which the critical factor appeared to be
legibility.

Other things, the first stage of this study had produced a comparative
analysis of 1 000 American riviews considered from the point of view of
their layout. A critical survey had then been made of other experimental
work which showed the limited impact of this research, particularly in
the field of lexicography. Attention had thus been turned to practical
investigation, illustrated by the work of Hardley (1978), which examined
in addition dictionaries and newspapers and showed the critical importance
of the use of space in the legibility of a text, and consequently in its
intelligibility.

With the development of the media under the influence of electronics,
this visual problem had become crucial. In addition the proliferation of
documentation which resulted from this development – both printed and
"grey" outup – made even more pressing the need for standarts to facilitate
communication. Studies carried out over 5 years of publication both by the
ISO in some 60 countries and in Great Britain showed firstly that one third

of countries had no standards and secondly that when such standards existed
they were not always respected because they were too costly or too rigorous.
Quite apart from the weight of cultural habit which needed to be changed, 4
or 5 years would be needed to institute more practical standards : there
was therefore no more to be lost.

The Bonnelex project presented by Mr Lenders and his assistants was the
result of two years comparative study of the various systems carried out
at the instigation of the Federal Ministry with a view to making lexicographical tools more efficient.

This objective involved the harmonization and computerization of the
dictionaries concerned and assessing them on the basis of size, content
vocabulary type and structure, which led to the selection of 11 applications. The details and conclusions of this analysis had been published as
a major report. Compiling the complementary elements of these various lexica
would produce the ideal lexicon, in which the authors distinguished the
mascrostructure, that is the index of entries, and the microstructure,
consisting of nine types of data attributed to each entry and covering
domains of phonetics, morphology, lexicology, syntax and semantics.
Broadly speaking, these elements had been taken mainly from the Condor,
Vari, Systran, Ham, Limas, and Plidis systems.

Implementation of this project had scarcely begun, but it met the requirements for the construction of both a lexicon a data bank which, though
monolingual, were likely to be use both to the lexicographer and to the
translator. The average user would not therefore need to be a computer
expert, nor would he need to be concerned about the internal structure of
the system which despite its complexity would appear completely transparent
to him and would operate in the purest conversational mode.

These papers drew a number of questions but several of these remained
unanswered in the absence of anyone to reply during the demonstration of
the Eurodicautom system which was being held at the same time.

As the result the calls for more light to be cast on the anarchical
situation in lexicography, its divorce from the academic world and the
necessary remedies were merely echoed by other speakers who confirmed the
difficulty of exchanges between researchers and users and more especially
the difficulty of defining the scientific requirements of a computer-based
methodology.

As for the problem of standards, doubt was expressed about the value to
lexicographers of the Mater referred to by the chairman.
Mr Ennis pointed out that his address had not been directed at such a
specific case and referred to the standards organizations, though he had
little hope of standards being produced which would remain compatible with
new technology. It appeared that in any event the norm in question was
so impratical that it was used by no-one. As a result it had recently
been updated by ISO-TC 37 and would shortly be submitted by the Member
States. For the time being it referred only to highly specialized
vocabularies and for a more complete inventory of standards relating to
terminology reference should be made to Infoterm Newsletter N° 4.
In no case was the simple transposition of conventional norms satisfactory
from the technical point of view, though it might appear adequate as regards
exchanges (as in the case of Mark used in libraries).

In view of the multiplicity of sources and objectives with which it was
concerned, the Bonnlex project appeared increasingly to be a purely
theoretical study. Mr Lenders defended himself, however against the
charge of pseudo-scientific obscurantism and explained that on the
contrary before juxtaposing dictionaries it was necessary to identify
all the questions which needed asking beginning, for example, with the
question of what modern lexicographers would consider as a word.

SESSION II
NEW TECHNOLOGIES

Introduction
  C. OITANA

An Attempt to Computerize Dictionary Data
Bases
  M. NAGAO, J. TSUJII, Y. UEDA and
  M. TAKIYAMA

A Hebrew-English Data Processing Dictionary
created On-Line
  Z. BUSHARIA, I. COHN, S. EYTAN,
  B. HARELI and S. YAGIL

Non-Roman Alphabet Usage in Online
Lexicography Output
  H.J. EHLERS

The Orthophonic Dictionary
  G. LURQUIN

LEXICOGRAPHY IN THE ELECTRONIC AGE
J. Goetschalckx and L. Rolling (editors)
North-Holland Publishing Company
© ECSC, EEC, EAEC, 1982

INTRODUCTION TO SESSION II : NEW TECHNOLOGIES

by C. OITANA, Chairman

At the beginning of the 1960s, when enthusiasm for research on automatic
translation was at its height, the motto was "what man can do, the machine
can do". Today, with greater modesty and accuracy, that motto can be turned
into "what man cannot do, the machine can do".
These are of course, not theoretical propositions but practical principles
in which the concept of possibility or impossibility is strongly influenced
by the cost benefit ratio.

What lexicography is called upon to do now is essentially to emerge from
its absorption with the past, and from its ivory tower in order to concern
itself with the present and the future by becoming the driving force in the
complex pattern of information and communication.

Without the help of modern electronic technology it is not capable of
meeting this challenge, but, a happy coincidence, electronics is now in a
position to meet the challenge to the full, within acceptable time-limits
and at acceptable costs, provided that the difficult problem of achieving
the necessary international organization and cooperation is solved.

Indeed, the present potential of electronic technology derives not so
much from individual discoveries or revolutionary innovations as from
the integration of existing techniques. There is, therefore, an integration of techniques which is only waiting for the integration of data
or information to take place.

If we survey what electronic technology can offer to lexicography today,
we can differentiate, in extremely simplified terms, two stages - a stage
of production or preparation,   and a stage of distribution or use. I
shall first list the services offered in the second stage, because they
are more obvious and easier to apply: fast data-transmission lines and
increasingly dense networks of information systems allow the final user
to put his requests for information to the appropriate file; suitable
message-switching systems direct the questions and replies to their
destination by the shortest or least encumbered route. There are already
systems capable of interpreting questions expressed in natural language
and of addressing them automatically to the most suitable file.
Incoming data can be made directly available to the user in word-processing
on text-processing applications; modern view data techniques make it
possible to receive the same data at home, on one's television screen to
store them and to recall them when required. With regard to the interrogation of on-line dictionaries, it should be pointed out that it is
possible not only to obtain the information on individual lexical headwords by feeding these headwords into the system, but also to obtain the
headwords by feeding into the system, during interrogation, the corresponding definitions or significant elements of them.
I would also point out the ability of modern information retrieval systems
to use the dialogue with the user as feedback for improvements.

The first stage - that of production and preparation - can be subdivided
into two aspects: firstly, collection and processing, and secondly,
management and updating.

Still working backwards, let us first look at the second aspect.
Present-day computer memories are capable of holding enormous masses of
lexicographical data, which can be managed by mini-computers with
dedicated lines on by large computers used on a time-sharing basis. However,
although, the integration of data is now an essential requirement for
lexicography, considerations of economy and convenience in management
and updating make it advisable to use decentralized files linked together
in a network.

I shall not dwell on the fact that an automatic file requires very little time and money to update, since I think this already very well known.

I would like to devote rather more attention to the services which electronics can offer in creating and drawing up lexicons, for these are less well-known and more problematic.

The vocabulary of a language undergoes changes of considerable soci - cultural interest, which no dictionary whether on paper or computerized, can adequately reflect. However, a lexicon entry - if it is not to be draw up "by ear" and therefore highly approximate - must take due account of at least the most important aspects of these changes.

A reliable assessment of the "information content" of a lexicon entry requires a systematic check on **its** effective use, measuring duration diffusion and morpho-semantic variation in both diachronic and synchronic context - checks and measurements which only electronic technology is capable of carrying out.

It is well known that the articles of the major daily newspapers exist in machine-readable form before they exist on paper. On this basis, the computer could carry out a systematic and comparative check at national level on the development of the 'popular' vocabulary used to form and inform public opinion.

Even specialized technical or scientific lexicons are subject to a process of change which is more rapid and far-reaching than is commonly believed. They begin as a 'jargon' in laboraties and design offices, in the form of labels or descriptions with precise meanings. They undergo a first morpho-semantic change - usually lexicographical - at the point when, instead of being merely labels, they become expressions in a text or in the language and a further -usually semantic- change in the popular literature of the field in question.

Provided that the difficult task of organization and coordination were carried out, electronic aids could be used, not only to check, but also to standardize, these lexicons at the international level.

The creation and centralized maintenance of sectorial thesauri, compiled
or partially financed by the Commission of the European Communities, is
an example of what can be done.

Among the stages which follow the initial formation of a lexical corpus,
I shall mention a few typical operations which are easy to carry out with
a computer. From a concise computerized encyclopedic dictionary drawn up
on the basis of uniform criteria, one can construct a thesaurus which
would contain, for each headword, a hierarchical structure with several
levels. From one or more thesauri one can automatically obtain a chart
of the distribution of the headwords in the lexicon around semantic
"condensation nuclei" and show disparities or similarities in the distribution for pairs or groups of languages.

Using an automatic dictionary containing an indication of the morpho-
lexical derivations, it is also possible to draw up a chart of the
derivations of the lexicon within a language or by groups of languages.

I have the impression that linguists, and particularly specialists in
lexicography, no longer have any deep or widespread prejudice against
electronic technology. On the other hand, there is a sense of bewilderment in the face of instruments which elude their control, increasingly
numerous and diverse initiatives and the high costs of applications.
This bewilderment can be dispelled only by a judicious and determined
effort at organization, to which this symposium can contribute.

LEXICOGRAPHY IN THE ELECTRONIC AGE
J. Goetschalckx and L. Rolling (editors)
North-Holland Publishing Company
© ECSC, EEC, EAEC, 1982

AN ATTEMPT TO COMPUTERIZE DICTIONARY DATA BASES

M. Nagao, J. Tsujii, Y. Ueda, M. Takiyama

Department of Electrical Engineering

Kyoto University

Summary

Two dictionary data base systems developed at Kyoto University are
presented in this paper. One is for a Japanese dictionary (Shinmeikai
Kokugojiten, published by Sansei-do) and the other is for an English-
Japanese dictionary (New Concise English-Japanese Dictionary, also
published by Sansei-do). Both are medium-size dictionaries containing
about 60,000 lexical items. This paper discusses two main topics.
The first is the problem of translating large, unformatted linguistic
data. Up to now no serious attempts have been made to solve this problem,
though several systems have been proposed to translate data in a certain
format into another. A universal data translator/verfier, called DTV, has
been developed and used for data translation of the two dictionaries. The
detailed construction of DTV is given. The other topic is the problem of
the data organization appropriate for dictionaries. It is emphasized that
the distinction between 'external structures' and 'internal structures'
is important in a dictionary system. Though the external structures can
be easily managed by general DBMS's, the internal (or linguistic) structures cannot be so well manipulated. Some additional, linguistic are
oriented operations have to be incorporate in dictionary data base
systems with universal DBMS operations. Some examples of applications of
the dictionary systems are also given.

1. INTRODUCTION

The computerization of large general dictionaries is significant for various reasons:

(1) dictionaries are rich sources of reference in the linguistic processings of words, phrases and text. Algorithms for natural language processing should be verified by a large corpus of text data, and plannege dictionaries should therefore be large enough to cover a large vocabulary.

(2) Dictionaries themselves are rich sources, as linguistic corpora. When dictionary data is stored in a data base system the data can be examined by making cross references from various viewpoints. This leads to new discoveries of linguistic facts which are almost impossible to achieve in the conventional printed versions.

(3) Computerized dictionaries have various applications in such areas as language teaching by computer, machine-aided human translation, automatic key word extraction, etc.(3)

We have been engaged in the construction of dictionary data base systems for three years, and have almost completed two such systems, one for a Japanese dictionary (Shinmeikai Kokugojiten, published by Sansei-do) and the other for an English-Japanese dictionary (New Concise English-Japanese Dictionary, also published by Sansei-do). Both are medium-size dictionaries containing 60,000 items. In addition to these two dictionary systems, we are now developing a system for an English dictionary (Longman Dictionary of Contemporary English, published by Longman Publishing Company, England).(4)

Two topics will be discussed in this paper. The first is the problem of data translation, i.e., how to obtain formatted data which are more suitable for computer processing than their printed versions. The second is the problem of data organization, how to organize the formatted data into data base systems. We will also give some examples of applications of these systems.

2. DATA TRANSLATION FROM PRINTED IMAGE TO FORMATTED DATA

We decided to input the dictionary contents more or less as printed, and to translate them into certain formatted structures by computer programs rather than by hand.

Ordinary dictionaries usually contain various types of information. In the English-Japanese dictionary, for example, the description consists of:

1. parts of speech
2. inflected forms
3. pronunciations
4. derivatives
5. compounds
6. translation equivalents in Japanese (Usually several equivalents exist, correspond to different aspects of meaning of the entry word)
7. idioms and their translations
8. typical usages and their translations
9. antonyms and synonyms
etc.

An entry may have several different parts of speech (homograms) and for each part of speech the other information 2-9 is described (even the pronunciation may change depending on the part of speech). 1 and 7, 8 and 9 are usually attached to one of the translation equivalents (see Fig.1).

In this way, the description for a dictionary entry acquires a certain structure and the various parts of the dictionary descriptions are related to each other. In the printed dictionaries, these relationships are expressed implicitly in linearized forms. Various ingenious conventions are used to distinguish the relationships, including several kinds of bracket, specially designed symbols (∥, ９ , β etc.) and character types (italic, gothic, etc.). However, in order to utilize these relationships in computer programs, we have first to identify them in the printed versions, and then to reorganize them appropriately so that the programs can manage them effectively. Instead of special symbols or character types, we have to use formatted records, links or pointers to express such relationships explicitly. We call this form of translation from the printed versions to computer-oriented formats <u>data translation</u>.

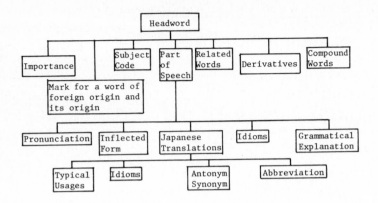

Fig. 1.   Relationships among Lexical Descriptions.

The printed version of a dictionary relies greatly on intuitive human understanding, and comprises many uncertain conventions. Gothic characters, for examples, indicate that the prases so printed are idioms, and italic characters show that the entry words are of foreign origin. In the input to the computer, these different types of characters are indicated by a set of shift codes. Shift codes, together with various special symbols such as (,), (,),ꝗ, etc., provide useful clues for the data translation. However, these codes have to be interpreted differently when they are used in different parts of descriptions For instance, " (" shows the beginning of the pronunciation when it appears immediately after a headword, but when it is used in the middle of an idiomatic expression it shows the beginning of an alternative to the immediately preceding expression. There are, however, many exceptions to such conventions. Moreover, the fact that there may be errors in the input texts makes the translation process more difficult.

If we use an ordinary programming language such as PL/1, the program becomes a collection of tricky mechanisms which is hard to debug. However, data translation of this kind is inevitable whenever we want to process unformatted linguistic data by computer. It would be very useful if we could develop a universal system for data translation (in fact, our system described below has been used not only for dictionary data translations but also for the translations of bibliographic data on ethnology at the National Museum of Ethnology).

2-1 Data Translator/Verifier - DTV

The data translation can be seen as a translation from linearized character strings to certain organized structures. The relationships implicitly
expressed in the linearized strings have to be recovered and explicitly
represented in the organized forms. This is basically a process of
parsing, and has many similarities with parsing of sentences in artificial
or natural languages. It has more similaries with natural language
parsings in the sense that both are defined by many uncertain rules. It
is therefore reasonable to expect that we can apply the same techniques
to this problem as have been found useful in natural language parsing.
Several proposals have been made to define data syntax by using ordinary
BNF notations (or CFG).(1, 2, 5). However, we adopted the ATN (Augmented
Transition Network) instead of CFG for the following reasons:

(1) CFG is essentiall a recognition model. Although it is possible to
    check the syntactical correctness of input texts by CFG rules, we
    need another component to transduce the parsed trees into the format-
    ted records we want. ATN gives us an adequate model of a data trans-
    ducer. It has provisions for setting up intermediate translation
    results in registers ATN registers are called 'buffers' in our
    system) and building them up into a single structure (BUILDQ oper-
    ation in ATN).

(2) CFG provides an adequate framework for managing recursive structures
    such as embedded sentences in natural languages. Though recursive
    structures are also found in dictionary data, they are not so con-
    spicuous. The structures in dictionaries are rather flat. In this
    sense CFG is too powerful to define data syntax of dictionaries.

(3) ATN provides a more procedural framwork than CFG. Because a CFG-based
    system assumes a general algorithm which applies the rules to the
    input text, the user who defines the rules cannot control the algo-
    rithm. This is a fatal disadvantage of CFG whenever the input text
    contains many input errors. It an input error is encountered during
    the translation process a CFG system fails to produce a parsed tree.
    The system or the human user has then to trace back the whole process
    to find the input error which has caused the failure. This is a
    formidable task.

2-2 Definition of Rules, Codes, Buffers and Files

On the basis of an ATN model we produced a modified version for data
translation. In this section we will explain the detailed syntax for
the DTV (the formal definition of the DVT syntax is given in (8)).

(A) Definition of Codes

In the case of syntactical analyses of natural language sentences, the basic units are parts of speech of individual words
or individual words themselves. Special checking functions such
as CAT and WORD are prepared in the original ATN model. On the
other hand, in the case of data translation, the basic units are
individual characters.

A restricted set of characters such as the character set defined
by ISO or ASCII is used and is sufficient for ordinary computer
applications. However, when we want to process real documents or
linguistic data such as dictionaries we need a much richer set of
characters. Although in principle a single type of bracket is
sufficient to express tree-like structures, several different
sorts of bracket such as (, [, ((,{ , , etc. are used to identify
different parts of descriptions in the published dictionaries. We
also noted that certain sets of characters, for example, phonetic symbols, appear only in specific positions (pronunciation
in the case of phonetic symbols) in the dictionary descriptions.
If we could identify the scope of the pronunciation parts, we
would not need to have extra sets of character codes for phonetic
symbols. We could interpret ordinary ASCII codes in the pronunciation part not as conventional predefined rules.

However, these redundant elements in the descriptions are especially useful for detecting input errors. Whenever we find the
codes for phonetic symbols in positions other than the pronunciation fields, or inversely, when we encounter in the pronunciation fields the codes for characters other than phonetic symbols, the input texts will certaines contain. Since we have over
10,000 different Kanji-(Chinese) characters in Japanese, a
standard code system such as ISO, ASCII etc. is no longer ad-

equate, and a special code system has therefore been developed (JIS Japanese Industrial Standard). The code system assigns a 2-byte code to each character. We have 752 extra codes which are not pre-defined by JIS and to which the user can assign arbitrary characters. Various types of brackets, shift code, phonetic symbols etc. have been defined by using these extra codes. Because each character, including alpha-numeric, Kanji, specifi-cally designed symbols, shift codes etc., corresponds to a.2 byte code, we can assign a decimal number to each character by inter-preting the 2.byte code as an integer representation. By using this decimal number notation, we can define arbitrary subsets of characters, as shown in Fig. 2. These subsets of characters play the same role in the data translation as the syntactical categories for sentence analysis. Note that a character is allowed to belong to more than one character set.

```
ALPHA-SMALL   =  9057 -  9082
ALPHA-LARGE   =  9025 -  9050
ALPHA         = ALPHA-SMALL, ALPHA-LARGE
KANJI         = 12321 - 20554
SHIFT-GOTHIC  = 10273
```

Note : The lower case alphabet characters are defined as the decimal numbers between 9057 and 9087. The al-phabet characters are defined as the union of ALPHA-SMALL and ALPHA-LARGE.

Fig. 2.   Code Definition by Decimal Numbers.

(B) Definition of Rules

A rule of DTV is defined by a triplet as:

(condition   action   next-state).

The condition part is specified by using the code sets defined in (A). Two forms of specifications are possible.

1. < subset-1,..., subset-n >
2. (subset-1,..., subset-n)

The first notation means that the characters in the specified subsets should appear in this order. The second is the notation for specifying OR-condition, that is, a character in one of the specified subsets should appear. Arbitrary combinations of these two bracketing notations are allowed such as

$$< \; (\; < \; >) \; (\quad) \; > .$$

The action part, which will be carried out when the condition parts are satisfied, are described by using a set of built-in functions. These are the functions for manipulating buffers and files. Some examples of such built-in functions are shown in Table 1. Several actions can be specified and they will be executed in sequence.

The next-state specifies the state to which the control is to be transferred after the current rule is applied. A typical state-diagram is shown in Fig. 3.

(C) Definition of Buffers and Files
We can define arbitrary numbers of buffers with various sizes as follows.

BUF-NAME	SIZE(BYTE)	IF-OVERFLOW-STATE
SPELLING	40	SPELL-ERROR
IDIOM	30	IDIOM-EXPAND
.	.	.
.	.	.
.	.	.

One typical input error is the omission of delimiters, which can cause serious problems in data translation. Various characters function as delimiters, such as shift codes, several types of bracket, etc., and are used in pairs (right v: left bracket, shift-in v: shiftout etc.) to delimit the scope of specific data fields. When one of the pair is missing two situations can occur: the buffers corresponding to the fields may overflow or illegal characters for the fields may be scanned.

The latter case can be easily detected because no transition rules are defined for such characters. DTV puts a message to the error message file, which identifies the position at which the

Function	Argument	Result
WRITE	*[-number] BUF(Buf-name)	the currently scanned character(or the 'number' preceding chracter) is witten in the buffer.
	RECNO BUF(Buf-name)	the ID number of the current input record is written in the buffer.
	PTR BUF(Buf-name)	the position of the scanned character in the input record is written in the buffer.
	'arbitrary character string' BUF(Buf-name)	the specified character string is written in the buffer.
	BUF(Buf-name) FILE(File-name)	the content of the buffer is written out to the external file.
	⋮	
MERGE	BUF(Buf-name1,...., Buf-name n) BUF(Buf-name)	the contents of the n buffers are merged into a single buffer specified by the second arguement.
CLEAR	CTR(Counter-name) or BUF(Buf-name)	the counter is cleared to 0 or the buffer is cleared by blank characters.
ADD	CTR(Counter-name) Number	the counter is counted up by the number.

Table 1. Built-in Functions in DTV.

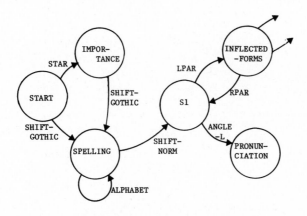

Fig. 3. Typical State-Diagram.

illegal character is found. The former case is rather more
difficult. Checking overflow conditions by rules makes the whole
definition very clumsy. We can specify in the definition of a
buffer the state to which the control makes a transition if the
buffer overflows. In that state a number of error messages is
printed out.

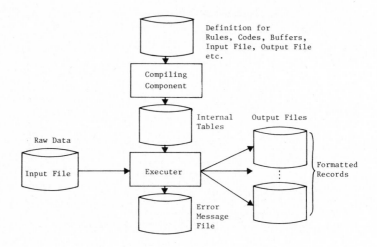

Fig. 4.   Overall Construction of DTV.

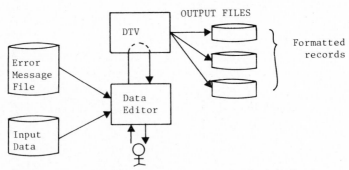

Note : Data Editor output an input record with the corre-
       sponding error message.   The human proofreader can
       easily recognize the input error and revise it.   After
       the revision, he/she can check whether the input record
       contain no more errors, by calling the DTV.

Fig. 5.   Data Editor Accompanied by DTV.

2-3 System Configuration

Fig. 4 shows the overall construction of DTV. With the compiling component the definitions of codes, buffers, files, formats of input and output and translation rules are compiled into several internal tables. On the basis of these tables, the executer scans the input characters from the input file one by one and applies the rules. During execution the system will report various error messages such as 'buffer overflow', 'illegal characters' etc. to the error message files. Because the detailed information, such as the position of the error in the input text, is associated with these messages, human proofreaders can easily recognize the input errors.

A flexible editor has been developed for correcting input errors. As this editor has a special command to call DTV the reviser can check the data syntax immediately after the correction (see Fig.5).

2-4 Experience with DTV

We used DTV for data translation of the English-Japanese dictionary. About 500 rules and 150 states were necessary to manage an exceptional description format of the dictionary. Because DTV has to scan and check every input character and because the dictionary consists of 6,500,000 characters, the whole process was very time-consuming (it took about 130 minutes to translate the whole dictionary by FACOM M200 at Kyoto University Computer Center).

In order to show the effectiveness of DTV, Table 2 presents the input errors detected in the initial input. Some can be corrected automatically only by augmenting DTV rules. Moreover, the data editor accompanied by DTV was so effective that all of the detected errors were completely removed by 3 man-mnths of work. However, DTV is capable mainly of checking the consistency of delimiting characters. There still remain a lot of input errors in the text, such as wrong spellings of words. The detection ofsuch input erros requires a certain semantic knowledge and cannot easily be done by DTV rules. A human proofreader has to do this. But while human proofreaders can

easily recognize these errors, they tend to overlook errors such as
omissions of delimiting characters. Effective co-operation between
man and machine seems therefore to be indispensable for the correction of errors in large linguistic corpora such as dictionaries.

Error Type	Explanations	Frequencies	
Missings of shift codes	Shift-out codes (the code for normal characters) are often missing.	792	
Confusions of similar characters	The phonetic symbol '3' is, for example, often confused with the number character 3.	5434	**
Fluctuations in character sequences	Certain functional character sequences can express a same thing. It is impossible to standardize them in the case that several key punchers work in parallel.	1166	*
Exceptional formats which were not expected beforehand	The description formats for acronyms, for example, are quite different from those of ordinary words.	550	*
Misunderstandings of key punchers	Though the key punchers consented to several standard ization rules for input, some of them misunderstood them.	1298	*
Miscellaneous errors		1276	
Total		10516	

Note 1: * shows that the errors of that type can be automatically
corrected only by augmenting DTV rules.
** shows that some of them can be corrected automatically
by augmenting DTV rules.
Note 2: The exceptional format errors are not input errors in a
true sense.

Table 2. Error Frequencies in the Initial Data.

Another point of interest is the relation between DTV and data entry
systems. Though our attempt here is highly batch-oriented, it will be
necessary in future to consider interactive data entry systems as a
means augment the dictionary data. An ordinary data entry system

usually guides the user as to what he should input next, by printing prompting messages such as 'input the next word', 'input the part of speech of the word', etc. However, when the input data have a wide variety of description format like these dictionaries, such a system becomes impracticable. Though some guidance by the entry system is necessary, it is natural for the user to whish to input data arbitranily. The data entry system should be capable of translating the texts into a certain formatted structure, and of checking the existence of input errors. Our data editor accompanied by the DTV is the first step toward developing such a data entry system.

3. DATA BASE SYSTEMS FOR DICTIONARIES

A dictionary description has a certain hierarchical structure, such as that previously shown in Fig. 1. such a structure can be well represented by a framework provided by ordinary DBMS's, since

it is merely a simple tree structure. However, the primitive data (or records) from which the whole structure is built have certain internal structures of their own. For example, idioms or typical usages in the English-Japanese dictionary are the primitive records which are located at certain fixed positions in the whole structure and are related to the other records such as translation equivalents, headwords etc. They can be accessed as basic units through usual DBMS operations. At the same time, they are composite expressions which consist of serveral component words. These component words are related to each other inside the idioms. We call such structures inside the primitive records 'internal structures' (see Fig. 6). In other words, the primitive records in a dictionary data base system are not primitive in the usual DBMS sense.

Though the external structures among primitive records can be managed by an ordinary DBMS, the internal linguistic structure cannot be so well manipulated. Moreover, what we want to do on the dictionary data base systems is concerned not only with external structures, but also in many cases, with their internal linguistic structures. Some addtional operations have to be incorporated with the usual DBMS operations in   to treat such mixed structures.

3-1 Japanese Dictionary Data base

The first thing we had to do was to incorporate a morpho/graphemic level of processing. Because Japanese has a very peculiar method of writing special techniques were required to utilize the dictionary consultation system arose from the fact that Japanese dictionary entries usually have more than one spelling. There are basically two different forms, Kana-spellings (using Japanese phonetic symbols) and Kanji-spellings (using ide ographs - Chinese characters). Corresponding to these two spellings, we have two types of printed dictionaries, one for Kana and the other for Kanji spellings. However, in actual sentences, there often appear mixed forms of these two spellings. (See Fig. 7). Though these mixed forms do not appear in

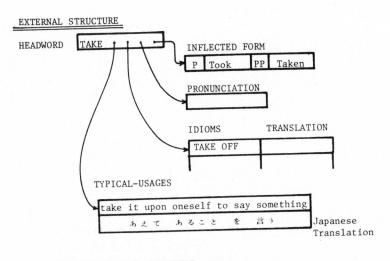

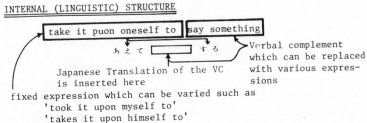

Fig. 6. External Structure and Internal Structure in a Dictionary Data.

Kanji-Spelling	Kana-Spelling	Mixed Spelling	Meaning
繰 返 す	くりかえす	く り 返 す	to Repeat
繰 り 返 す		繰 か え す	
		繰りかえす	

Fig. 7. Various Spellings of a Single Word.

the ordinary, printed dictionaries of both types, human readers are able to convert them into one of the two basic spellings. In a computerized dictionary system, a certain graphemic level of processing is necessary to allow the system to be consulting from these mixed forms.

In our system, the intermediate indexing structures are provided for both Kana and Kanji-spellings (Fig.8). The dotted line shows the access path for Kana-spellings and the bold line for Kanji-spellings. The relationships among GCT, FFCT, SCT and IT are illustrated in Fig.9, and the required memory spaces for these structures are given in Table 3..

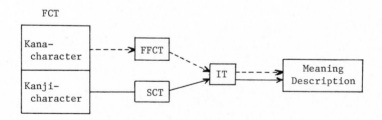

```
FCT : First Character Table
FFCT : First Five Characters Table
SCT : Second Kanji Character Table
IT : Item Table
```

Fig. 8. Intermediate Indexing Structure for Japanese Dictionary.

Mixed spellings are normalized into one of these basic spellings. We
can obtain Kana-spellings from mixed ones by systematically changing
the Kanji-characters in the mixed spellings into corresponding
Kana-strings. However, because each Kanji-character corresponds to
three or four (or more) different Kana-strings (each Kanji-character
has several pronunciations), the resultant Kana-strings have to be
matched against the Kana-spellings in the dictionary. Some example of
retrieval results are shown in Fig. 10.

Another problem is the incorporation of the morphological analysis
component. Because the word inflection system in Japanese is much
richer than in English, the morphological analysis component is
indispensable in the Japanese dictionary system.The morphological
analysis program developed for another of our projects, i.e., the
Machine Translation Project (7), has been incorporated into the
system. The retrieval program contains Japanese inflection rules and
can convert inflectional variants to their infinitive forms. The
rules are almost perfect, and more than 98% inflectional variants can
be converted correctly to their infinitive forms.

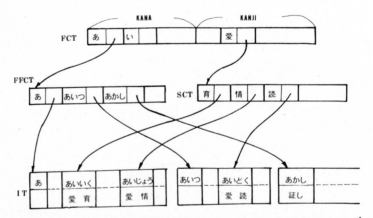

Note : Each record in IT(Item Table) contains a pointer to the
meaning description of the word. IT, FFCT and SCT are blocked
and stored in the secondary memory (disc file). Each block
contains 50 records. A SCT record contains a set of Kanji-
characters which follow the same (first) Kanji-character.

Fig. 9. Relationships among FCT, FFCT, SCT and IT.

Index Table	Storage Requirement
FCT	24　KB
FFCT	18.6 KB
SCT	700　KB
I T	4.3 MB

Table 3.　Required Memory Space.

(1) Input spelling by KANA-charecter

KANAMOJI = あいじょう ◄─────── Input

あい　じょう　　　　　　　　　　　　　　愛情 ◄─ Retrieved entry

≡－ジャウ｛愛情｝　　こ自分の身近に有る人や、自分より弱い
何とか（尽く）してあげたいと思う心。「母（へ）の一」こ異性
でなければと思い、親しむ心。「一を打ち明ける」

あい　じょう　　　　　　　　　　　　　　愛嬢 ◄─ Retrieved entry

≡－シャウ｛愛嬢｝　　かわいい（と思っている）娘。まなむす

Note : Two entries are retrieved because they have the
the same spelling.

(2) Input spelling by a Mixed-spelling

KANJI = あい色 ◄───────── input

ONKUNI BL USED
色　しき；じき；しょく；いろ；
あいしき
NOT FOUND IN KOMOKUTBL
あいじき
NOT FOUND IN KOMOKUTBL
あいしょく
NOT FOUND IN KOMOKUTBL
あいいろ
KOMOKUSU =　　　　　　1；
MATCHING_KOMOKUSU=　　　　1；
あい　いろ　　　　　　　　　　藍色

The Kanji-character '色' is
replaced systematically by its
corresponding KANA-strings.

An entry which has the
the mixed-spelling is
found.

Fig. 10.　Retrieval Results of Japanese Dictionary.

3-2 English-Japanese Dictionary Data Base

The morpho/graphemic processing required for the utilization of this dictionary is much simpler than for the Japanese dictionary. Because most of the derivatives are adopted in the dictionary as headwords, the processing for derivational suffixes is not necessary. We can retrieve the corresponding lexical entries from their own spellings. To obtain the original word from which the derivative is derived it is only necessary to traverse the external structure (i.e., a record for a derivative always contains a pointer to its original word). Therefore, the current system only recognizes the inflectional suffixes of English so as to convert the inflected forms to their infinitive forms. As for irregularly inflected words, all the inflectional variants are extracted from the dictionary, and are stored in the inverted files (all the headwords are also stored in the inverted files). Some retrieval results are shown in Fig.11.

As we described at the beginning of this section, some linguistic operations have to be incorporated in a dictionary data base system in addition to the usual operations provided by ordinary DBMS's. Morpho/graphemic processing is one such operation. Another example

1) An Example of Regularly Inflected Words

ARMIES ←——— input word

a r · m y

重要度	2	←— importance
品詞	名	←—P.O.S.
発音	ármi ／ á:－	pronunciation
語義1	軍隊；陸軍．≥	Japanse translations
2	団体．	
3	【虫】ヨトウムシ≤群をなして作物を害する≥．	
4	男子の名．	
用例＊	an ～ of ants	
	アリの大群．	usage example

73 MSEC USED.

2) An Example of Irregularly Inflected Words

ASHMEN ←——— input word

a s h · m a n

品詞	名	← P.O.S.
発音	æ ʃ m æ n	← pronunciation
語変	pl.‡ーmen [－men]	
語義	《米》ごみ取り人夫．清掃員．	

39 MSEC USED.   Japanese translation

Fig. 11. Retrieval Results of Inflected Variants.

is the retrieval of 'similar' expressions. The English-Japanese dictionary contains English idioms and their translations, and typical usages of each word and their translations. The effective utilization of these by computer is a very interesting topic, because this is one of the essential "raisons d'efre" of the dictionary. We have been developing some elementary programs to utilize the idioms in the dictionary. The system can retrieve idioms or usages which bear certain similarities to the input phrases. For example, when the user inputs a sentence such as 'He wore a long face' the system retrieves the idiom 'pull (make, wear) a long face' which has the highest similarity with the input. In this process, all of the words in the input are reduced to their infinitive forms (in this case, 'wore' is reduced to 'wear'), and all of the idioms and typical usages in the individual word entries are retrieved for the comparison with the input phrases. The comparison is currently performed as follows:

1. Each word in the retrieved idioms and usages is reduced to its infinitive form.

2. Literal string matching is performed. In the matching process, extra words in the input and retrieved idioms or usages are ignored. Only the order of words is taken into consideration.

3. Similarity value is computed for each idiom and usage.

The expressions with the highest value are printed out. In the current system, the similarity value is determined by a simple formula as

(the number of matched words) / (the number of words in idioms or typical usages).

Some results are shown in Fig. 12. We have to develop a more sophisticated method of computing the similarity value. Especially, information about semantic relationships among words must be taken into consideration. Computerized thesauri will be useful. Certain words in idioms and usages the role of variables. 'Oneself' in such a idiom as 'be a law unto oneself' is regarded as a variable, and should be able to be matched with 'myself', 'himself' etc. 'Person' in 'take a person about a town' should

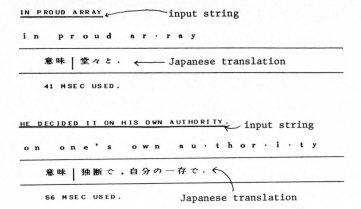

Fig. 12.　Retrieval Results of Similar Expressions.

file HEADWORD

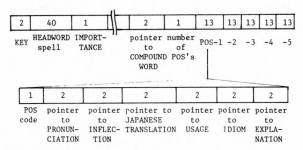

NOTE: 1) Numbers in boxes are numbers of CHARACTERs.
(1 CHARACTER = 2 bytes)

2) For example, 'pointer to JAPANESE TRANSLATION'
stands for the pair illustrated below.

file JAPANESE-TRANSLATION

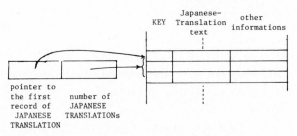

Fig. 13.　Examples of Formatted Records.

be matched with any person, such as John, he, and so on. In the latter
case, 'town' can also be replaced by many other words which have certain
semantic features in common, for example, 'place'. We are now designing
such semantically guided pattern matchings.

3-3 Data Structure for English-Japanese Dictionary Data Base

The formats of records which are obtained as the result of data
translation are shown in Fig. 13. The records in these formats
contain a large number of extra spaces, because they are of fixed
length and because, on the other hand, the length of the descriptions
in the dictionary varies greatly, depending on individual words. The
necessary memory size for these records amounts to 150 Mbyte, and we
have reorganized them with a view to reducing the memory size. The
actual data organization is shown in Fig. 14, in which the required
memory size is 35 Mbyte. All kinds of text data of variable length
are maintained in the same place (the Text Data File) in this organization.

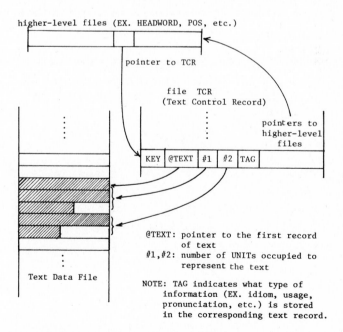

Fig. 14. Data Structure of English-Japanese Dictionary.

The information which is necessary for managing the records in the
Text Data File is contained in a TCR. A TCR consists of a pointer to
the corresponding text rec ord, the number of occupied text data
records, a tag field, etc. The tag field indicates what kind of text
data is stored in the record. Arbitrary numbers of text data can be
linked together. The memory efficiency of this data structure is
obvious. Moreover, the average time for retrieving and displaying
the result on the screen is 320 msec. About half of the time is spent
on the display control (about 120 msec - 160 msec, depending on the
data size). To access a headword from its spelling requires only 3
msec. The remainder is spent on retrieving the other records such as
pronunciation, P.O.S. idioms, etc.

4. CONCLUDING REMARKS

All the systems described in this paper have been implemented on a
FACOM M-200 (Kyoto University Computing Center), mostly using PL/1.
As the computing center introduced an MSS (Mass Storage System) and
began the service last summer, these systems are to be maintained on
it. Several other groups in our university, especially a research
group of the Faculty of Leterature, are very interested in utilizing
the dictionary systems for their own researches. A set of utility
programs has already been developed. We hope that such a joint effort
between computer scientists and linguists will lead us to new,
fruitful research areas.

ACKNOWLEDGEMENT

We would like to thank the other members of Prof. Nagao's laboratory,
and in particular, Mr. Yukinori YAMAMOTO for his efforts in implementing the first version of DTV and for his valuable suggestions the
data organization of the Japanese dictionary data base.

REFERENCES

(1) Fry, J.P., Frank, R.L. et. al. : A Developmental Model for Data Translation, ACM SIGFIDET Workshop on Data Description and Access, 1972.

(2) Fry, J.P., Smith, D.P. et. al. : An Approach to Stored Data Definition and Translation, ACM SIGFIDET Workshop on Data Description and ccess, 1972.

(3) Michiels, A., Moulin, A., Mullenders, J., Noel, J. : Exploiting the Longman Computer Files for MT Lexicograhy and other Purposes, Technical Report, University of Liège, Belgium.

(4) Michiels, A., Moulin, A., Noel, J. : Working with LDOCE, Technical Report, University of Liège, Belgium.

(5) Liu, S., Heller, J. : A Record-Oriented, Grammar-Driven Data Translation Model, ACM SIGFIDET Workshop on Data Description, Access and Control, 1974.

(6) Nagao, M. Tsujii, J. : Data Structure of a Large Japanese Dictionary and Morphological Analys   is by Using It, Journal of Information Processing Society of Japan, Vol. 19, No. 6, in Japanese.

(7) Nagao, M., Tsujii, J., et. al. : A Machine Translation System from Japanese into English, Proceedings of the 8th International Conference on Computational Linguistics, 1980

(8) Ueda, Y. : A Study for an English-Japanese Dictionary Data Base, BS THesis, Kyoto University, 1980, in Japanese.

LEXICOGRAPHY IN THE ELECTRONIC AGE
J. Goetschalckx and L. Rolling (editors)
North-Holland Publishing Company
© ECSC, EEC, EAEC, 1982

A HEBREW-ENGLISH DATA PROCESSING DICTIONARY CREATED ON-LINE

Authors:

Z. Busharia,	The Academy of the Hebrew Language	(Z.B.)
I. Cohn,	Ministry of Defence	(I.C.)
E. Eytan,	The Academy of the Hebrew Language	(E.E.)
B. Hareli,	Chairman of the Committee	(B.H.)
S. Yagil,	I.B.M. Israel Ltd.	(S.Y.)

Summary

The authors are members of a committee charged with establishing a Hebrew-English data processing dictionary, based primarily on the I.S.O.'s extensive English-French vocabulary. The committee is sponsored by the Israel Institute of Standardization (I.I.S.) and the Academy of the Hebrew Language. In order to expedite the committee's work, a time-shared,text processing system has been developed, using bilingual Hebrew-English screen terminals and a laser printer. The committee's decisions are immediately keyed into a terminal located in the conference room, and are stored in a computer file, available for current updating and improving, leading up to the dictionary's edition.

Particular features of the Hebrew language are: Special script, right -to-left writing, diacritical marks for vowels, frequent dual spelling. Therefore special programs provide line inversion, bilingual indexing, and partial vocalization. These features are illustrated in the paper.

The system may be of interest to those concerned with automated creation of multilingual, multiscript dictionaries and glossaries, involving numerous diacritical marks and/or non-Latin scripts such as Greek, Arabic or Russian.

(S.Y.)

Contents:

1. INTRODUCTION

The modern Hebrew language is the major official language of the State of Israel.   It was revived some 70 years ago, after lying dormant for many centuries, while serving for religious and literary purposes only, somewhat like Latin, Ancient Greek, Sanskrit, etc.

Israel's Academy of the Hebrew language has assumed the task of introducing the necessary technological terminology into the revived language.

Lately the subject of Terms and Definitions has in many countries become part of standardization activities.   Accordingly the International Standard Institute (I.S.O.) is issuing the International Standard No.2382 called "Data Processing Vocabulary".

Sample

ISO 2382/III-1976 (E/F)

03.01.07
delay line
A line or network designed to introduce a desired delay in the transmission of a *signal*.

03.01.07
ligne de retard
Ligne ou réseau conçu pour introduire un cer la transmission d'un *signal*.

03.01.08
pulse
impulse
A variation in the value of a magnitude, short in relation to the time schedule of interest, the final value being the same as the initial value.

03.01.08
impulsion
Variation de la valeur d'une grandeur, brève l'échelle de temps considérée, la valeur finale la valeur initiale.

In Israel the Israel Institute of Standardization and the Academy of the Hebrew Language have jointly undertaken to coin the Hebrew data processing terminology, having chosen as a basis the English version of the said standard.

Thus, these two organizations have formed a Standardization Committee for this subject , with representatives from universities, suppliers, and users actively participating, among them the authors of this paper.

2. HEBREW LANGUAGE FEATURES

2.1 - General

There are a number of characteristics distinguishing the Hebrew lang-

uage from Indo-European and other languages and posing special problems
for machine treatment.   For purpose of illustration, in this section the
Hebrew word "kotev" is used, meaning "pole".

2.2 - Script

Hebrew script is completely different from Latin script.   It contains 27 letters, without the duplicity of upper and lower case.   There
exists ample typing and printing equipment for Hebrew script, but for computer use the letters of the Hebrew alphabet have to be represented by the
26 letters of the Latin alphabet, in the same order.   The one surplus
Hebrew letter (the first one) is in most computers represented by the '&'
sign.

Example (the first letters):   א ב ג ד ה ה ו ז ח ט י

                                         I H G F E D C B A &

2.3 - Direction

Hebrew writing runs from right to left, excluding the numbers. Since
standard input equipment, such as display terminals, is built left-to-
right, the transliterated texts have to be inverted, line by line, for
Hebrew use.   Any numbers or Latin-lettered words within the line have, of
course, to be excluded from the inversion.

Example: Original Hebrew: ק ו ט ב   ("kotev")
                             ⟵
             Transliterated: A H E W
                                 ⟵
             Inverted in machine: W E H A
                                   ⟶

2.4 - Vocalization

Hebrew texts and words appear in either of two forms:

(A) Unvocalized, i.e. they show the consonants, with certain vowels
represented by additional characters inserted between the consonants; this
is called "plene" spelling, and is the form used in everyday texts.

Example: ק ו ט ב

(B) Vocalized, i.e. most characters represent the consonants only, and
are supplemented by diacritical marks or signs (diacritics) for the vowels.
Many of the marks are simple dots.   The marks are placed below, within, or
above the characters.

This spelling form is called "defective" spelling.

Vocalization, with the ensuing defective spelling, is mostly used for
special purposes, such as the Bible and other religious books, poetry,
printing for children and immigrants, dictionaries, and occasionally for

particularly difficult words.

    Example: ק ֹ ט ב

2.5 - Dual spelling

Thus, many words (roughly a fifth) permit dual or even triple spelling, thereby presenting occasional puzzles for some of the users of the
Hebrew language. The remaining words have one unitary spelling only.

    Example, taken from general-purpose dictionary:

       Pole ....   ק ֹ ט ב , ק ו ט ב
                             (kotv)   (ktv)
                         (= plene) (=defective)

It should be noted that even in plene spelling the vowel "e" of
"kotev" is not represented, but must be inferred from the context.

2.6 - Homographs

Another result of unvocalized spelling is a multitude of homographs,
as can easily be understood from the foregoing example. The three-letter
defective "ktv" could also be pronounced "kitev", meaning "he has polariz-
ed".

2.7 - Identification of roots

Various lexical and grammatical elements frequently are prefixed, in-
fixed, and suffixed to the root or stem of the word, as it appears in a
text. E.g. the equivalents of the particles "and", "as", "from", etc.,
are prefixed; other prefixes denote conjugation and tense in verbs; nominal and verbal suffixes express person, gender, number, etc. These af-
fixed elements make the kernel of the word hard to identify.

3. DICTIONARY FEATURES

3.1 - Index

In a dictionary organised by a subject-matter, the alphabetical index is a most important tool, and particularly so in a bilingual or multilingual dictionary. For an efficient index, redundancies have to be el-
iminated, and unique alphabetical access has to be assured. The following paragraphs point to the main considerations, whereas the technical
solutions are dealt with in sec.6.

3.2 - Redundant material

The time lag between inception of the ISO-standard (late 60's to early 70's) and the anticipated publication of the Hebrew-English Data-Processing Dictionary (mid 80's) produce some redundancy due to obsolescence,

triviality, and over-specialization.   In these cases the committee,after careful deliberation, has not given the English term a Hebrew translation, but an indicative sign ("....") instead.

3.3 - Auxiliary words

Auxiliary and explanatory words - such as "to" preceding English in-finitives, or "(abbreviation)" and "(deprecated)" - have been marked for exclusion from the alphabetical index by enclosing them in the sign " | ". This is done during "proof-reading" on the terminal, a method easier and cheaper than programmed determination of appropriate cases.

3.4 - Synonyms

In both languages, synonyms have frequently to be admitted, although in technical language uniqueness of term is desirable.   Synonyms (e.g. tag, label) are listed under the same item number, and therefore do not present any technical problem.

3.5 - Homonyms

Homonyms, listed under separate, but sequential item numbers, have been given a "private" serial number, occupying the lemma's leading two positions.   They,of course,have to be suppressed from the leading column of the alphabetical index, in order to place the lemma proper in its cor-rect alphabetical position.   In the quotation column, however, the serial number is retained, e.g.

Are................... Who are you? 04.05.07
Automation ....   1 Automation 01.01.05
                           2 Automation 01.01.06

Frequent classes of homonyms are: Noun and verb ("copy"), action and method ("data processing"), and process and object ("documentation").

3.6 - Dual (plene and defective) spelling

The inserted characters - representing vowels - in plene spelling frequently alter the term's position in precise alphabetical sequencing. For easy use of the alphabetical index, both spellings must therefore be included.   In our dictionary, only the lemmata, i.e. the terms themselves are vocalized, and therefore printed in defective spelling.   In cases of dual spelling (about 20%), the unvocalised term in plene spelling is added to the masterfile as an extra line, preceding the one in defective spell-ing.   This extra line is not printed in the dictionary, but is used for the index only, as explained in sec.6.

4. SYSTEM DESCRIPTION

4.1 - General

The system software comprises the following main parts:

Data files: Masterfiles, one for each chapter.

                Concatenated files for comprehensive index.

                Print files.

Private programs: Bi-lingual editor.

                Vocalization printer.

                Page editor (text processor).

                Index writer.

Installation services as described in section "The on-line system" (5.1).

4.2 - Masterfile

The masterfile is screen-oriented, and of simple, unsophisticated type, every line being one technical record.   Each chapter contains about a hundred items.

Sample

```
01.03.02                                    01.03.02|A item number
01.03.02                              מעבד נתונים  |◊ lemma (unitary)
DATA PROCESSOR                                      |◊ (contd.)
PROCESSOR              מכשיר המבצע עיבוד נתונים, כגון: מכונת |D definition
                      חישוב, ציוד לעירוד כרטיסים מנוקבים |D     "
                                           או מחשב. |D     "
                   הערה: מעבד הנתונים אינו כולל בהכרח מעבד |_ note
                             המוגדר בפריט 01.03.50. |_     "


01.03.03                                    01.03.03|A item number
01.03.03                              מכונת חישוב |a lemma (plene)
                                      מכונת חשוב |◊ lemma (def.)
CALCULATOR
                     מעבד נתונים לפעולות מתימטיות, המצריך |D definition
                             השתתפות מתמדת של אדם. |D     "
                       הערה: ראה הערה בפריט 01.03.04. |_ note
```

4.3 - Items

Each item is identified by a 6-digit, 3-level item number, (04.07.02 e.g.).   The item could be considered a logical record, though technically it is not accessible as such, for lack of a proper record key.

The item is composed of a varying number of "lines" of equal size (72 bytes or characters).   The lines are of different "types", such as: "Item number", "Term", "Definition", "Example", "Notes", etc.   The "type" is expressed by a control character in position No. 1, constituting the hinge of the entire program logic.

4.4 - Lines

The lines are bilingual, the left side allotted to the English term, and the right side to Hebrew in all the "types". Irrespective of side, however, the choice of font (English or Hebrew) and of direction, is the main task of the bilingual editor.

4.5 - Programs

(A) The bilingual editor, written in Assembly language, works under EDGAR with all its text-processing capabilities, as explained in sec.5.

(B) The page editor, written in PL/I language, is of standard type, with the added feature of controlling page ejection by dictionary logic. This logic requires, that at page bottom no new item is started, unless there is sufficient room for item number, all lemma lines, and at least the first definition line.

(C) The remaining private programs - Vocalization printer and Index writer - are described in secs. 7 and 6 respectively.

5. TECHNOLOGIES APPLIED

5.1 - The on-line system

The system runs on an IBM 370/158 computer, under the VM/CMS time sharing system, with the DES editor (Display Editing System, also known as EDGAR).

The editor serves for entering, editing, modifying, storing, and deleting text, using bilingual Hebrew-English screen terminals (models 3277 and 3278).

Printing is done on an IBM 3800 Laser Printer, which allows generation of arbitrary character sets.

Utilizing this capability, a full bilingual character set has been prepared, consisting of upper and lower case English letters, full Hebrew script, including all diacritical marks, besides of the 10 digits and some special characters.

It is noteworthy that character set for other scripts, such as Arabic and Cyrillic, have also been prepared.

5.2 - Operation

(A) Of the 14 chapters of I.S.O.'s Data Processing Vocabulary so far published, seven have by now been keyed and stored, each chapter in a seperate file. The files contain every English term, together with a proposed initial Hebrew translation of the term and of its definition.

(B) Whenever the committee convenes, a terminal is placed in the conference room.   The chapter under discussion is fetched from storage and
displayed on the screen.   The committee's decisions, i.e. new Hebrew
terms and their definitions, are immediately entered and stored, replacing
the initial existing ones.

(C) The editor's search feature allows location of all occurences of
any English or Hebrew word in the dictionary, whenever this is required
for the committee's deliberations.

(D) At the session's end, the modified version of the chapter discussed is submitted for printing on the central Laser Printer.   The printout
is usually available after several hours, sometimes within an hour, depending on the computer's current workload.

(E) Whenever required, an up-to-date version of the alphabetical index (Hebrew and English) can be obtained with the same ease.   This serves
as a powerful tool for detection of technical errors in spelling and in
system grammar.

(F) The printout, together with the index, is then taken for proofreading and addition of special technical features described later in this
paper.   The file is processed on the terminal, and an updated version of
the printout made ready for the committee's next session.

(G) The final edition of the dictionary is printed on the laser printer, with the lemmata in traditional Hebrew script.

6. THE INDEX WRITER

6.1 - General

The purpose of the index feature is to allow alphabetic search, in
both languages, for complete lemmata or for individual words contained in
them.   The bulk of the dictionary text, such as definitions, examples,
notes, as well as section headings, are not indexed.   The index is printed
without diacritics.

6.2 - Format

The index is produced in two versions, automatically following each
other: First in Hebrew and second in English.   Each of the two versions
is composed of three columns, with no diacritical marks added:

(A) Leading column, showing single words in alphabetical order; the
words are in defective spelling;   in cases of dual spelling, the same word

in plene spelling appears in another line.

(B) <u>Quotation column</u>, showing the complete term or terms - in plene spelling - in which the leading word is contained.

(C) <u>Number column</u>, showing the item number for each term quoted.

Sample

Item Number	Quotation (Complete term)	Leading word	
01.02.04..	.............................גדיר	גדיר	
01.03.07..	....................מחשב בו-זמני	בו-זמני	
01.06.06..	.....................חקר ביצועים	ביצועים	(plene)
01.06.05..	...................בעזרת מחשב...	בעזרת	
01.01.02..	...........(מידע (נעיבוד נתונים	עיבוד	
01.06.06..	.....................חקר בצועים	בצועים	(defective)
01.06.08..	.....................בקרה מספרית	בקרה	
01.06.08..	......................בקרה נומרית		
01.03.24..	................בקרה סדרתית עוקבת		
01.01.08..	..........הנדסת בקרה אוטומטית		
ADMINISTRATIVE	ADMINISTRATIVE DATA PROCESSING..................01.06.04		
ADP	ADP (ABBREVIATION)............................01.01.09		
	ADP (ABBREVIATION)............................01.01.10		
ALGORITHM	ALGORITHM.......................................01.04.10		
ANALOG	ANALOG..01.02.07		
	ANALOG COMPUTER.................................01.03.13		
ANALYSIS	OPERATIONS ANALYSIS...........................01.06.06		

6.3 - Processing

(A) Word-Records - For each word (unless marked for exclusion by the "|" sign) in each term in each language - and in Hebrew for each spelling - a separate record is created. The record contains the three elements just described.

(B) Sorting - At the end of the file or the chapter, a standard sort-routine is called, which alphabetically sequences the records, for each language, in the order mentioned: word, term, number.

(C) Editing and Printing - On return from the sort routine processing is concluded by printing the sorted records line by line, suppressing repeated lemmata in the leading column, and with addition of page headings and headings for leading letters.

6.4 - Dual spelling

(A) This paragraph deals with the minority of lemmata in dual spelling. In the dictionary body, only the lemmata (terms) are to appear in

defective spelling, and as such each of their individual words must appear
in the index.   If, however, they are looked up from an ordinary text, they
must be found in plene spelling.   To make the quotation column readable
without vowel marks, it must in both cases be taken from the plene masterfile line.   For this purpose, the plene line always precedes the defective one.   Now, each word-record obtains its quotation part (the complete
lemma) from the first masterfile line encountered: Plene or unitary, as
the case may be.   This is then attached to the two different leading
words: plene and defective, and to their common item number.

(B) The transformation of spelling forms is not yet computerized, for
reasons outside the range of this paper.

6.5 - Words to be excluded

This situation has been explained in the section on Dictionary features, 3.3. The index program does not create word-records for words enclosed
in vertical bars ("|"). On the other hand, these words cannot be dismis-
sed from the quotation part, so that only the sign "|" itself is omitted
from the complete term, which is then left-adjusted by the program.

7. VOCALIZATION PRINTER

7.1 - General

The problem of vocalization in Hebrew has already been mentioned in
Secs. 2.4 (vocalisation) and 5.1 (on-line system).   It may be sum-
med up as follows: The lemmata - as opposed to the remaining text - are
to be printed with diacritics added, and in defective spelling.

7.2 - Techniques

Vowel-diacritics can be added to the letters by two techniques:

(A) Special fonts, incorporating a dot within or above the letter.

(B) Marks only, printed in an extra line below the character line.

7.3 - Codes

The application of either technique to each letter appearing in the
masterfile's lemmata is controlled by a code-character attached to the
"target"-letter.   For this purpose, a set of code-characters has been defined, including all digits and a few special characters, not utilised in
the Hebrew lemmata.   The codes are either preceding or following their
target-letter, under parametric choice.   The remaining special characters
are used as usual, except a few substitutions such as turning the '¢' into
a '|'.

7.4 - Fonts

The special fonts include the letters eligible for a dot placed within or above the letter or both, and a few exceptional cases not covered by the above solutions. Altogether there are now 6 fonts:

(A) Regular Hebrew letters without any marks.

(B) Letters with a dot within.

(C) Letters with a dot above.

(D) Letters with a dot within and above.

(E) Letters with exceptional position of marks.

(F) The marks to be printed in the extra line.

7.5 - Line height

The regular character line is printed in pitch 10, i.e. 10 lines per inch. The extra line is printed pitch 15. The alternation of pitch is under program control.

7.6 - Sample print
    (not final)

01.01.11   01.01.11

electronic data processing   עיבוד נתונים אלקטרוני

EDP (abbreviation)   עיבוד נתונים אוטומטי הנעשה באמצעים

אלקטרוניים.

01.01.12   01.01.12

integrated data processing   עיבוד נתונים כלולי

IDP (abbreviation)

7.7 - Example

To illustrate the vocalizing principles used for this dictionary, the Hebrew word for "transmission" has been chosen, which is called "timsoret" (containing the five phonemes "ti-m-so-re-t"). The description, for clarity, is broken down into five phases.

(A) The item as recorded on the magnetic masterfile, printed out without any editing, running from left to right, and in Latin characters only. It shows the Hebrew dual spelling, and the English. Position No.1 shows the lines' control characters, to be omitted from the final dictionary print:

@   Z   N   Q   E   X   Z   (plene)

¢   Z   N   Q   X   Z   NOISSIMSNART   (defective)

(B) The same two lines as displayed and/or printed for the committee's deliberations, and for subsequent improving:

ת מ ס ו ר ת   @ (plene)

TRANSMISSION   ת מ ס ר ת   ¢ (defective)

(C) The Hebrew word, in defective spelling, with vocalization codes:

C @4Z ON 9Q 6X   Z   (defective)

Explanation

C   =   control character for this "type"

@4Z =   "ti" (each of the two codes @ and 4 producing a different dot)

ON =   "m" with "shwa" (pronunciation without vowel)

9Q =   "so"

6X =   "re"

Z   =   "t" pronounced without vowel, but being the last letter left without "shwa"

(D) The result, character by character, as it would appear without re-inversion; this phase is shown for illustration only, since in practice vocalization and re-inversion are executed together:

תּ רָ סֹ מְ תּ   (defective)
———————→

(E) The final result, as printed in the dictionary:

TRANSMISSION   תּ מְ סֹ רָ תּ

LEXICOGRAPHY IN THE ELECTRONIC AGE
J. Goetschalckx and L. Rolling (editors)
North-Holland Publishing Company
© ECSC, EEC, EAEC, 1982

NON ROMAN ALPHABET USAGE
IN ONLINE LEXICOGRAPHY OUTPUT

H. J. Ehlers

Director Corporate Planning,

Ernst Klett, Publishers and Printers

Stuttgart, F. R. Germany

Summary

The standard Roman character set used today in most information media does not answer the strong demand for multi-lingual information transfer. The adaption of computer applications to include all character sets of the main European languages, at least of the official UN languages is essential, but poses problems especially for Arabic or even Chinese. Line printers use formed character sets, and any expansion of it involves replacement or addition, whereas matrix printers, which use dots to form characters, can be adapted more easily to form new symbols within the matrix limitation. Most VDU terminals also use the matrix method. Some small diacritics cannot be handled adequately as yet. Sophisticated photocomposition devices cover many different character sets, but alone are not suitable for all fields of computer assisted lexicography.

Programs for bi-lingual output (on a line printer, VDU and photocomposing unit) using Roman and Arabic character sets with diacritics have been developed successfully by Klett/Interpart and other printing and software firms. Arabic, written from right to left, was difficult; other character sets, such as Greek or Russian, will cause less problems.

0   INTRODUCTION

0. 1   Coded character sets

An early draft of this paper was written in China during the first plenary meeting of an ISO Technical Committee which has taken place since the People's Republic of China joined the ISO, the International Organization of Standardization. Only in the Far East, we Europeans realize how much we take for granted that the output of computer stored coded information uses a character set, based mainly on the Latin alphabet. As we as publishers are used to talk of non-books when we want to describe various modern information media like micro-film or video disc, etc. we have to use the clumsy 'non Roman alphabet' form when we want to denote the wide field of 'unusual' character sets we learnt at school, be it Greek, Russian or the dozens of general characters, including space, punctuation marks, the many mathematical or chemical symbols etc. The non Roman alphabet covers also the 169 Japanese Kana characters, or the more than 300 graphics needed for high quality Arabic, and last but not least the 6763 Chinese graphic characters defined and coded in the new Chinese National Standard for Information Interchange we discussed in Nanjing this spring.

We cannot cover in todays presentation all the non Roman alphabet character sets which are important for computer aided lexicographic work. We have only taken some samples to show the problems we have to face.

For data-base applications or for any computer aided information interchange or even for the most simple manipulation in a micro chip processor, any graphic character that needs visual representation for output, be it on a line printer, a visual display unit or a photocomposition device, must first be binary coded in a prescribed manner. By means of this code combination transmitted from the processor to any output device, the graphic display form of the character in question will be recalled, either from a character memory for a matrix output or by choosing the metal or plastic letter in a line printer.

Diacritics are small signs above, below or at the side of characters. They denote phonetic and often semantic functions and are an integral part of any language, whether in Roman, Greek or Arabic alphabet. Lexicography cannot dismiss diacritics, and such small graphics seem very difficult to represent visually on computer output devices.

Since January 1981 when Greece joined the EEC, the Greek language has introduced for the first time a non Roman character set. Though, some Greek letters are similar to Latin, it is a rather complicated character set. It has upper and lower case alphabet, and characters such as capital T, M, N or E, small 'o' or 'a' are identical to Latin, but may have other meanings (P = Rho). Hyphenation and punctuation take the same form as in the Latin set. Diacritics, however, are context sensitive and include grave, accent, circumflex, dieresis and aspirate. They precede a character if it is capital; aspirates and accents are often combined. The iota subscript is placed under small letters and after capitals.

We already mentioned the general characters not usually language based, like marks to structure a text, or the scientific and technical symbols. These characters are as necessary as the special phonetical transcription graphemes we find in most dictionaries.

0. 2 Alphabetical ordering arrangement of entries

Though already the word 'alphabetization' points to another language with non Roman letters, we generally take for granted that lexicographic entries follow the Roman letter alphabet. In a computer based text surrounding we want to use this tool's ability in helping to collate textual items into a predetermined order.

The widely used ASCII or EBCDIC binary codes have a collation value only as far as the 26 standard letters are concerned. For diacritics or other symbols special conventions are needed. For non Roman characters we need programmed sorting fields based on the coded information of the linguistic units we want to arrange for easy retrieval.

I cannot go into details here. I only wanted to mention this problem which causes a lot of, as yet, unsolved questions not only in a non Roman alphabet character representation.

1 COMPUTER OUTPUT

In this survey we cannot cover all aspects of computer output. We have to leave out the methods developed recently for voice response as we have to neglect the different output methods used for the various types of video discs. COM or ink jet output, too, we cannot cover today. These and other devices using electrographic principles in another form we will deal with briefly in our section on photocomposition units.

As for output medium that has to cope with non Roman characters we will mention impact printers using formed characters or matrix, then the VDU, that is, the CRT display terminals, and finally the photo-composition units. Based on examples, we hope to demonstrate how the different output media cope with non Latin alphabet letters, diacritics or special character sets.

1.1 Line printer

The modern typewriter or a Daisy Wheel terminal may serve as suitable example for a formed character printing device. Each character is preshaped and will convey its visual face form, character by character, via the ribbon onto paper.

Normally the character set of a typewriter is between 88 and 96 characters. Some of these printers like the golf ball typewriter, allow a change of the character set by a replaceable printing device like a Daisy Wheel. Twin print head models may have a 192 character set. Letters with diacritics can form a separate face character, other accents can be placed below or above a letter that is typed with a second typestroke. The character set of those formed character line printers is limited. If needed, some characters not often used can be replaced by others, e. g. phonetic symbols, as we did in our lexicography department at a time when the computer was not yet used for aiding lexicographic work.

Instead of formed characters where some type designer translated a type font onto a metal or plastic master, a matrix printer has a standard dot matrix and for each character the combination of dots forming a graphic symbol is stored. The quality of these **matrix** printers depends on the size of the matrix and the size of the smallest unit, the dots, forming the character. A matrix of 5x7 is sufficient to produce legible Roman characters, but no diacritics. An extremely high resolution matrix as we find in some photocomposition units, allows high quality graphic representation. For this Greek lambda an 80 high by 46 wide matrix has been used. Most line printer matrixes are relatively primitive using only a 7 high by 5 wide dot matrix, low case **descenders** or underlining are only possible with 9x7 wide matrix. A big advantage of matrix generated print output is the possibility of defining new symbols within the matrix limitation. The characters needed for the new form can be recalled from memory and used for output.

1.2 VDU terminal

Most terminals for visual display on a CRT also use the matrix method. Very often, the resolution here is even less than with dot matrix impact printers. As video text is in at the moment, we might demonstrate the 7x9 matrix used there for coded character representation. The main weakness of most CRT displays is their inability to differentiate the usually small diacritics. The German Umlaut with its two dots is no problem, but the Greek iota subscript or the differentiation of the Arabic fathah (a) or dammah (u) result often in almost insurmountable problems. Very slowly high resolution, bit map display screens are being introduced on the market. In December 1980 here in this building we could see the Xerox 8010 Star information system using such a screen which offers a choice of type fonts from 8-24 point and many other graphic elements.

1.3 Photocomposition unit

Due to the exploding use of word processing, photocomposition devices are now coming into use, not only in the printing industry, but also in offices and places where lexicographic work is done. As type-written documents have replaced the handwritten letter, typesetting is likely to replace the typewriter in many areas. Typeset documents are more legible, use less paper space and most systems allow differentiation of characters through small or bold face, italics and, so important for lexicographic work, a much higher choice of subscripts and super-scripts.

Within our context, it is important to note that photo typesetting devices, at least some of them, can also cope simultaneously with non Roman alphabets. As we need in almost all lexicographic work at least three character sets, this ability to mix a wide range of graphics, including capital and small letters, accented letters, etc., is very important. Modern photocomposition units retrieve digitized fonts which are usually stored on a disc and can be called into memory when needed. Laser imaging allowing high resolution digitizing produces high quality output. Modern line printers use the same electrographic principle. Microprocessor controlled manipulation of the stored data is also often possible. Even such extremely complicated character sets as Chinese can be handled by these devices. Not the full set, of course. It might be mentioned here that in 1313, more than 100 years before Gutenberg, a Korean ruler ordered a moveable typefont containing 60.000 characters. In the last years it has also been possible to adapt photo-typesetters, these originally graph by graph devices, to cope with script which is not formed by putting one letter next to the other, but by calligraphic word units, as is needed for Persian or Arabic cursive script. This aspect will be covered later.

2 INTERDEPENDENCE OF THE THREE OUTPUT MEDIA

From what has been said so far, one might presume that for quality output of Western European languages which use the Latin alphabet and other texts with non Roman characters as we need in lexicographic work, only photocomposing units are really suitable. This is true, but as anybody knows who already works in this field, we need all three output media. For an online search in a lexicographic data base, for example, a VDU is irreplaceable. The same is true for online updating. Keying in of coded textual material, using a non Roman character set, is inconvenient but feasible. But updating without a display screen is impossible, as we know from our long practical experience in this field with bilingual Arabic text. For the next 5 years it seems that we will also be unable to manage without line printers. Not all experts using lexicographic database are willing to work with the display unit. Others would gladly use such a modern device, but cannot, due to circumstances where it would not be economically or technically possible to connect a CRT screen online to the database. What we need therefore is more insight into the problem by R + D experts in the field of video display terminals and line printers to adapt their units so that they can be used not only with our Western world Latin character sets, but also with others based on non Latin characters. Chip manufacturers offer boards that can generate different character sets and emulate some typographic functions on the screen and a corresponding line printer. For Cyrillic or Greek this problem has almost been solved, though, as said, the diacritics still pose problems.

3 MULTILINGUAL OUTPUT

In my third part, I hope to demonstrate how we at Klett, but also other printers and publishers, work in a multilanguage context. I have chosen Arabic, an official United Nations language, but also one of the most widely used written languages of the world.

Text handling (that is data processing of coded information for human comprehension which is intended for presentation in two- dimensional form and consists chiefly of words and character strings) and communicating of Arabic is difficult. There are many reasons: The Arabic alphabet involves considerable difficulties, not usually found with the Latin alphabet. Arabic is read from right to left and uses no upper or lower case characters. Up to today it is still a penman's script in which the shape of each letter is dependent on the context, not only immediately preceding and succeeding characters, but on the entire alphabetic content of the letter string forming the word. There is no 'please print' in Arabic, letters cannot stand in isolation. The shape of Arabic letters, the intercharacter fit, the strings of characters and the optical spacing forming words and lines, are subject to definite rules of orthography and calligraphy. The importance of the written language is not only caused by centuries of Koran studies which virtually ossified the calligraphic form of language, but this written language is - here the parallel to China is obvious - very often the only way of communication for people living in different parts of the world where Arabic is spoken.

Arabic, like Hebrew, is a semitic language, based on a root system; the roots consist entirely of consonants of which there are 29, but the vowels are not normally written in daily use, in the Koran and also in educational, scientific, technical and of course lexicographic context, they appear as diacritics above or below the consonant vowelled. Whereas the Latin alphabet was in its early form made up of isolated almost geometric characters, written Arabic has been cursive from the beginning. In Arabic it is not a question of forming single letters well, but creating groups of letters to form words or letter combinations and ligatures, that look well formed and beautiful.

As in all cursive script, Arabic has different variants of most letters according to its position within a word. Some of you may still recall the old German Fraktur script where we also differentiated between an S at the end of a word with an S at the beginning of a word

and an S in a combination with a ligature. An Arabic reader expects
different letter forms according to the position of the letter (initial,
medial, final and isolated). For a number of consonants the form is
identical and they are distinguished only by diacritics, small cubes which
vary in number and position.

Last but not least, Arabic script is further enriched and made more
complicated by a great number of ligatures. (That is, a combination of
two or more letters forming a new graphic). The letter 'm', for example, can be found in over fifty different shapes. So the number of
different character forms rises easily to over 300. Not all of these
character forms were used in the old lead typesetting, but high quality
work was achieved in many places, though the process was very time-
consuming and expensive.

Computer-based lexicographic bilingual output where Arabic is
source or target language, needs high quality type face of good legibility
and harmonic proportions, both within a character and in combination
with others. It is also necessary that the output allows a combination of
a Latin script with Arabic and to combine numerals which run, also in
Arabic, from left to right, rather than, as Semitic language texts, read
from right to left. Anyone who wants to do lexicographic work, or is
like the Klett daughter company Interpart, active in Arabic terminology
work, has to realize that all vocalization is done by 'pointing' or diacritical signs. We had to program our photo-typesetting equipment to be
able to cope with diacritics, ligatures and the other specialities of
Arabic - no hyphenation at the end of lines. To do this in the KITAB
program for high quality Arabic photo-typesetting, we had to combine
the computer power of our Digiset photo-typesetting machine with a big
main frame, so that the electronic beam of the typesetting machine
imitates on the high resolution CRT screen the working of a calligrapher.
After carefully analysing the context, our KITAB programs calculate
where diacritics should be placed, what letter forms to be used and
where ligatures would be necessary.

Even with smaller computer power, for example the microprocessors in a powerful mini-computer, it was possible to output
acceptable Arabic on typesetting equipment, as can be seen by the
samples of Worldwide Languages, London, or CIMOS, Paris. But it
has proved impractical to rely only on photo-typesetting for bilingual
Arabic output, especially in a data-base terminology surrounding. So
Klett/Interpart and others had to adapt the software for Arabic script
in combination with Latin character sets, numerals etc. for an output
on a specialised VDU screen. The high resolution digitalisation data
which are used in the Digiset CRT typesetter had to be reformated to
fit the 12x10 combineable matrix in an intelligent display terminal or in
a matrix line printer. A very complicated process which took a long
time and which is still not finished. Fortunately due to video text there
is worldwide a lot of research going on in regard to legibility aspects
for textual material presented on a CRT screen and on a matrix line
printer. Klett is very active in this field, too, especially as far as typography for multilingual use is concerned.

As we know from lexicographic work there is an increasing group
of readers which has to and is able to switch very fast from one vocabulary and character set to another. Even if those languages use similar
character sets, a bilingual reader must be able to manipulate in his
mind symbols forming words of different languages with different
grammar and word order. It gets even more complicated if two distinct-
ly different sets of symbols, Roman and non Roman characters, are used.
Some words or letter combinations have identical or very similar character shape, but very different contextual meaning. The Arabic numerals
are well known examples. These strings and ligatures have to be recognized and arranged mentally to the language set to which they belong,
only then reading and deciding in which direction the eyes should move
is possible. One last example: The presentation of an Arabic diacritic
like the shaddah (double consonant) will look different on VDU when the
other language context is German with its 'Umlaute', whereas to an
English reader similar dots above the letter are not common.

4 FUTURE TRENDS

Text communication in the future that will meet users' requirements cannot limit itself to one language or only one character set. The
interdependencies in text processing and communication in multilingual
communities demand extensions to cover special character sets and non
Roman alphabets that are compatible with established character coding
standards. The ISO was able to achieve this for the Chinese. Other
languages, like Arabic, will follow.

LEXICOGRAPHY IN THE ELECTRONIC AGE
J. Goetschalckx and L. Rolling (editors)
North-Holland Publishing Company
© ECSC, EEC, EAEC, 1982

THE ORTHOPHONIC DICTIONARY

G. LURQUIN

Summary

For translators and translation services dictionaries are an will remain
the primary lexical resources; the question is whether, for scientific and
technical terminology, they will be capable of meeting future needs in the
context of the new order for information and communication.

Existing dictionaries are many and varied but have in common their orthographic basis, that is their entries are based on the written language. This
system presupposes that the user is familiar with the precise spelling of
the required word. However, particularly when the user is not a native speaker, or when the term is one of specialist vocabulary, only the approximate
spelling may be known. Our proposal is therefore to compile orthophonic dictionaries, with phonetically-based entries. Such entries can moreover be
grouped together according to their roots.

This innovation can be justified in a number of ways. At a time when a new
world order is being established for information, the documents which the
latest applications of data processing can make available to the peoples of
the Third World, in international languages of which they frequently have
an inadequate command, must be capable of being conculted by as many people
as possible. Compiling orthophonic dictionaries now would in addition be an
investment for the future, for the day is no longer far off when man will
be able to converse orally with computers.

0.   The word "innovation" seems to be significant in the name of the Directorate General responsible for organizing this colloquium. This paper is
an attempt to meet one such objective: progress in and through innovation.

1.0   For translators and translation services dictionaries are and will
remain the principal lexical resource: the question is whether, for scientific and technical terminology, they will be capable of meeting future
needs in the context of the new world order for information and communication described in the Sean McBride report 1 and elsewhere.

1.1   Existing dictionaries are many and varied: encyclopaedic or language-
oriented general or specialist, alphabetical and/or analogical, explanatory
or translational, descriptive and/or historical, monolingual or multilingual. As Jacques Cellard has recently shown in an article in <u>Le Monde-
Dimanche</u> [2], they also differ individually: language dictionaries of approximately equal volume can vary widely in the ways in which they define and
illustrate the meaning of a particular word. The same goes for multilingual
translational dictionaries.

1.2   Many though they are, they are all orthographically based: lexical
entries or headwords are taken from the written language. This system presupposes that the user is familiar with the precise spelling of the required
word. However, particularly when the user is not a native speaker, or when
the term is one of specialist or technical vocabulary, only the approximate
spelling may be known. Finding the word may thus be difficult from the
start. Someone hearing a term in English may not know its French equivalent,
and to find it in a bilingual English/French dictionary or to interrogate
a terminology bank he must know its spelling. Spelling is well known for its
deceptive nature, and 'illogical' spellings exist in every language: we are
all familiar with the 'idiotic' irregularities which make written French a
minefield. The spelling does not correspond to what it purports to represent.
The spoken word and the written word are not one and the same [3].

1.3   Whether they are teachers or linguits, professors or managing direc-
tors, experts are unanimous in deploring everyone's poor spelling French.
To take some recent examples, let us look at a number of articles which

appeared in the press at the end of May: firstly from <u>La Libre Belgique</u> on
25 May 1981.

(<u>La Crise de l'orthographe</u> by Claude Thomas): "... recently a Brussels
borough undertook the courageous experiment of testing the spelling ability
of a number of schoolchildren. In June 1980 a test dictation was given to
51 primary schoolchildren aged 11 to 12. The same test was given again the
following December, this time including 10 to 11 year olds, a total of 348
children. One conclusion of the test was as plain as a pikestaff: no child
made fewer than three mistakes". Secondly, from <u>Le Monde</u> dated 22 May:
"... for the launch of 'Top' (= toute l'orthographe pratique), his new dictionary of practical spelling, Jean-Jacques Nathan invited linguistic specialists, journalists and personalities to a spelling lunch: the pre-lunch
drink was accompanied by a dictation composed by the compiler of the dictionary, André Jouette, which tripped up every participant (except, of
course, those who prudently slipped out during the test)... the number of
mistakes ranged from seven, the best (by an assistant lecturer at the CRNS
who is specialist in spelling) to 31. Proof that even those whose profession
it is to write or study language are not immune to the pitfalls of French."

Thirdly, in <u>Médias et langages</u>, No 10–11 of May and June 1981, the publication of "Fourteen measures for our language", the edict of the Haut Comité
de la langue française. The French spelling system has never been properly
mastered either by the whole of the literate population or by the whole of
the intellectual classes, or even, at any time in history, by a majority of
them. "How many Frenchmen today can write and spell without faultlessly and
hesitation? One in ten? Certainly not. One in one hundred? Most unlikely.
One in a thousand?"[4]

1.4   This concerns not only French, but also English, which is spreading
further and further beyond the shores of the United States and Great Britain.
I quote from <u>Le Monde</u> of 23 May 1981 (page 31): "The British were somewhat
surprised to find that they had among them two million illiterates, not
counting immigrants". Other languages with easier spelling, less riddled
with traps, do exist, such as Italian and Spanish. More and more people,
however, will continue to speak the principal international language even
though they are not native speakers.

2.0   If we replace normal spelling with a phonological alphabet, representing each element in the phonetic chain by a single unequivocal sign,
we are replacing something artificial with something natural. Phonology has
given us the ability to have a more detached view of the written form
through which we must pass in order to arrive at the language itself5. Our
proposal is therefore to compile orthophonic dictionaries, with phonetically-based entries. If a term can be taken in its spoken form, the form in
which it is heard, and with spelling no longer a problem, dictionary-sear-
ching is facilitated and the term is more easily found.

2.1   In an orthophonic dictionary the entry is shown in phonetic script.
We recommend use of the International Phonetic Association (IPA) alphabet,
which is unique in that it permits vowel tones and consonant articulation
to be noted precisely. It is not difficult to read: all students of foreign
languages learn to decipher it, and although the script is not less suited
ideal for certain languages it has the advantage of being universally used.[6]
Words are classified in alphabetical order of their phonetic form, which is
to say the order of ordinary dictionaries with the vowel symbols a,a,ä,e,E,
etc having the value of separate letters following a,e,o, etc. The orthographic representation (spelling) of the term or word is also given, since
it has the effect of permanent tangible object 'a more suitable form than
the sound for establishing the unity of the language over a period of time'
(Saussure), since it follows the orthophonic representation which makes a
more natural, more real and less artificial connection.

Exemples.   En : si:nou'dzenisis = caenogenesis; 'si:sifɔ:m = caeciform;
                  'si:ziəs = caesious.
            Fr : siRkɔmdyksjɔ̃ = circumduction; ɛlmɛ̃tɔlɔzi = helminthologie;
                  tRikɔfitɔ̃ = trichophyton.

2.2   Another way in which the orthophonic dictionary is new is that it is
a closer approximation of what is believed to be the mechanism of the mental
dictionary, i.e. of that part of the human memory in which our vocabulary
is stored. Organized for the sake of understanding, the memory index makes
a correspondence between sound and meaning in respect of each word. A recent study on slips of the tongue carried out by Anne Cutler at the Univer-

sity of Sussex in Brighton showed that phonologically similar words are
located close to each other in the dictionary and that the mental dictionary is consequently organized by sound, on the basis of the similarity of
similar-sounding words. The study also shows that 'words are not catalogued
at random in the dictionary but classified according to their roots'. One
can therefore conclude that a word's place in the dictionary is determined
by the sound of its root. For each dictionary entry there may be a number
of words classified as root plus affix. 'It is clear that the mental dictionary is an extremely complex analythical system. It contains all the
information about all the words we know: their pronunciation, their meaning
and the relationship between them'. Other studies confirm this sound-based
organization of the mental dictionary, which is more concerned with comprehension, that is with using the sound to determine the sense, than with
production, which means using the sense to arrive at the sound. Thus, according to D.A. Fay[8] , errors in tonic stress in English, when the stress
is shifted from one syllable to another within a word by analogy with
another word from the same root, show that words are classified according
to the sounds which make up their roots. This would seem to be borne out
by the processes used by poets in generating nonsense words (e.g. the work
of Henri Michaux and Maurice Blanchard), by children in the creation of
private language, and by certain glossomanic aphasics[9].

Exemples : *En* si:k- : 'si:kəl = caecal...; 'si:kəm = caecum...;
                            si:'kɔtəmi = caecotomy... Voir si:s-.

                     ...

                  si:s- : 'si:sidi = caecidae...; 'si:sifɔ:m = caeciform...;
                            si:'silən = caecilian...; si:si'li:idi = caecilii-
                            dae... Voir si:k-.

                     ...

          Fr kɔl(e)- : kɔlɑgɔg = cholagogue...; kɔlǎjiɔgRafi = cholanqio-
                            graphie...; kɔlesistit = cholécystite...;
                            kɔlesistɔstɔmi = cholécystostomie...; ... melɑ̃kɔli
                            = mélancolie...; etc.

3.0   This innovation can be justified in a number of ways.

3.1   At a time when a new word order is being established for information,
we must abandon our Europe-centred attitudes and have more consideration
for the peoples of the Third World: the developed nations have a duty to
make scientific and technological information available to them, for that
is the only way in which they will be able to improve their economic and
human conditions[10]. The documents which the latest applications of data
processing can make available to the peoples of the Third World, in international languages of which they frequently have an inadequate command,
must be capable of being consulted by as many people as possible. Twenty
years from now there will be as many French-speaking 15-year-olds in Africa
as there are in the whole of France, Belgium, Luxembourg, Switzerland and
Quebec together[12].

This orthophonic system has already been tried out for teaching French
children to read and write their own language. A dictionary has recently
been published [13]. Phonetic notation is even being used to teach French to
the children of immigrants[14]. In other words, culture and writing are no
longer one and the same thing, as they were 30 or 40 years ago.

3.2   Compiling orthophonic dictionaries now would in addition be an investment for the future, for the day is doubtless not far off when man will
be able to converse orally with computers, and when there will be talking
translation machines[15]. There has been enormous progress in this field since
the "Speak and Spell" machine developed and built by Texas Instruments gave
so much pleasure to the children who were learning to read and write with
its help. Speech synthesizers will benefit from progress in circuit minia-
turization, large-scale integrated circuits and the development of new micro-
electronic components. In addition, the world's largest computer manufacturers are becoming interested in speech recognition systems, and the amount
of research being undertaken in universities and other institutes makes it
plain that before long presentday equipment will seem as primitive as an
old typewriter seems to us today[16].

3.3   Finally, the linguistics of speech, on which new research into artificial intelligence is being based, points towards the question of compiling
new dictionaries.

4. Notwithstanding the advantages of the orthophonic dictionary not just I have already described, but many others as well, such as the speed advantage in understanding a word with a short phonetic spelling rather than a long conventional spelling, the possibility of the system's use by individuals who are unable to use a keyboard, etc. - it is true that there are still a large number of obstacles in the project's path. The prestige of visual form, the written word, is far from being least of these. In addition, although practically all words have only one spelling [17], a single word may be read in several different ways [18]. It is also true that machines capable of listening to and understanding continuous speech, with its intonation, its rhythm and its inflections, are not going to be built next week: what we are proposing is achievable, however, since we are concerned with isolated terms [19].

Such difficulties should not limit our determination to make progress and to envisage a new kind of dictionary for our languages. The orthophonic dictionary has the undoubted educational advantage of giving easier and wider access to information and communication. Though the path from the researcher to the final user may be long, there is no doubt about the ultimate result: a dialogue between man and machine. Talking to a machine which understands you and does for you the work it is designed to do is no longer a dream!

Notes and references

(1) Voix multiples, un seul monde. Communication et société aujourd'hui et demain

La Documentation française, 1980, 368 p.

(2) 25 January 1981, p. XVIII

(3) 'Writing masks one's view of language: it is not so much dressing up as disguise. This is well demonstrated by the French word oiseau, in which not one of the sounds of the spoken word (wazo) is represented by its own symbol; nothing of the language remains'. (Ferdinand de Saussure, Cours de linguistique générale, p. 52).

(4) Le Monde de l'Education (supplément to Le Monde): L'orthographe.

(5)   'A letter is not strictly speaking a basic sign, but merely a transi-
       tional sign, an intermediary link between the two signs which are ac-
       tually used: the phoneme – the unit of spoken language, of what is
       said, and the word, the visual unit of written language, of what is
       read'. (Ferdinand de Saussure)

(6)   The reasons given by André and Jeanne Martinet for preferring Alfonic
       to IPA apply only to the French language.

(7)   Anne Cutler, La leçon des lapsus in La Recherche N° 112 (June 1980),
       p. 686–692. V.A. Fromkin (Ed.). Errors in Linguistic Performance:
       Slips of the Tongue, Ear, Pen and Hand (Academic Press).

(8)   D.A. Fay in Linguistic Inquiry, 8, 505, 1977.

(9)   Pierre-Marie and Guy Lavorel, Cortex et cortèges de jargonautes in
       Le Language et l'homme N° 45 (January 1981), p. 53–57.

(10)   'The right to communicate is a logical extension of progress towards
       freedom and democracy ... It is a double right: the right to receive
       a communication, and the right to pass on information ... New techno-
       logy is going to lead to an enormous increase in the amount of infor-
       mation available, and to make its transmission easier ... Information
       and communication are regarded as a human right (...)' (McBride report,
       p. 215).

(11)   In his book Le Défi Mondial, Jean-Jacques Servan-Schreiber writes that
       the Third World must be made computer-conscious, and allowed to bene-
       fit from the spinoff of the electronic and telematic revolution. He
       maintains that information is accessible even for those countries which
       are backward educationally. 'Its role is precisely to enable them to
       make a step forward. With talking computer terminals they should even
       be able – in some cases – to bypass the need for literacy'.

(12)   The report by the Haut Comité de la langue française states that
       'by the end of the century there will be more children taught in
       French outside France than inside France' (Le Monde, 17 January 1981,
       p. 1).

(13) <u>Alfonic, dictionnaire de l'orthographe</u>, André & Jeanne Martinet, SELAF, 1980.

(14) Speech-therapy students at the Institut Libre Marie Haps have presented papers describing their methodology and the results obtained with Turkish children. Entires in Hungarian proper-name dictionnaries are compiled orthophonically.

(15) See <u>La Recherche</u> N° 118, January 1981, p. 81, <u>Les Machines parlantes en plein expansion</u>, and N° 99, April 1979, <u>La reconnaissance de la parole</u> (JP Haton and JS Liénard); <u>Speech recognition by computer</u>, by Stephen E. Levinson & Mark Y. Liberman, translated as <u>La reconnaissance de la parole par ordinateur</u> in <u>Pour la science</u>, June 1981; <u>The synthesis of speech</u>, by James L. Flanagan in <u>Scientific American</u>, February 1971.

(16) A great deal of research is being undertaken in Europe, and a dozen or so teams in France are working on effective systems for oral communication between man and computers, among others the Centre de Recherche en Informatique in Nancy and the Laboratoire d'Informatique pour la Mécanique et les Sciences de l'Ingénieur in Orsay. This research is nonetheless some way behind that being undertaken in the USA and Japan. With all this research, progress is being made on making recognition is less dependent on the speaker and the sound environment.

(17) <u>Goulache, goulasch ou goulach</u>? by Jacques Cellard in <u>Le Monde Dimanche</u> 31 May 1981, p. 14.

(18) See Martinet & Walter, <u>Dictionnaire de la prononciation française dans son usage réel</u>, France Expansion, Paris 1973

(19) Jacques Girardon; <u>La parole est aux robots</u> in <u>l'Express</u>, 28 March 1981, p. 72; Jean Camion in <u>Le langage et l'Homme</u> N° 45, referred to by Jacques Houbart, <u>Jean Camion: quatre signes pour transcrire et synthétiser la parole</u>, in <u>Industries et techniques</u>, 1 April 1981; and Daniel Lacotte <u>Machine à parler: Inventeur cherche industriels</u>, in <u>Usine nouvelle</u>, N° 10, 5 March 1981.

PANEL DISCUSSION

Session II - NEW TECHNOLOGIES

The Situation in Greece
  S.E. DIAMESSIS

Language Barriers and Scientific
Communication
  Dr. A. GRYPDONCK

Discussion of the Session II by
  R. HAAS

LEXICOGRAPHY IN THE ELECTRONIC AGE
J. Goetschalckx and L. Rolling (editors)
North-Holland Publishing Company
© ECSC, EEC, EAEC, 1982

THE SITUATION IN GREECE

(PRESENTATION OF S.E.DIAMESSIS)

1. It is with great pleasure that I take this first opportunity to speak
in Greek, the seventh official language of the E.E.C. I shall start
with some background information and then say a few words about work
in my country Greece, in this field.

As a point of personal introduction although I am here as an individual I work as a Counsellor for the K.E.M.E. - the Center for Educational Research and Teacher-in-Service Training of the Ministry of
Education of Greece. The KEME is the advisory board to the Minister of
Education, the educational planning body.

2. In the above capacity the KEME, established in 1975-6, has been the
instrument for the implementation of the recent 5-year Educational
Reform of Greece.

Part of this reform has been the establishment of the so-called
"Demotiki" language (the 'people's language') as the official language
of the country - as against the formerly used 'refined' form of
'katharevoussa' (puristic Greek).

KEME has come up with new Grammar and Syntax books for Demotiki -
guidelines, besides all other uses, for present and future efforts in
lexicography (and machine translation).

3. Concerning Lexicography in Greece, it must be said that generally,
over the years, there have been numerous but rather scattered efforts on
both and organizational and a personal basis by various individuals-
lexicographers who have worked independently on Terminology, etc.
Examples : El. Engineering, Mathematics, Physics, etc.
It should be noted that there is still a large gap in this field.
Greek (a language with a 24-letter alphabet) is not a very easy
language) Yet, it constitutes a very intereting field for the linguist

111

to explore. We shall mention the better known formal (or semiformal) attempts at solving the lexicographic and terminological problems of Modern Greek (the order is not necessarily either chronological or one of importance regarding the respective work done the status of the institution involved). On the other hand, work on Machine Translation (or computer utilization) has been very limited. One effort we can cite specifically is a published paper (1975) describing a 'new Grammar' employing transliteration methods on translating, on a limited basis, between English and Modern Greek (the method was tested on the authors Dictionaries-glossaries in Electronics). This as well as some other such work on, we believe, ancient Greek were conducted at the 'Democritos' Research Center of Greece.

Furthermore, however, there have been some other efforts abroad, especially with ancient and biblical Greek.

4. Among the better known institutions, agencies, etc. involved or interested, to our knowledge, in Lexicography and linguistic work of one sort or another over the years are the following - the list does not claim to be exhaustive nor should it create the illusion of excessive work in the field :

    The K.F.E. - Center for Philosophical Studies
    The Greek Standards Association - 'ELOT'
    The Greek Technical Chamber
    The Greek Academy of Sciences (Committee on Neologisms, 1971,etc.)
    The Univ. of Thessaloniki's Manolis Triandafyllidis Institute
    The Min. of Coordination's Agency for Scientific Research and
    Techn.(YEET)
    The Min. of Education's KEME
    The Nuclear Research Center 'Democritos'
    The Univ. of Athens (work on etymology, etc.)
    etc.

5. Some of the areas in which there has been, and is presently being, conducted work by teams or individuals, formally or informally, in this field are :

a)   a Greek version of the EUDISED Thesaurus

b)   contacts with Eurodicautom and Infoterm for work on Glossaries and Terminology in Greek

c)   independent glossary and dictionary work in various fields (e.g. Computers, Math., Philosophy, Education - proposal on the former pending (YEET).

6. There are still a number of linguistic issues involved with modern Greek, the resolution of some of which is connected with deveopments that could further simplify some aspects of related Lexicography and/or Machine Translation work (as has happened, for example, with the recent abolition of subscripts. Development in view : abolition of all accents - aspirates but ones). In this light, as well as in view of the fact that Greek, because of its own characteristics, is a very interesting language perse for both Greeks as well as non-Greeks, we believe that the road is open for scientific collaboration as well as exchange of ideas in both Lexicography and Machine Translation (and/or the use of the computer for lexicographic work) - inclusive of the field of Speech Recognition (and Artificial Intelligence, as related to the Greek language specifically, as a more extensive field of work and of original Research).

Our research teams are open to and willing to establish such collaboration (in the form, perhaps, of joint Projects) and should warmly welcome such an interest for joint research.

LEXICOGRAPHY IN THE ELECTRONIC AGE
J. Goetschalckx and L. Rolling (editors)
North-Holland Publishing Company
© ECSC, EEC, EAEC, 1982

Language Barriers and Scientific Communication

Dr. A. Grypdonck

The aim of this contribution to the discussion is to consider language
barriers in scientific communication and to highlight some of the problems they create.(1)

Science needs communication, and scientists - like anyone else - are
dependent on communication. It is a question not just of the (social)
right to information, but also of the symbiosis which can develop from
scientific communication; moreover, communication is intended to achieve
economies through avoiding duplication in research. However, communication is possible only through a common language, and shortcomings in
this common basis create language barriers.(2)

Language barriers in scientific communication may take the form of
semantic obstacles between scientists of the same disciplines (the
problem of diversity within the specialized language, as is particularly
the case in the non-exact sciences), and more so between scientists of
different disciplines (the problem of progressive specialization and a
lac of interdisciplinarity). In addition to this, of course, there is the
problem of comprehensibility between scientists and students and semi-
laymen, or more generally between science and society (science as public
property). In many cases, however, all this is aggravated, and the
communication problem made even more complex, by the international

diversity of languages. The situation is made worse by a fairly wide-spread carelessness in the use of language. (3)

One major aspect of this problem of international scientific language barriers is the fact that, because of political, economic and scientific factors, English is the language most used for scientific publication. This raises the question of the need for a scientific 'interlingua'.(4)

Several factors militate against the idea of English as an 'interlingua':

- English is not the language of the majority in Europe; in fact, no one language in Europe is spoken by more than 15% of the population; (5)
- the level of knowledge of English, and opportunities to learn it, vary widely throughout Europe and the world; (6)
- there are continuing chauvinistic and nationalistic pressures against the use of a foreign language as a means of communication; (7)
- English itself is not a uniform language; within the geographical limits of English as a mother tongue there are wide variations in grammar, vocabulary and spelling. (8)

Translation is naturally one way of tackling the problem of international language barriers. Apart from the delay in publication this involves (loss of time), there are two major aspects involved in translation.

Writing and reading in a foreign language both involve a loss of information, and this loss of information content naturally also occurs in the case of translation. In this case the situation may be further aggravated by the translator's lack of specialized knowledge of the discipline which is the subject of the text to be translated. An incomplete knowledge of a language, but also an incomplete knowledge of a specialized language and a specialized terminology, add to the semantic problems, with particular reference to polysemy. This applies even more to scientific publications since, particularly in the case of the humanities and social sciences, scientific language requires not only a precise terminology but also a precise and careful choice of words. The problem is not quite so great in the case of the exact sciences, since they frequently use an intern-ally recognizable specialized terminology which is an established part of a language. Another phenomenon is the untranslatability of certain concepts because of the differing social and cultural contexts of the author and reader. (8)

All this means that writing scientific texts in a foreign language and translating such texts require the assistance of experts. In the first case, experts in a language, in the latter case experts in both the language and discipline involved. Editing and translation can be done properly only by someone who not only has an excellent knowledge of the original language and the language into which it is being translated, but also has an adequate knowledge of the discipline involved.

Having to call in experts considerably increase costs, and this aggravates the economic problems involved in publishing and disseminating (scientific) books and journals. A balance therefore has to be sought between the accounting requirements on the one hand, and the quality and (international) readability of the publications on the other. (10)

There is another consideration which must be added to this economic approach. That is the exponential growth in the volume of scientific information, i.e. the information explosion and the accompanying growth in specialization and spcialism. However, it would appear that relatively little of this volume is used in practice. This raises the question as to whether there is any point in publishing and - in many cases - translating this volume of information. Essentially, this is also an economic aspect. (11)

Finally, and quite apart from any chauvinism - there is distinctiveness (including the scientific distinctiveness) of each cultural community. The pursuit of unity and cooperation at European or world level must not be a barrier to distinctiveness. For anyone whishing to make a scientific contribution to the advancement of the community in which he lives and in which his scientific research has its roots, it is also important that he should be able to do this by publishing in the language of his own country, in his mother tongue. (12)

A number of conclusions can safely be drawn from these few very brief considerations:

- There is a rational basis for efforts to find an international medium
  for scientific communication. Three aspects are involved here: the
  quality of the information, the costs and the convenience (for both
  author and reader) of this international medium.
- English as a world medium for scientific communication is an impracticable proposition. Under the present circumstances, however, if scientific communication is to be promoted, it is advisable that scientists
  should have a relatively good knowledge of English - passive knowledge
  in the case of the consumer and active knowledge in the case of the
  producer of information. (13)
- Publishing in one's own language is of continuing importance for the
  (development of the) cultural community in which one lives; One must be
  able to communicate with the community (even with a broad public).

- Scientific communication (particularly at international level, but at
  national level as well) can be improved by rationalizing the stream of
  superfluous scientific information. This can be done, for instance, by
  first of all publishing in oen's own language within one's own (restricted) language area, followed by publication at international level
  - and hence is one or more languages of international importgance, or
  even in an 'interlingua' - of abstracts or, better still, of synopses,
  since these latter give a better picutre of the content ofthe publication. This would reduce the sheer volume ofthe stream of informatin.
  It would same money and in most cases would provide adequate basic
  information. The accessibility of science would be maintained, and
  anyone wanting the complete text could then request it and, if necessary, have it translated. (14)
- Scientific language and its use must be rationalized between scientists
  of the same discipline, across the frontiers of disciplines and countries, and through efforts to achieve uniformity (santdardization) of
  terminology (semantic problem) and of the codes and symbols used, as
  well as by promoting interdisciplinarity, which can only be of benefit.(15)

One other thing should be added in conclusion. Promoting scientific
communication, which in the final analysis is of importance for the whole
of society, is a task for the individual scientist. He must contribute
towards it and remember that there is no point in publication for publi-

cation's sake. What he publishes must be oriented towards the consumer of the information. (16)

Notes

(1) In the wider context of language as a communication medium, see also:

A. Grypdonck, Taal - Taalbarrières - Taaleenheid in 'Taal en de communicatie van kennis' (ed. A. Grypdonck), to be published in 1981. This publication contains several other articles on the same subject (including one by A. A. Manten).

See also the report of the discussion group Editing in a multilingual environment at the Second International Conference of Scientific Editors (Amsterdam October 1980) (Chairman:A. Grypdonck; rapporteur: J.M .Marx). (The papers have still to be published).

(2) All human communication is a 'dialogue' and must take account of the fact that the reader (or listener) alone gives this communication genuine substance and meaning. Communication must be oriented towards the consumer of language.

It is estimated that 9 to 10% of all R&D expenditure in the USA and UK is lost through faulty communication, i.e. through unsuspected and unwanted duplicatin of research (see H.D.L. Vervliet, Wetenschappelijk publiceren : problemen, tendensen, alternatieven, Brussels 1980, P. 14).

(3) There are many kinds of language barriers:
- historical: to understand Erasmus or Goethe we must read them in the context of their times;
- the geographical macro-barrier;
- the micro-barriers between the standard language and dialect, and even within the standard language because of differences in form and emphasis;
- socio-cultural barriers (in all human existence, including education and the working environment);
- semantic barriers (polysemy);

- the interdisciplinary language barrier;
- the language barrier between science and society;
- the superabundance of information (substantialism).

(4) Some historical elements - which show the vicissitudes - in connection with the concept of an 'interlingua':

- In the past, the fact that a language has gained importance beyond national frontiers has frontiers has frequently been based on the radiation of knowledge or skills or trading activity (e.g. the influence of the works of Jan Ympijn Christoffels and Simon Stevin in England and Sweden in the 17th century).

- the role of Latin: Middle Ages and later Modern Latin.

- The 'lingua franca', a language of commerce derived from several languages and of importance for trade relations around the Mediterranean from the time of the Crusades right into the 19th century.

-'Pidgin', a mixed language used in the Far East between Chinese and Europeans (a corrupt form of English).

- French, the language of diplomacy and international literature from the 17th century until before 1940.

- German as a language of international communication in the first half of the 20th century in scientific and other sectors.

- The shift in favour of English just before and later through the Second World War.

P. Stevens refers to English as 'the lanuage of most extensive publication' (British and Amercan English, London 1972). M.D. Frank (Internationaal Uitgeven in 'Het geheim van de uitgever', ed. A. Nuis, Amsterdam 1978, page 80) goes s far as to say that the proportion of scientific literature published in English is estimated at 85% of the world total.

The various efforts to establish artificial languages of an international nature have failed to achieve convincing results. However, moves now appear to be afoot to set up a universal language, 'European', for the EEC, which will be a sort of mixture of the different Community languages (see D. van Bergeijk, De taalbarrière in de informatievoorziening in 'Open', 12th year, No 6, June 1980, page 320 et seq.).

Since 1935 the proportion of English publications in the total literature consulted has beeen rising rapidly both in English-speaking regions and in European countries (see A. Manten Taalbarrières en)intrnationale) wetenschappelijke communicatie in 'Taal en de communicatie van kennis'; see Note (1).

There are, however, other factors. A Dutch survey (see A. Manten ibid.) indicates that sociologists read and publish in their own language to a greater extent than other scientists. It would also appear that prac- titioners of the exact sciences and engineers are increasingly asking for access to the Japanese and Russian literature.

There are sometimes differences within one and the same country (possibly because of cultural affinities). In the case of Belgium, French speakers are more likely to publish in French (even at international level), while Dutch speakers are more likely to publish in English for international distribution (see a communication from A. Cockx in Taal en de communi- catie van kennis mentioned in Note (1).

(5) See 'Le Néerlandais' (ed. 'Ons Erfdeel'; Rekkem 1981) page 7. Accord- ing to data published by Strevens (ibid.) 300 million people through- out the world speak English as their mother tongue, and the same number again use it as a second language (which is not regarded as a foreign language).

(6) The diversity of mother tongues and the differing opportunities for learning English, as well as the differences in the degree and extent of knowledge of that language, pose serious obstacles. Outside those regions where English is the mother tongue, we can distinguish between three categories: regions where English is not the mother tongue but the second official language, regionswhere English is not even learnt as a second language. There are thus major differences in the opportunities for learning English successfully. In this connec- tion, there are even differences betwen the Netherlands and Flanders. In Dutch-speaking Belgium, English is frequently not the second language learnt at school.

(7) See, for example, J.P. Abadie The publication of scientific journals in France, in 'Scientific Information Transfer - The Editor's Role'

(ed. M. Balaban), Dordrecht 1978, pages 377-383.

(8) For an analytical illustration of these differences see P. Strevens, ibid. Any generalized (internation) use of English can only increase the erosion and heterogeneity of the language.

(9) For a remarkable example of untranslatability - the English word 'perspective' compared with the Japanese 'no tan', as illustrated by the different ways of representing three-dimensionalism in a flat surface - see R.L. Ackoff On purposeful Systems (e. N.J.T.A. Kramer; text of a lecture, Interuniversitaire Interfaculteit Bedrijfskunde, Delft 1974) page 15.

(10) The costs involved in scientific communication are already relatively high, amounting to an estimated 30% of total R&D costs betwen author and user (creation 7%; publication, distribution, storage 11%; use 13%). (See H.D.L. Vervliet, ibid.)

(11) Some figures to illustrate this:
- Over a period of twenty years (1959 - 1979) the number of articles published in the professional and practical literature in the USA increased nearly fivefold, whereas it had not even doubled over the period 1929 to 1959 (see C.G. Benjamin in 'Publishers Weekly' of 24 April 1981).
- Nearly 90% of all scientific authors in the history of mankind are currently alive (according to H.D.L. Vervliet Wetenschappelijk publiceren : Problemen, Tendensen, Alternatieven Brussels 1980).
- There are currently 50 to 60 000 scientific and technical journals throughout the world. Two million articles are published each year. A full 98% of natural science articles is of no further importance ten years after publication (see P.J. Vinken De wetenschappelijke onderzoeker als producent en gebruiker van informatie in 'Universiteit en Hogeschool', 24th year, No 6, March 1978, page 319 et seq.).
- The average scientist reads only 10% of all the articles he receives (300 per year out of 3000). (See P.J. Vinken, ibid.)

(12) It happens not infrequently that scientists of the same mother tongue read (and interpret) each others' texts in what is for them a foreign language, usually English. In itself, this is an uneconomic procedure which can only involve a double loss of information value. The fact is that scientific works are written and published in English, perhaps simply for reasons of prestige, even when this may not be necessary in view of the intended of distribution.

(13) History shows that the importance of a language is determined by political, cultural and social (and even scientific and technological) trends. The importance of English is thus probably also transient, just as was the case with Latin as the language of science at one stage in history.

Apart from the essentially less acceptable obstacle of chauvinism, any international predominance of one language will, in particular, come up against the cultral individuality of the many people for whom that language is not their mother tongue. Nor will it be able to translate all the cultural peculiarities of the different cultures on which it has been imposed. Artificial languages have not had the expected success, despite the fact that htey have frequently been internationally oriented and have been aimed at wide areas of human existence.

It is in any case not necessary to have <u>one</u> international language, although it would appear useful to have a generalized second -or perhaps, for some, the third - language, to be acquired during the course of normal education, the aim being to have it available not for literature, but as an instrument for international communication, which is essentially communication between cultural communities.

(14) A synopsis is more extensive than an abstract an always contains the central ideas and the main conclusions of a study. A translation of this is thus in itself of great importance, since it communicates the major elements of publication to someone who is not acquainted with the original language.

One example is the Journals of Chemical Research (published by the
Société Chimique de France, The Chemical Society and the Gesellschaft
Deutscher Chemiker). The manuscripts are submitted either in French,
German or English, but the author must always add a synopsis in
English. (FOr the importance of this journal, see H. Gruñewald De
toekomst van het wetenschappelijke tijdschrift, in 'Universiteit en
Hogeschool', 24th year, No 6, March 1978, page 340 et seq.). More-
over, there are a number of scientific books and journals in Dutch-
speaking countries which contain the full texts in Dutch and abstracts in English.

Another possibility, of course, is publication of the full text in
English, with abstracts or synopses in several languages. One
example of this is the journal for sociology, ethnology and anthropology, Current Anthropology', published by the University of
Chicago Press.

That publishing synopses is effective in avoiding useless publication and translation, and thus saves money, is substantiated by
the fact that, of the 10 000 subscribers to the synopsis journal
'Journal of Chemical Research', an average of only five ask for the
full text (see H. Gruñewald, ibd., page 345).

(15) There is the semantical labyrinth of the use of scientific language.
Some examples: culture ('Culture is one of the two or three most
complicated words in the English language' states R. William in
'Keywords', London 1976, page 76) model, system, information,
communication, informatics, management (for the latter, L. F. Urwick
quotes the word in nine different meanings for one complex sense; in
all, he found some twenty meanings; The Problem of Management
Semantics in 'California Management Review', Spring 1980, No 2/3,
page 77 et seq.).

There is a confrontation between the individuality of the use of
language and the presence or absence - or partial presence - of
collective standards of meaning. The way in which the stadards of
meaning are laid down in aids such as dictionaries is also sometimes

an obstacle. Sometimes incomplete, sometimes not clear-cut, and frequently out of date.

It is sometime necessary to incorporate reduncy, i.e. superfluity of relevance or function, so as to give a clearer representation of what is meant.

Unity in the use of scientific language is intended, above all, as a search for a reasonable and comprehensible stock of terminology, as a search for common features, as a search for an interdisciplinary understanding, and as promoting an opportunity for communicating with a wider public.

For both normal language ans specialized messages, unity of language implies that there is unity between the 'language use' of the 'transmitter' and the 'language potential' of the 'receiver', so that the language used - if necessary, by including redundancy - is completely clear and adapted to the public to which one whishes to give information.

(16) Ultimately, it must be borne in mind that a text can only be effective if it reaches the reader in a form which he can understand. The sense of language lies in hearing the spoken word, in reading the written word, but above all in understanding the word. The speaker and the writer have an important task in this: the way in which he chooses his language, the way in which he translates his thoughts into language and the extent to which he applies the rules of language and accepted or familiar standards of meaning largely determine, right from the outset, whether he will be understood and to what extent the public he is aiming at will understand him - even though he will not always be able to establish whether the 'receiver' of his report has understood him.

On the other hand, it is also one of the scientist's tasks to inform the 'general public'.

LEXICOGRAPHY IN THE ELECTRONIC AGE
J. Goetschalckx and L. Rolling (editors)
North-Holland Publishing Company
© ECSC, EEC, EAEC, 1982

Discussion of the session II

New Technology

by R. HAAS

Although it is my duty as rapporteur to give as objective a picture as possible of the way the discussion went, I cannot help pointing out that the
contributions to the discussion by the members of the panel were somewhat
wide-ranging and could not always be clearly ascribed to the subject area
of new technologies. It should be mentioned, in addition, that there was
only little evidence of a real willingness to enter into discussion.

The following is as brief a summary as possible of what was said:
It was pointed out that recourse to artificial intelligence was only in its
infancy. The use of computers is primarily restricted to those activities
which exploit two of the computer's characteristics, namely

- speed
- accuracy of operation.

The problems dealt with are such that they are in principle simple to sys-
tematize. Special attention was devoted to the treatment of non-Roman characters in the broadest sense of the term.

In addition to those activities which could more or less be described as
routine, future programmes were presented, such as the development of the
next generation of terminological data banks and further development of machine translation or the automated compilation of translation aids (lexica,
glossaries etc.).

Two contributions which lay somewhat outside the subject area of new technologies were "Language barriers and scientific communication" and the
"Description of the present language situation in Greece". On the first
topic the main factors which lead to the establishment of such barriers
were outlined and proposals were made for economically viable ways of, if
not removing, at least lowering them. Heavy emphasis was laid both on the

127

English language and on international and interdisciplinary cooperation, although with respect to English we were warned against being too optimistic about its chances of becoming an "interlingua" (lingua franca).

Two main problems were raised in describing the present language situation in Greece.

- firstly, the changeover to a "modern" Greek involving the introduction of a new grammar;

- secondly, the need to fill the gaps in Greek vocabulary, particularly in the scientific and technical fields in their broadest sense.

True discussion was limited to a few points. The main points which should be mentioned are those I have discussed above and the doubts expressed with regard to an orthophonic dictionary.

SESSION III
TERM BANKS

The Terminological Activities at the
Commission of the European Communities
    J. GOETSCHALCKX

International Efforts of Termnet towards the
Recording of Terminologies in Machine-
Readable Form
    H. FELBER and Ch. GALINSKI

Linguistic Criteria to Evaluate Terminology
Banks
    R. GOFFIN

Specialised Lexicography in the Context of a
British Linguistic Data Bank
    J. McNAUGHT

Software for Terminology Data Banks
    A.E. NEGUS

Discussion of the Session III by
    P. FRANÇOIS

LEXICOGRAPHY IN THE ELECTRONIC AGE
J. Goetschalckx and L. Rolling (editors)
North-Holland Publishing Company
© ECSC, EEC, EAEC, 1982

THE TERMINOLOGICAL ACTIVITIES AT THE COMMISSION

OF THE EUROPEAN COMMUNITIES

J. GOETSCHALCKX

Adviser

Medium and Long-Term Translation Service

Head of Terminology Bureau

Commission of the European Communities

Abstract

The European Community, which is a Community of various nations speaking
different languages, is a multilingual organization. This multilingualism
is carried to extremes for acts of primary and secondary Community law,
particularly when such acts must be published in the Official Journal.

In order to cope with the problems of translation and terminology this
entails, Community linguists turn to the lexicographical works available
on the market, to index card systems and glossaries compiled by the
Community's own language services or by organizations which play a more
or less similar role in other fields or within other geographical or
political areas, and lastly to a term bank or to machine translation.

The time would now appear to be ripe for studying the ways and means by
which traditional lexicographical activities and the creative terminological activities of such organizations could become of mutual benefit.

When the father of the European Community, Jean Monnet - after whom this building is named - declared 'we do not want to ally states but to unite peoples', he not only laid the foundations for the Community's and its institutions' progress towards unity and integration, but also provided the basis for this organization's multilingualism. It is, however, the job of the Community's linguists to ensure that this concert of nations does not develop into dissonance.

Once one has multilingualism one needs translation, and if one has translation one needs terminology. It is therefore not surprising to find this even mentioned in the Treaties. It is in fact laid down in the Treaty establishing the European Atomic Energy Community, under Article 8, that 'It (the Joint Nuclear Research Centre) shall also ensure that a uniform nuclear terminology . (is.) .. established'.

What was felt to be necessary at the time in the nuclear field, which was relatively new and thus an exciting and somewhat frightening focal point for industry and research, is no less necessary in all other fields, even traditional ones. Broadly speaking, the same activities and professions exist everywhere, but they have not always developed in the same way, have not always been based on the same models and do not always operate within the same social, economic or legal context. All this, added to the fact that each language has its own specific character, has led to differences between the various terminologies.

There are nonetheless exceptions to the above remarks, for example there are no coalmines or vineyards in Denmark. Similary, there are professions which exist in the North and not in the South, to mention only the post of ombudsman.

Terminological difficulties in translation can naturally occur at two levels. Firstly, when trying to understand the original text, and secondly when drawing up the translation in the target language. The specialized terminology which occurs in the source language may be so esoteric that the meaning of the sentences loses its clarity and becomes ambiguous or even totally unfathomable. Quite apart from cases in which the text - written by an expert for an expert - keeps the translator guessing by using ellipitcal expressions. When an article on printing refers to a 'touche 3 mm', it is not obvious that this means a contact pressure produced by a 3 mm gap between the two parts in question, although this seemed perfectly clear to the expert.

On the other hand, the technical terms used in the source language may turn out to be perfectly comprehensible even though they do not belong to the everyday vocabulary of the language, either because their etymology is crystal-clear or because the sentence (micro-context) or the whole text (macro-context) sufficiently clarifies the meaning. However, this does not mean that the translator, who is often of necessity a 'jack of all trades', will know the corresponding terms in the target language even if this is his mother tongue. Sometimes, he may be able to get away with using a circum-locution. Should a translator write in his text that basalt 'deteriorates', this is not serious because the expert, who is expecting the verb 'weather', will correct it himself. However, this is not always possible. To come back to the printing industry, it is clear that, in order to translate the term 'cahier', one has to know that this is translated into English as 'signature', since simply translating the word 'cahier' would in most cases make the translation indecipherable.

A specific and familiar problem to all those who deal frequently with legal texts is that of ensuring that uniform and consistent terminology is used, once again in order to avoid ambiguity in the interpretation of the text.

This concern to find the precise term is important in making texts more intelligible. Naturally, ambiguity can never be completely avoided. However, when a translator, in a text on mines, covers the concept of depth by the specilized term 'Teufe' in German, and not by the general word 'Tiefe', the informed reader will know that he is dealing with an expert and that he can trust his judgement. Once the problem had been posed and more or less understood by those concerned, solutions had to be found.

The first solution was obviously that of compiling index card system, both on an individual basis and collectively for use in the early termino-

logy departments. These index card systems, which still exist, are
basically the result of selective searches by translators and terminological difficulties which inevitably occur day to day translation.

Very early on these selective searches produced, in addition to feelings
of satisfaction at a successfully completed search, feelings of frus-
tration at unsolved terminological requests, or at least at requests
which had not received what could be called a satisfaction answer from
the terminologist's point of view. This is in many cases a matter of
time, because one is often aware that the answer to a question exists
somewhere. The real problem is having the time to reach the person who
has the answer to your problem.

The above observation led to the conclusion that the ideal solution would
be to pre-empt questions by ensuring that the answer was available before
the question was put. This is what led to the compilation of thematic
glossaries.

Such glossaries are based on a comparative assessment of original documents in each language. The information can be presented either in
phraseological format or with terms backed up by definitions and further
explanation. The source of each piece of information must be clearly
noted even if this is not mentioned in the published version of the
glossary.

It is clear that the above method is particularly applicable to scientific and technical terminology, Glossaries aimed at ensuring the use of
uniform and consistent language, such as the glossaries on the Treaties,
on Staff Regulations or the Budget, are based on the translated texts
which have been officially recognized and adopted.

Terminological work is not restricted to the Terminology Bureaux alone.
For example, the Commission department responsible for Euronorms has also
undertaken to define certain terms and to standardize their equivalences.
The Business Cooperation Centre has just published a glossary in seven
languages on sub-contracting in the metals sector, and the department
responsible for the removal of technical barriers recently published a

glossary of the main terms used in national legislation on the building sector. The division responsible for approving electrical apparatus used in potentially explosive atmospheres is also intending to standardize to some extent the terminology used. The Secretariat-General and the Office for Official Publications apply certain rules on the use of abbrebiations for currency units etc.

Sometimes such work is done in collaboration with the Terminology Bureaux. The work on electrical apparatus is done for example in conjunction with Brussels, and on the building sector in conjunction with Luxembourg.

But all systems have their limitations. Once a certain volume of input, and especially a certain number of languages, is reached, a traditional index card system becomes unwiedly. It should not be forgotten that one term in seven languages should produce, in the simples hypothesis, seven index cards. Should the term be complex and require cross-referencing then this number can be greatly increased. An if there are several synonyms in different languages then total confusion may ensue. There are fish which have 7 or 8 names in one language alone.

The same is true of glossaries. When one has a cupboard full of glossaries, one no longer knows which one to consult, in spite of the attempt at classification made in the publication called 'Fil d'Ariane'.

The use of the computer, therefore, ultimately became inevitable. The first attempts a this were Euroterm and the KWOC lists for texts concerning the legislation and regulations of the European Economic Community. The Dicautom of the High Autority of the European Coal and Steel Community was the first attempt at producing phraseological glossaries and starting a term bank which could also be consulted via a praseological formats. The Euratom Glossary, produced because of the legal obligation imposed by the Euratom Treaty, was also published using a computer.

For various reasons, these first attempts were not followed up. However, these projects were not fruitless. As approaches and systems design matured they led to the creation of a real terminological data bank called EURO-DICAUTOM. As its name implies, this data bank is specifically based on experience gained with Dicautom and on regular exchanges of views with colleagues from the other institutions within the Interinstitutional Terminology Group (GIIT).

A multilingual organization's terminological data bank but cannot be multilingual, with all the advantages and drawbacks that this entails. At present, the six official languages are represented to varying degrees. Greek will be added to the bank as soon as the technical difficulties involved in including the Gree alphabet in the computer and displaying it on the terminals have been solved.

Terminological data is either displayed in a phraseological form or as a term backed up by a definition or accompanied by an illustrative context, or the two combined. Sometimes, there will even be term representation. This is a makeshift solution which we accept as a second best, with the firm intention of upgrading such items as soon as possible by adding a definition or an illustrative context. A note is often extremely useful. Amongst other things, it may contain what we call the 'semantic word', i.e. a word which indicates in uncoded form the field in which the term being sought is used. As an example of what I mean, 'biophotolysis' as term (VE) with 'biomass' as note (NT), tells the user in what context the term was found. It is always possible that a term will be translated differently in a different field.

The note can also be a source of further information, such as etymology, unusual plural form, local usage, technical or political context etc.

The bank may be accessed either in batch processing mode or on-line. The terminologists who manage the system normally use batch processing because this enables them to tidy the bank up on a more or less permanent basis.

When people other than terminologists consult the bank, the system has been designed so that this can be done on-line, directly by the end user, which in practice means the translator or any other person who actually needs terminological data.

There were two main reasons for this decision: firstly, one has to admit that only the translator has full knowledge of the broad context of the terminological problems he has to solve. Therefore, he is best placed to assess just how relevant the answer provided by the system is.

The second reason was that, as terminologists are few and far between, their workload should be reduced as much as possible, and that therefore they ought not to act as intermediaries between the translator and the system. On the other hand, it did not seem wise to entrust the consultation of the terminological data bank to non-linguists. Firstly, because it would be even more difficult for such a person to assess the relevance of the answer given, and secondly because the standard search involves five or six questions which have to be rapidly answered. There would thus not be time, for example, to interrogate the computer a second time giving a closer definition of the problem.

Having made this decision, a system had to be brought into operation which would be extremely simple to access, even for someone who is not at all familiar with computers, and which would also not force the translator to completely change his working methods.To a certain extent, therefore, the system is modelled on the normal proceding used by the translator. This is the basic principle behind one of the characteristics of the system, which is the part reply.

The translator searching for a complex expression, such as 'charge nominale de rupture finale', and who does not obtain a straight and complete answer, will be very glad to have the following part replies
charge de rupture finale
charge de rupture
charge nominale.

Similary, if a translator is seeking the complex expression 'aéroglisseur à jupe souple', he will certainly be pleased to find on the terminal jupe souple
jupe souple
aéroglisseur à jupe rigide
aéroglisseur.

Using the above information, he can piece together without difficulty a complete answer to his query.

Should the part replies not be relevant, the user can stop interrogating the system, in the knowledge that, because the answering is weighted, the term bank will subsequently provide a fuller answer.

The anomalies which occur from time to time are the outcome of program hitches which are now being ironed out.

Eurodicautom has also been available via Euronet for approximately one year. Roughly 90 institutions or individuals have a link. This raises different problems. The users are no longer a uniform group. It is no longer just translators but also documentalists who use the system. In general, the documentalist is not a layman in computer matters. In addition, he has working habits and a way of thinking and approaching a problem which are not the same as those of the translator. The translator is always worried that he will not find an answer. It is common knowledge that one never really finds what one wants in dictionaries either. The documentalist, on the other hand, is always scared that he will get too many answers and takes steps beforehand to pinpoint his questions more clearly. What is more, Euronet links operate on 300 bauds. This means that passages which take only a fraction of a second to appear on the screens of Community translators take whole seconds or even several seconds to reach the distant screens of Euronet users.

Once the system has been used regularly for at least a year by the translators of the Community institutions, the experience gained could lead to a new, faster version of the software for experienced users.

The major problem of any data base is naturally its input, and the same is true for terminological data banks. In my view, there are two possible approaches. Firstly, one could provide mass input and rely on the law of averages to provide a high hit rate. The other approach is based on noting terminological problems which occur in texts for translation, so that these can be systematically solved and used as input for the system. This means that each term search will only be carried out once for each pair of languages.

The two approaches could be complementary rather than mutually exclusive. In addition, mass input is feasible only for those fields in which the Communities carry out their activities, and translator feedback only becomes useful when a certain volume is reached. In a multilingual system, the second input method is, however, much less viable than in a bilingual one. Documents are not always translated into all the Community languages, and the difficulties encountered by translators are not always the same in the various languages.

One pitfall which mut be avoided is redundancy. It makes the search unnecessarily longer, increases machine time and annoys the user. Eliminating redundancy cannot be achieved solely by programming and therefore requires a lot of qualified and scarce personnel. What is more, some sets of terminology which are in the form of a nomenclature, such as the Common Customs Tariff, the Nimexe and others, often have to be kept as they stand. In such cases, slight redundancy would appear inevitable.

In the final analysis what is the point of a terminological data bank?

Its major advantages are its more or less unlimited storage capacity and its unrivalled search speed. We only need to think of the time required to consult a traditional index card system: first of all, look for the drawer which contains the section of the alphabet required, then look for the index card, read the card, and return it to its original position. Compare this to the same process at a computer terminal, whilst bearing in mind that it is infinitely quicker to copy the contents of a screen on the printer connected to the terminal than to photocopy an index card.

Since, in addition, all the information is centralized, there is no need to wonder where to look for it. Where input is concerned, a single card is used for all the languages, and there is no longer any need to deal with multiple entries. There is no problem involved in adding languages or other data, definitions or notes for example, at a later date, since what has already been put into the system does not need to be rewritten. No card will ever disappear because of an oversight or a deliberate user essor, or be put back out of alphabetical order.

At the 'Bundessprachenamt', after more than 20 years of operation, the
average number of requests per day is approximately 1 500. At the Communities, the translators have not yet become used to considering Eurodicautom as a front-rank aid. On the contrary, they only use it as a last
resort after having exhausted all the other data sources, as is shown by
the Negus Report. Under such circumstances, an average hit rate of 20 to
30% - the figures most commonly quoted - is more than respectable,
especially if one considers that the Bundessprachenamt term bank contains
1 400 000 pairs of terms, mainly English, German, Russian and to a lesser
extent French, Dutch and Italian. Eurodicautom, on the other hand,
contains only 1 100 000 pairs of terms in the 6 languages. Their proportions are as follows, French 98%, English 95%, German 57%, Italian
48%, Dutch 42%, Danish 40%.

There is therefore still massive development potential, since with only a
few terminals and trained users there were already some 100 questions per
day in 1980. What then is the way forward? I have already referred to the
possible use of a more direct and faster interrogation procedure, as soon
as enough users have mastered the system to an extent which makes such an
improvement feasible.

As for input, ways should be found of recovering the results of the
terminological searches carried out by translators every day, particularly by those who, by character or inclination, prefer to pursue their
own research.

Mass input should also be continued. In this connection, however, the
question is whether terminologists and lexicographers ought not to
combine their efforts. There are programs which make it possible to
extract thematic glossaries from the main corpus of a lexicon. We are
working on programs for tidying up the raw output from glossaries retrieved in this way using word processing equipment.

Similary, many editors of lexicographical works use data processing aids
in order to produce their dictionaries. The computer, the word processor
and photocomposition have at ready made their appearance here too.

Cooperation on such matters therefore seems both logical and desirable. Now is perhaps the time to discuss this, when we are all gathered here in this building which is named after the orginator of sectoral integration.

International organizations are cooperating. Mr. Lewandowski, assistant Secretary General of the United Nations, stressed this once more at the FIT Congress in Warsaw. They are also seeking ways of cooperating with national organizations. Specialized national and international organizations could help us in their specific spheres of interest. I am thinking of the International Union of Railways or the International Telecommunication Union, the mention only two.

My conclusion will be on the same note: this task is far too great for us to hope to accomplish it alone. This is not our aim, quite the contrary. But it would seem fair to assume that each organization can make its own contribution, the European Communities like other organizations and, if possible, together with them.

LEXICOGRAPHY IN THE ELECTRONIC AGE
J. Goetschalckx and L. Rolling (editors)
North-Holland Publishing Company

INTERNATIONAL EFFORTS OF TERMNET TOWARDS THE RECORDING

OF TERMINOLOGIES IN MACHINE-READABLE FORM

H. FELBER and Ch. GALINSKI

International Information Centre for Terminology (Infoterm)

Summary

This paper gives an overview of the activities of Infoterm and
TermNet in the field of computer application to terminology
work. Especially TermNet programmes two and three are
dedicated to this task. In preparation of an international co-
operation of producers and users of terminological data,
conferences were convened by Infoterm and studies carried out.
It has become an inevitable necessity to record terminological
data in machine readable form and process them by computer.
The management of the terminological data flow by electronic
means requires international guidelines and standards and
an intensive collaboration of all parties concerned.

1. INTRODUCTION

The rapid progress taking place in all fields of human activities causes and will cause in future an enormous increase of the number of new concepts which are to be expressed by linguistic signs and symbols, i.e. terms, letters, graphic symbols etc. This phenomenon is common to each language spoken by people who want to participate in the advancement of human knowledge and skills. In order to be able to cope with the implications of this development, terminology was developed as a scientific discipline and terminological activities have escalated both on an international and national level during the last few decades.

Terminology has been recognized by more and more scholars, scientists and practitioners as a basis for:

- the ordering of knowledge (development of systems of concepts for each subject field)
- the transfer of knowledge, skills and technology (especially in training and education)
- the transfer of subject information and knowledge from one language to another (translation and interpretation)
- the formulation of subject information
- the abstracting and condensing of technical information
- the indexing, classifying and retrieval of information (thesaurus construction and usage).

At the beginning of this century quite a number of enormous terminographic undertakings were launched such as the "International Electrotechnical Vocabulary" (IEV) (from 1909 onwards), Schlomann's "Illustrierte Technische Wörterbücher" (1900-1932), the "Technolexikon" of the Verein Deutscher Ingenieure (VDI) (1900-1905) and many more (1).

In 1936 the preparation of terminological principles and methods was taken up by the International Federation of Standardizing Associations (ISA). This work is carried on by Technical Committee 37 "Terminology (principles and co-ordination)" of the International Organization for

Standardization (ISO), the Secretariat of which is held
by the Austrian Standards Institute (ON) (2). The International Information Centre for Terminology (Infoterm) which
is affiliated to the ON, was established in 1971 with the
task of co-ordinating terminological activities around the
world.

During the last decade a number of terminological data
banks was established by national and transnational organizations in all parts of the world and there are still many
more in development or planning.

2. INFOTERM AND TERMNET (3)

With a view to promoting terminological activities
Unesco established within the framework of UNISIST as part
of the General Information Programme the International
Information Centre for Terminology (Infoterm) which is
financed by the Austrian Government, the Federal Chamber of
Commerce, the Austrian Standards Institute and Unesco.

UNISIST is a Unesco intergovernmental programme to encourage and guide voluntary co-operation in the exchange of
scientific and technical information at national, regional
and international levels.

The activities and tasks of Infoterm are:
- to collect and analyse terminological information
- to collect standardized and other specialized
  vocabularies and compile bibliographies of them
- to offer information services
- to give advice on the application of terminological
  principles
- to teach the general theory of terminology
- to function as author and/or editor of the Infoterm
  Series, the Infoterm Newsletters, the TermNet News
  and many other publications and documents
- to function as co-editor of the international
  periodical "Fachsprache"
- to prepare studies of the development of terminology

- to launch and carry out pilot projects (sometimes in co-operation with other TermNet partners
- to hold university courses and provide in-house training
- to organize international meetings and conferences
- to promote the standardization of terminology.

At the First Infoterm Symposium (Vienna 1975) (4) it was decided to create an international network for terminological activities, with the name "TermNet". At the time being this network is in the process of being developed on the basis of a study which was prepared by Infoterm in 1976 and was approved by a special advisory group of Unesco in 1977 (6).

In order to secure a harmonious and co-ordinated development of all aspects of terminology three working programmes have been set up for TermNet:

Programme 1: Developing the scientific basis for terminology (General theory and principles of terminology)

Programme 2: Establishing closer co-operation in preparing terminologies and in recording them in machine-readable form

Programme 3: Establishing closer co-operation in collecting, recording, processing and disseminating terminological data and information.

A graphical scheme of Infoterm's activities and the TermNet Programmes is attached as Appendix 1.

3. <u>THE NECESSITY OF PREPARING TERMINOLOGIES AND OF RECORDING THEM IN MACHINE-READABLE FORM</u>

The rapid progress in all areas of human activity requires, as a consequence, unceasing terminology work. In the present and future society in which subject information plays an important role, the exact meaning of concepts used in science, technology, economics and the humanities has to be determined and known before any useful

communiction can be established. In other words, terminology
is the prerequisite of any scientific activity. The number
of newly created concepts increases at such a rate that the
formation of new terms from word elements (terminological
morphemes) will become extremely difficult. The number of
concepts is about a thousand times larger than the number
of word elements available in each language to form terms.
Due to this unfavourable relation between concepts and word
elements, methods such as the combination of word elements
and transfer of meanings have been applied, which in many
cases have caused ambiguities and confusions in the respective system of concepts.
The only way out of this dilemma is the strict observance
of terminological principles and guidelines.

The preparation of terminologies and their updating at
regular intervals should be a common effort of all learned,
professional and specialized organizations and subject
specialists of the world. If they are not willing to make
this effort, they will sooner or later not be able
to disseminate the knowledge and the skills of their disciplines and professions in an efficient way. This would have
repercussions in the way of duplication of efforts in
research, development and innovation resulting in a large
scale waste of human skills and talents.

4. A NEW TERMINOGRAPHIC APPROACH

The times when terminologies for many a specialized
field were prepared by single terminographers and were
based on the lexicographical rules of common language
vocabularies have passed. Instead a new systematic approach,
which is based on the teamwork of subject experts, terminologists and computer experts within terminology committees
and commissions has been developed (7).

The characteristic features of this new approach are:
- the strict application of internationally acknowledged terminological principles and methods which make a decentralized terminology work possible and the products compatible
- the application of computer-aids for the recording, storage, exchange and dissemination of data
- the cooperation of data producers (e.g. specialized organizations), of data processing agencies (e.g. data banks and computer centres) and of information disseminators (e.g. data base hosts, publishers)
- the worldwide planning of terminological activities which allows a coordinated development of terminology in all subject fields.

5. TERMNET PROGRAMME 2

This programme is designed to begin a co-operative project involving subject specialists and terminologists in a joint effort to prepare terminologies and to record their terminological data in machine-readable form in all branches of science, technology, economics and in various professions, to keep these records up-to-date and develop terminologies which do not yet exist, with due consideration of user needs and of the development of the disciplines concerned. This is a comprehensive undertaking which requires the co-operation of specialized and professional organizations (subject specialists), organizations processing terminological data (terminological data banks, computer centres) and organizations for the dissemination of terminological data (terminological data banks, information systems, publishing houses). Infoterm could provide terminological advice to and management services for the project.

These terminologies are to be prepared as far as possible in accordance with international terminological principles by subject specialists (e.g. terminology commissions) from competent specialized and professional organizations with the co-operative guidance of terminologists and kept-up-to-

date. They are to be recorded in machine-readable form in
an agreed format to be standardized by ISO. They are to be
distributed via terminological data banks, information
systems and networks or publishing houses in a form
(magnetic disc or tape, microfiche, book or others) that
will meet the needs of different user groups. Modern technology will make it possible to supply these data on microfiche or in book form, directly accessible via monitor from
data banks on small magnetic discs with a large storage
capacity. The use of microcomputers will enable the user or
small co-operative groups of users to have access to a terminological data base, consisting of small discs, the holdings
of which will, of course, be kept up to date.

Since various user groups (subject specialists,
language mediators, information specialists) have different
needs, optimal machine-readable terminological files are
to be designed in accordance with these needs. This requires
research and its practical application in pilot projects,
e.g. files will have to be modelled on the basis of Wüster's
General Theory of Terminology in order to meet the needs of
subject specialists.
The objective of TermNet Programme 2 is the recording and
updating of the existing terminologies in machine-readable
form of as many subject fields as possible so that the
terminological data are easily available and accessible to
the users and can serve as the basis for scientific
communication.

5.1 Unified guidelines and formats

There are special principles laid down for the preparation of terminologies which have also been published as ISO
Recommendations and ISO Standards. For the recording of
terminologies in machine-readable form an international
format based on unified terminological data elements will
have to be created. In preparation of such a format a
comparative study on terminological data elements was

carried out and an expert meeting was convened by Infoterm
with the assistance of Unesco (8).

5.2 Plan for recording terminologies in machine-readable form

A plan will have to be made outlining the actions to be
taken by all parties concerned. This will comprise the
following five stages:

(1) preparatory work

(2) creation of terminological vocabularies by
    subject specialists

(3) recording of terminological data in machine-
    readable form

(4) data processing

(5) data dissemination

In addition proposals for pilot projects will be worked
out. Furthermore a discussion of the possible presentation of
terminological data on various data carriers and of possible
distributors of terminological products will be necessary.
In regard to the marketing of these products, terminological
data banks, information systems as well as publishing houses
will have to be taken into consideration.

5.3 Co-operation in the field of data processing

Terminologies prepared by subject specialists and recorded in machine-readable form are to be processed by
computer centres specializing in terminological data (i.e.
mostly terminological data banks). The output of these data
banks in form of magnetic tapes and discs serves as the
basis for the production of other data carriers (i.e. microfiches, books, etc.).

5.4 Implementation of TermNet Programme 2

In preparation of this project the following activities
are required:

(1) the application of international guidelines and
    standards for compiling, structuring, systematizing,
    recording, processing and disseminating terminologies.

(2) consultancy services to organizations with respect to the recording of terminological data and to the possibilities of processing these data by competent institutions.

(3) the co-operation with existing terminological data banks.

(4) the organization of international training courses on the application of terminological principles to be offered to specialists.

As a first step an attempt will have to be made to convince the foremost international professional organization of the necessity to record terminologies in machine-readable form. As a matter of fact, terminologies are already recorded in a number of organizations.

6. PREPARATORY WORK

Infoterm has already begun to implement TermNet Programme 2.

On the one hand efforts are being made to create the necessary working tools for terminologists, i.e. standards, guidelines, directories, bibliographies, etc. Special mention has to be made in this connection of the computerization of the "World Guide to Terminological Activities" (9) which includes data on terminological commissions, committees and projects. On the other hand meetings and conferences have been convened by Infoterm in order to provide a discussion forum for the experts concerned. The following events were pertinent to this work:

(1) The First International Conference on Terminological Data Banks was held in Vienna in 1979. Terminological data banks require reliable terminological data from the disciplines concerned in order to become efficient and worthwhile.(10)

(2) An international meeting of experts on terminological data elements was held in Vienna in September 1980. The unification of terminological data

elements and the creation of a format for the
recording of terminological data are basic for an
international cooperation of term banks.(11)
(3) A joint meeting of Infoterm with the Union of
International Technical Associations (UATI)
was held in Vienna in November 1980. The TermNet
Programmes, in particular Programme 2, were
presented and discussed there.(12)

A keen interest in an international co-operation for recording terminological data in various subject fields has been
indicated to Infoterm by several universities and specialized organizations such as some standards organizations
which have terminological data banks or which develop such
banks. A concrete co-operation is coming into existence
in the field of civil engineering.

7. THE ROLE OF INTERNATIONAL GUIDELINES AND ISO-STANDARDS

For the preparation, recording, layout, exchange and
dissemination of terminological data international guidelines and ISO-Standards are required (13).

7.1 Preparation, layout, exchange, dissemination

A set of international standards (ISO-Recommendations
and ISO-Standards) and of national standards for the
preparation of terminologies, for the layout of vocabularies and for the exchange of terminological data are in
existence. A bibliography was prepared by Infoterm which
is kept up to date in form of the revised Infoterm Newsletter nr. 4. (14)

7.2 Recording

The most important standard to be issued is a catalogue
of unified terminological data elements. This standard will
have to include a set of mandatory data elements which represent the minimum set of information necessary for the

identification and description of concepts. Preparatory
work for this was done by an expert meeting on terminological data elements which was convened by Infoterm with the
assistance of Unesco (see above under 6). In addition to
it, a standard on the recording of terminological data in
machine-readable form is required. Infoterm, in co-operation
with Unesco, intends to convene expert meetings on these
topics.

8. PREPARATION, RECORDING, PROCESSING AND DISSEMINATION OF TERMINOLOGICAL DATA

The implementation of TermNet Programme 2 will have to
be considered under two aspects: the technical and the
organizational aspect.

    (1) The technical aspect concerns the preparation of
        terminologies,i.e. the compilation, systematization,
        recording, processing and dissemination of termino-
        logical data as well as the application of standards
        to this work.

    (2) The organizational aspect concerns matters such as
       - convincing specialized organizations of the
         necessity to prepare terminologies and keep them
         up to date.
       - to assist in the organization of joint projects
       - to give advice to organizations on how to prepare
         terminologies, how to apply principles and
         standards, how to record terminological data in
         machine-readable form and finally how to
         establish a data bank.
       - to organize and offer international training
         courses on the application of terminological
         principles;
       - to organize and convene meetings and conferences
         dedicated to the specific problems concerning
         the implementation of TermNet Programme 2;
       - to ensure that the computerized "World Guide to

Terminological Activities", including data on
organizations, institutions, committees, commissions, data banks and on projects in progress is
constantly updated;
- to ensure that the International Bibliography of
  standardized vocabularies and the International
  Bibliography of Mono- and Multilingual Specialized
  Vocabularies is kept up to date and made available
  to users in machine-readable form or in microform;
- to provide an information service about all
  magnetic tapes available which contain terminological data.

Since the creation of terminological data banks is very
expensive, the various specialized organizations and their
groupings (e.g. ICSU, UATI, etc.) will have to examine very
carefully whether it is necessary to establish individual
data banks. In most cases it will be more economical to
render the magnetic tapes which carry the terminology of a
subject field to a terminological data bank already in
existence or to data base hosts and use their services.

9. FUTURE WAYS OF CO-OPERATION BETWEEN DATA SUPPLIERS AND DATA DISSEMINATORS

Terminological data should be offered in such a form
as is most useful to the various types of users. Specific
forms of co-operation between data suppliers and data
disseminators (publishers, data banks, data base hosts,
etc.) will have to be established and organized on an
international level.
As a consequence, specific forms of co-operation between
data suppliers (e.g. spezialized organizations) and data
disseminators (e.g. publishers, data banks, data base hosts)
will develop which will require a permanent dialogue between the parties involved.

In analogy to the field of information and documentation, joint efforts will have to be undertaken with respect to training of users and producers of terminological data as well as to research and development of the science and methodology of terminology.

10. OUTLOOK INTO THE FUTURE

The TermNet Programme 2 is a long term project which requires good will, co-operative spirit as well as moral and financial support by those benefitting most from it. A set of pilot projects will have to be carried out to create the tools for its functioning. Infoterm is prepared to function as catalyst for the realization of this programme. The process will, however, depend on the amount of work and effort with which individual organizations will support this programme. Whoever is capable of contributing to it is invited to do so.

References:

(1) WÜSTER, E. Internationale Sprachnormung in der Technik, besonders in der Elektrotechnik. (Die nationale Sprach- normung und ihre Verallgemeinerung) [The international standardization of language in engineering, especially in electrical engineering. (The national standardization of language and its generalization)]. 3rd rev.ed. Bonn: Bouvier, 1970, 160x230 mm, (Sprachforum, Beiheft Nr. 2), p. 206 ff.

(2) FELBER, H. Die internationale terminologische Grundsatz- normung - Rückblick und Ausblick [The international standardization of terminological principles - retro- spective and perspective view].
In: FELBER, H.; LANG, F.; WERSIG, G. Terminologie als angewandte Sprachwissenschaft - Gedenkschrift für Univ.-Prof. Dr. Eugen Wüster [Terminology as applied

linguistics. Homage to Prof. E. Wüster]. München/New York/London/Paris: K.G. Saur, 1979, p. 61-69, A5.

(3) FELBER, H. Infoterm and TermNet. Plans, Activities, Achievements. International Classification 7 (1980), nr. 3, p. 140-145; and TermNet News 1 (1980), p. 21-62.

(4) INFOTERM. First Infoterm Symposium. International Co-operation in Terminology/Premier Symposium d'Infoterm. Coopération internationale en Terminologie. München: Verlag Dokumentation, 1976, 332 p. A5 (Infoterm Series 3).

(5) FELBER, H. Study on the development of a network for terminology information and documentation. Wien, 1978, 45 p., A4. (Infoterm 1-78).

(6) UNESCO. Report on the meeting for the evaluation of the study of the development of a network for terminology information and documentation, prepared by Infoterm. Vienna, 1977 (unpublished), 12 p., A4.

(7) FELBER, H. Theory of terminology, terminology work and terminology documentation. Interaction and world-wide development. Fachsprache 1 (1979), nr. 1-2, p. 20-32.

(8) FELBER, H. Draft - A comparative study on the termino-logical data elements of the general theory of termi-nology and on those data elements used in terminologi-cal data banks of the world, 39 p., A4, (TermNet 1-80).

(9) KROMMER-BENZ, M. World Guide to Terminological Activi-ties/Guide mondial des activités terminologiques. München: Verlag Dokumentation, 1977, 311 p., A5 (Infoterm Series 4).

(10) INFOTERM. Terminological Data Banks. Proceedings of the First International Conference convened in Vienna, April 2-3, 1979, by Infoterm. München: Verlag Dokumentation, 1980, 207 p., A5. (Infoterm Series 5).

(11) INFOTERM. Report on the meeting of experts on termino-logical data elements. Vienna: Infoterm, Sept. 1980, 29 p. (TermNet 4-80).

(12) UATI - WORKING GROUP 1 "TERMINOLOGY". Minutes of the
     meeting held in Vienna (Austria) on 7 November 1980/
     Procès verbal de la réunion qui s'est tenue à
     Vienne (Autriche) le 7 novembre 1980 - 4ème session.
     Paris, 1980, 14 p., A4 (UATI - WG 1-12-80 (E) + (F)).
(13) FELBER, H. International standardization of terminology
     - Theoretical and methodological aspects. International
     Journal of the Sociology of Language. Special issue
     "Standardization of Nomenclature", 1980, nr. 23,
     p. 65-81.
(14) Infoterm Newsletter 4. List of "Terminological principles
     and methods of terminological lexicography". Lebende
     Sprachen, 22 (1977), nr. 2, p. 93-95, updated 1981-04-21.

LEXICOGRAPHY IN THE ELECTRONIC AGE
J. Goetschalckx and L. Rolling (editors)
North-Holland Publishing Company
© ECSC, EEC, EAEC, 1982

LINGUISTIC CRITERIA TO EVALUATE TERMINOLOGY BANKS

by

R. GOFFIN

Commission of the European Communities

Terminology Bureau (Brussels)

SUMMARY

The aim of this document is to present some observations resulting from
an attempted critical analysis of the methods for evaluating - on the
basis of linguistic criteria - a terminology data bank for translators.

Such a data bank quite naturally falls within the dynamic translation
process and this factor must be taken into account for the evaluation
plan. Evaluation must take account upstream of various parameters concerned with terminological density, extraction from context and break-up
of source text; at the transfer stage, of several parameters concerned
with the various permutation models; finally, downstream, of parameters
concerned with reinsertion into context and reactualization in the target
text. The central problem is that of the relationship between the neutralized terminologism and the consistency of the discourse. Thus it is not
solely the number of references which determines the wealth of a data
bank but the relevance and possible permutations between the information
items stored.

1. Data processing serving terminological research

The application of data processing to the language fields has been a
fairly recent venture and yet it is a subject which has already
acquired its myths and preconceptions; it has had its prophets and
high-priests and has its theorists and its practitioners its own
technical vocabulary and its jargon (linguisticians, mediatize and
didacticial). Its holy cities (Montreal and Luxembourg) are recognised, its filibusters and grand wizards feared and it will soon be
claiming its first martyrs.

Data processing was first harnessed for the purpose of lexicology in
1949. The computer was in the first place a machine for storing,
sorting and retrieving information and a way of drawing up alphabetical lists, frequency indexes and correlation tables and thus of
studying prallel terms. The task of putting Saint Thomas Aquinas's
work on the computer was started in 1949. Father R. Busa analysed a
total of 10 660 000 words. The Institut de la langue française, first
at Besançon and then at Nancy, entered 70 million words taken from the
works of major French authors. Computer lexicology was off to a good
start.

Terminological research has been bound up with data processing since
the end of the 1960's. The LEXIS system developed by the Federal
Languages Office in Hürth, the Siemens TEAM system Terminologie -
Erfassungs -und Auswertungsmethode), the Montreal University terminology bank set up on 2 October 1970 under the name TERMIUM and handed
over to the Ottawa Translation Bureau in 1975, the Quebec Terminology
Bank, the NORMATERM system and the EURODICAUTOM terminological data
bank together constitute adequate proof that computerized terminology
is alive and well.

2. Multilingual terminology banks

Nowadays we have scientific and technical data bases, legal data
bases, economic and financial data bases, biblical data bases and even
equestra in data bases for racing enthusiasts. Linguistic data banks
are characterized by their own specific information structure and by
the nature of linguistic matter processed. N. Pasa the first linguistic

data banks were the word or term banks containing data taken from the lexical field. Projects are now in hand to create textual data banks and orthographic and grammatical data banks.

Depending on the nature of the unit being processed several types of lexical data banks may be distinguished:

1. The word bank: the word is regarded as a simple or complex lexical unit taken from general vocabulary;
2. The term or terminology data bank: the term is a word from a specialist language belonging to a set defined by a field of experience. As Rondeau, Grégoire and Tessier demonstrated the term 'terminology' should really be used in the plural, in contrast to the accepted usage, since what is put into the memory is terms or series of terms, not the discipline called terminology.
3. The terminological data bank: in which the terminological unit - uniterm or multiterm - is accompanied by semantic data (definition, explanatory context or note) illustrative data and documentation (reference or sources, subject code or field of application similar to the indications for usage in dictionaries).

The terminology data bank should not be confused with the automatic dictionary, which is a dictionary which may be consulted by remote means (teledictionary) and results from a machine adaptation of existing dictionaries in which alphabetical order has been changed to numerical order. Indeed, the bank is, to use the expression coined by B. Quemada, a non-dictionary. The advantages and disadvantages will be examined.

Current multilingual data banks have files based on the matching up of terms in two or more languages, frequently accompanied by definitions or information on context, files containing single-language subject terminologies (nomenclatures) accompanied by standard definitions plus the equivalent in another language.

1.Unidirectional files which provide in a specific target language; an equivalent for a term from one or more source languages; English is the pivot language in the two Canadian data banks;

2. Multidirectional files which provide equivalents in one or more target languages from a variety of source languages, so that each language may be the source language or the target language as required.

Each of the five existing multilingual data banks was designed to meet the immediate needs of specific user groups, which has meant that they all have their own particular structures and operating methods, custom-produced software and word stores reflecting actual needs. The corollary of this is almost total incompatibility as regards data structure and calculation of the number of units.

Computerized terminology is faced with rather delicate problems since the machine is not able to go too deeply into context and everyone knows the importance of context, in particular of context in translation. Whereas the human translator frequently translates 'across the meaning', the computer, often regarded as a rather clever dumb animal, is unable to adopt a reflective approach and has no access to extra-linguistic, factors. It has been said, not without foundation, that in machine translation the role of the computer is comparable to that of a man asked to translate a text without understanding it from a language he doesn't know into another language of which he has no knowledge.

Multilingual terminological and lexical data banks are affected by the following factors:

1. The lexicon constitutes an open class and a flexible set which is estimated to have 6 million units. Since the memory has such vast capacity it might eventually be possible to incorporate all the lexemes of a specific language.
2. The number of signifiers is lower than the number of ideas. Terms are stored according to homographic structure and not as polysemants.
3. There is frequently no reflexive one-to-one correspondence between the specialist language lexicons; a term may have several corresponding terms in another language.
4. It is not possible to resolve the question of equivalents at the level of the single unit, but only at the l ~l of the complex lexical unit - Example:

Lame de scie, à ruban à denture unilaterale

Life insurance company building fire escape regulations

Charrue pour labour à plat à traction animale sans avant-train.

This document is intended to present some observations and uncertainties which arose during a (rather tentative) attempt at critically analysing the methods required to evaluate terminology data banks in accordance with linguistic criteria. Evaluation of a system involves the value and the cost of that system plus an objective judgement, based on countable if not quantifiable criteria, and measurement of efficiency - that is the cost effectiveness ratio. The data currently available on hosts and producers are too fragmented and not sufficiently clearly defined to allow a truly scientific analysis of efficiency; this point will therefore be left out of account.

The value of a terminology data bank does indeed depend on many factors other than linguistic ones's;

a) technical factors: reliability and flexibility of material, response time, memory capacity, reliability of lines;

b) data processing factors: software quality, command sequences and file structure;

c) psychological factors: some people regard the computer as a rather low form of life and a nosey parker, whereas others think it a revelation for the human sciences;

d) organizational factors: whether the data base is to play the role of an 'also ran' and be consulted only after the manual file;

e) documentation factors: in particular classification by subject fields;

f) finally the purpose of the terminology bank, which for this paper we shall restrict to translation.

A data bank designed as a translator's search aid may also be useful to other users. The variety of its objectives and hence the wide-ranging circle of users and their requirements will further complicate the evaluation process.

The ground covered by this paper needs to be restricted on two fronts: 1) description of a bank for use by translators and 2) consideration of the single case of consultation in direct conversational mode.

3. The termininology bank at the centre of the translation process

It would be over simplistic to regard the terminology data bank as a sort of barn accessible by terminal from which the required bundles of hay may be extracted by means of a pitch fork. A terminology bank for translators will naturally become part of the dynamic translation process which must be taken into account for evaluating the effectiveness of a bank.

It is known that the translation process consists of three stages:

a comprehension, analysis or decoding stage, a transposition, confrontation or transcoding stage and a reformulation, synthesis or encoding stage. Although these stages are quite distinct they are frequently closely linked and interdependent.

Upstream of the bank any evaluation must take account of a certain number of parameters connected with the nature of the source text:

1) the terminological density of the source text: a text may be made up solely of terms in a nomenclature with a single meaning, i.e. it can be 100% terminological; it may contain only some such terms;
2) the choice of terms to be the subject of the question: is the translator to interrogate the bank following an initial reading for all the words of which he has no immediate active knowledge or only after he has unsuccessfully consulted traditional resources?
3) division of the terminological unit: four criteria have in fact been retained - formal, quantitative, semantic and taxonomic - all interwoven and interdependent.
4) partial or total context neutralization: the translator encounters the terminologism within the discourse, then removes it from its context, i.e. neutralizes its environment.

When making a terminological analysis, the translator locates the unknown terms in the source text and divides the text into terminological units. These units are most frequently synaptic and thus consist of at least two elements since statistics show that specialist vocabularies use 80% syntagmatic combination. This consists of a series of lexical elements (or syntagmata), collocations in English, compound terms in German and synapses in French.

Examples:

D. Druckwasserstoffbestañdigkeit : F. résistance à l'hydrogène sous pression

E. non-dispersive ultra-red gas analysis : F. analyse non dispersive des gaz aux ultra-rouges

F. charrue pour labour à plat à traction animale sans avant-train

D. Gespannkehrpflug ohne Vorderkarre : E. animal drawn reversible plough with front wheel assembly

At the transfer stage, the translator, who has taken on the role of initiator/receiver, consults the bank in conversational mode and compares a draft target text with the possible equivalents which the bank presents out of context. (see figure)

This stage involves several parameters:

1) acceptability of the responses having regard to the text;
2) possible syntagmatic combination.

Some permutation models are set out below:

The case of the monoseantics LD

M (LD) $\equiv$ (LA) in language terms

m (TD) $\equiv$ (TA) in textual terms

Reflexive one-to-one correspondence exists in all contexts and the transfer may be made without reference to the field denoted : chemical nomenclature, botanical classification, biological taxinomy (one-to-one correspondence).

M (LD) = M_1, M_2, M_3, (LA)

m (TD) = m_1, (TA)

This shows the case of synonyms : there are several synonyms corresponding to a term in the target language.

M (LD $\approx$ M (LA)   possible equivalence in language terms

m (TD) $\equiv$ m (TA)   acceptable equivalence in the text

M (LD) : $\emptyset$ (LA)   no correspondence in language terms

m (TD) $\approx$ x + y + z (TA) paraphrase in textual terms

Case of polysemant LD

Reduction of the polysemant by CM or definition

$$P \text{ (LD)} \begin{cases} m_1 \text{ (TD)} \equiv m_1 \text{ (TA) and thus } \dfrac{P}{m_1 \text{ (TD)}} : m_1 \text{ (TA) 1:1} \\ \\ m_2 \text{ (TD)} \equiv m_2 \text{ (Ta) and thus } \dfrac{P}{m_2 \text{ (TD)}} : m_2 \text{ (TA) 1:1} \end{cases}$$

Reduction of polysemant by collocation or lexical/   solidarity/co-text
Syntagmatic where the word appears in the same field.

$$P.\text{(LD)} \begin{cases} m_1 \text{ (TD) x } m_1 \text{ y = } m_1 \text{ xy, x } m_1 \text{ y, xy } m_1 \text{ (TA)} \\ m_2 \text{ (TD) x } m_2 \text{ y = } m_2 \text{ xy, x } m_2 \text{ y, xy } m_2 \text{ (TA)} \end{cases}$$

Thus the wealth of a term bank is not merely a question of the number of
references but the relevance and possible permutations of the item's of
information and the nature and scope of texts interrogated. Fragmented
answers may also prove useful and form the basis for an appropriate
complete answer in the target text. There are several types of response
(1) relevant complete response (2) relevant partial responses; (3)
suggestions; (4) interference (5) silence.

Relevant complete responses are those which correspond exactly to a
question based on a uniterm or a multiterm. They presuppose a reflexive
one-to-one correspondence - i.e. m (LD) is equivalent to m (LA) for a
uniterm and m_1 + m_2 (LD) is equivalent to m_1 + m_2 (LA) or m_2 +
m_1 (1A) for a multiterm where there are no homographs. These may be
avoided by quoting the field of application and neutralizing the source
context without any semantic shift.

Relevant partial responses are those which contain one or two lexemes from the multiterm. They presuppose a one-to-one correspondence, a single field of application and the same partial division.

Suggestions are those which produce accepted interference in which the onus is on the user to reinsert the terms in the context on the basis of a series of possible responses. The problem is soluble in the target context only where data are provided with a neutralized context.

Interference

The user is buried under an avalanche of responses when expecting a few well chosen responses from the system. The Eurodicautom software contains a search strategy for responses in relation to their terminological value. (See P. François, Interrogation en mode conversationnel de la Banque de données terminologiques Eurodicautom October 1980).

Silence

The bank does not contain the data item requested.

Downstream evaluation should take account of two parameters:

1) reinsertion in the context;
2) reactualization in the target text - the translator produces his own discourse.

The central problem is the relationship between the neutralized terminologism and the consistency the discourse. If, as L. Guilbert has shown, terminologism denotes objects and refers to an element of reality ('semantics by allusion'), it necessarily operates as an element in the sentence and thus at the sytagmatic level, except in nomenclatures or subject terminologies; it may this only be defined in relation to a set of terms for a specialist field.

Terminological analysis and synthesis are two-way processes which lead from the text to the terminologism and back again whilst preserving the meaning intact.

The translator consults the computer with a word picture in his mind, but for the machine the word is simply a string of characters. It is true

that interrogation is by ideas but on the basis of their graphic representation (signifiers). It might be said that the transfer 'to things and to
phenomena' is not part of the plan.

It is also possible to distinguish the requirements of the linguistic
context and those which stem from the extra-linguistic context which
cannot be determined. This then leaves us in a paradoxical situation :
the more contextual and extra-linguistic indications there are in the
file - that is the more the key term is accompanied by its paradymatic
and syntagmatic parameters and the narrower the field for its equivalent
- the more difficult it is to neutralize the term and re-insert it in a
non-repetitive target text.

It is sometimes difficult to sort out the upstream parameters from the
transfer downstream parameters since terminology and translation are so
closely bound up with one another

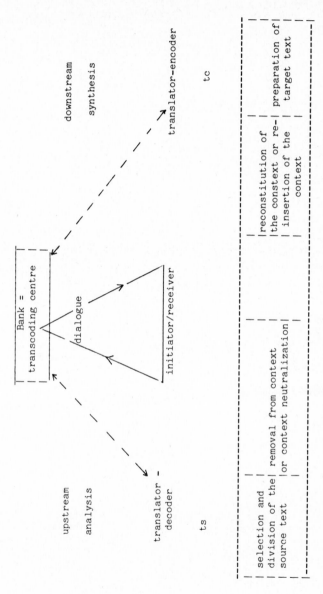

The terminology data bank at the centre of the translation process

LEXICOGRAPHY IN THE ELECTRONIC AGE
J. Goetschalckx and L. Rolling (editors)
North-Holland Publishing Company
© ECSC, EEC, EAEC, 1982

SPECIALISED LEXICOGRAPHY
IN THE CONTEXT OF A BRITISH LINGUISTIC DATA BANK

John McNaught
Centre for Computational Linguistics
UMIST

Abstract

The status of specialised lexicography is examined: the
roles of publishers of dictionaries, and of terminological data
banks are investigated. The impact of the information explosion, the varied needs of users for multilingual terminology, the problems of interlingual transfer and the development of new data base technology and lexicographical working
methods are considered. A British Linguistic Data Bank is
described, which represents the first model of its kind based
on substantial market research. This LDB will serve many
different user groups, providing varied services for technical
writers, translators, publishers, information scientists and
standardization agencies. The nature and role of specialised
lexicography will be markedly affected by such developments,
for which the British LDB is taken as a model.

This paper is based on the results of a feasibility study of the establishment of a linguistic data bank in the United Kingdom, carried out during 1980 by the Centre for Computational Linguistics of UMIST, with the support of the British Library (1,2,3).

For the purposes of this study, a Linguistic Data Bank (LDB) was defined as follows:

- a collection, stored in a computer, of special language vocabularies, including nomenclatures, standardized terms and phrases, together with the information required for their identification, which can be used as a mono- or multilingual dictionary for direct consultation, as a control instrument for consistency of usage and term creation and as an ancillary tool in information and documentation.

This definition is wide enough to cover all existing term banks, as well as machine dictionaries and also such tools as documentation thesauri in machine readable form. More importantly, it covers a multitude of different functions. The study itself was both far ranging in scope and detailed in selected areas. It lasted 12 months and involved several phases, of which the three most important were a) a comparative and critical survey of existing LDBs - their modes of organisation, operation and contacts with users; b) an in-depth study of the circumstances of potential users and contributors in the UK; c) design of a model LDB suitable for a British market. a) was partly carried out by study visits to the major European LDBs; b) was accomplished via questionnaire action, interviews, consultation and presentation of conference papers. The study has therefore been extremely thorough, and conclusions based on valid evidence. Experience gained from the study has led us to propose a BLDB which will be a single national centre containing much more information than, and fulfilling different functions to, the traditional term bank, which normally limits itself to providing information on terms and phrases to one particular type of user. BLDB will be flexible, multifunctional, multidisciplinary and multilingual.

1. The State of Specialised Lexicography

The decision to recommend the establishment of a LDB with such characteristics was taken after careful ana⁻ysis of the

state of special lexicography in Britain and abroad, especially in relation to the information explosion in the fields of
science and technology, the need for fast, reliable interlingual communication, the growth of telecommunications and of
data base technology, and the increasing need for collection,
harmonisation and dissemination of special language vocabularies. There are many creators of terminology, and many
users working in the same or different fields, or mediating
between fields or across language boundaries. In recent years,
the terminologist has assumed a key role, standing between the
creators and users/mediators, attempting to collect, regular-
ise and distribute terms. Terminological research is aided,
and its results made known, via the techniques of specialised
lexicography. Thus specialised lexicography lies at the heart
of the whole matter. Fundamental improvements in the whole
process of special language communication are then seen to be
dependent on improvements in special lexicography.

Several important observations were made during the course
of this analysis:
a) Automation has been introduced into the tasks of sorting,
updating and especially photocomposition of dictionaries, with
the consequence that dictionaries can now be produced more
quickly, more cheaply and above all more frequently than ever
before. Unfortunately, this new data base technology has not
been significantly employed to the direct benefit of the user,
who is given no choice in how to access information, or as
regards its presentation. Today's information needs are wide
and varied, and a particular dictionary format may be found
useful by some users, but time-consuming to use and unin-
formative by others. The form of dictionary entries, manners
of cross-referencing, ways of indexing compound words, idioms
and phrases all differ from dictionary to dictionary, thus
requiring the user to be familiar with the organisation of his
dictionaries. Moreover, publishers have spent most of their
efforts on producing general language dictionaries, whether
mono- or bilingual. There are few publishers in the UK active
in publishing specialised dictionaries. Yet we have noted

that there is a growing need for such tools, as much as a
means to achieve rapid, efficient interlingual transfer as to
provide information on one's own language terms.

It is noteworthy that the techniques and methods applied
to general language vocabulary are relatively indifferent to
differences between vocabulary items, or the existence of
synonyms and variants. General language dictionaries differ
substantially in form and content, and this is normally seen
as beneficial, as it can be argued that these dictionaries
complement each other, and that the semantics of general
reference can never be exhaustively covered. However, special
languages have as their raison d'être efficient communication.
That is, any divergence in information on terms of a particular
field automatically entails a breakdown of communication. The
ultimate objective of specialised lexicography is then seen as
that of univocal designation. This implies widespread, easy
access to terminology in ways that suit users' ends, for only
users can validate terminology through voluntary acceptance
and use.

This objective cannot be achieved by dispersed, unco-
ordinated efforts, resulting in tools which, although produced
quickly, reliably and cheaply, differ little in format and
mode of use from the conventional dictionary produced by manual
methods. Other considerations to be taken into account are:
the problems of quality control of terminology; the fact that,
in volatile fields, terminology evolves and changes constantly;
the perhaps limited number of users of a particular, but important, terminology; the importance of feedback mechanisms
between end-users and the producers of specialised dictionaries.

Thus, while automation has proved of great benefit in the
production of general language dictionaries, the particular
nature and demands of modern specialised lexicography require
much more of data base technology, especially in relation to
end-users.

b) In response to the needs of users, especially for multilingual terminological information, a few large user groups,

mainly on the Continent, and mainly active in the field of
translation, have established automatic dictionaries and term
banks, not only to collect their own terminology, which is in-
adequately catered for by published dictionaries, but also to
provide their translators with new specialised lexicographic
tools, which are far removed from the conventional dictionary.
Output formats and modes of consulting these data bases are
tailored to the perceived needs of their translators, according to the type of work done, etc. Thus the Bundessprachenamt,
one of the first to set up a LDB, provides its translators
primarily with various batch listings, whereas the CEC's
EURODICAUTOM was conceived from the outset as an on-line tool.
Both organisations are equally active in terminology, and so
their banks benefit from the services of terminologists who
continually input, validate and update many thousands of terms
per year. The study revealed that translation is differently
organised on the Continent to Britain. Continental companies
often support large translation departments. This is not the
case in Britain, where the largest translation unit in industry
does not exceed 20 members. On the other hand, there is a
widespread and active network of freelance translators. It is
therefore unrealistic to expect any individual British company,
government department or industry to set up its own term bank.

c) Two divergent tendencies in specialised lexicography were
noticed: publishers have employed new techniques and basic
routines to hasten production of general dictionaries, while
neglecting, it must be said, the varied and urgent needs of
specialist users in a multilingual technological society; LDBs
abroad have concentrated more on developing tools for specific
users, mainly translators, and on collecting and disseminating
highly specialised terminological information in particular
fields. Thus the number of LDBs capable of answering the
diverse lexicographical needs of many different user groups is
very small. There is no true national LDB in Europe, hence no
LDB capable of coordinating total terminological control over
all the special languages of a linguistic area. In order to
fill this gap, some existing centres are expanding their

services and their collections to meet the demands of a wider range of user groups. However, this inevitably causes problems, and will take some considerable time. The recent connection of EURODICAUTOM to EURONET-DIANE is to be welcomed in this respect.

d) There is a case to be made for the fusion of the roles of publisher of dictionaries and TDB. This has not as yet taken place to any great extent, due to the different objectives pursued by both parties. Only two centres have successfully managed to combine a term bank role with a publishing role. One, TNC of Stockholm, has a longstanding program of rationalisation in terminology and lexicographical production, called TERMDOK. Over the years, TNC have produced a number of multilingual specialised glossaries from data base holdings. Recently, their dictionaries have been implemented on a large multi-user machine, and will be available for batch and online consultation. The other centre is that of Siemens of Munich, which has developed over some 20 years now a data bank primarily for the translators of Siemens Linguistic Services Department. Recently, though, this LDB has expanded its functions to offer data base management services to publishers and other firms and organisations, to set up a network of users and contributors of many kinds, from several countries, and to produce its own full-scale specialised dictionaries, complete with definitions, sources, foreign language equivalents and so on. From decision to publish to distribution of the finished product takes some six weeks. Most of this time is spent on human administrative affairs. Actual machine processing of the data is fast, efficient and reliable. A large number of output formats and media are available so that output may be customised to a great extent.

2. The Advantages of a Single, National British LDB

The advantages of having a single national data base will benefit users of English terminology both at home and abroad. Should the proposed LDB be closely associated with BSI (as undoubtedly ought to be the case with any national LDB and the corresponding standards institution, and as is the trend with e.g. DIN/Siemens, TNC/SIS, etc.) then such publications as BS glossaries may be produced on a regular basis, constantly updated and in line with current terminology. Other publications may include dictionaries of definitions, simple word lists, mono-, bi- or multilingual dictionaries of a general, technical or specialised interdisciplinary nature. Terminological data will increase in reliability, accuracy and relevance. A single, comprehensive LDB can have a wider scope than existing conventional dictionaries, and can, through implementing a large, complex, machine-manipulated term record, reproduce subsets of information, with varying degrees of detail and specifications. Aided by the computer, terminologist, lexicographer and user will be able to eliminate discrepancies in term records, thus helping to refine lexicographic tools.

In addition, the LDB will be able to be consulted directly, in on-line or batch mode. It has been recommended that the utmost flexibility be available to allow the user to construct the search profile best suited to his task. Concomitant parameterisation of output modes and formats will also be available, with 'packages' being provided, suited to the needs of different user groups. As the process of harmonisation leading towards efficient special language communication is based on widespread knowledge of terminology, and the existence of diverse lexicographical tools containing this terminology, other modes of consulting the LDB's contents have been proposed, such as the use of customised microfiches, or floppy discs containing subsets of term records in a particular field.

The benefits to the users of English abroad, are that a BLDB will be able to direct the process of harmonisation of designation and usage, so that agreement may be achieved and maintained on English use of scientific and technical terminology at home and abroad. English is the national language of a number of countries, a second official language in many others and one of the main vehicles of international scientific communication. Its unity is particularly threatened by the

information explosion. English terms are the basis for
'internationalisms' in other languages. Appropriate designation in English therefore has far-reaching consequences for
effective communication in other languages, and between these
languages and English. It is to the UK that non-native users
of English look for guidance, British English being the preferred variant. In areas where designations and usage are
first created in non-English speaking environments there is a
great danger of deficient designation, harmful both to effective communication and the natural creativity of English. Many
LDBs abroad have large collections of English terminology, not
all of which has been created or validated in an English-
speaking environment. The existence of a national BLDB will
aid these centres to validate their English terminology, and
will contribute to effective communication between foreign
languages and English. Correspondingly, foreign language
equivalents established by BLDB for its own terminology should
be carried out in cooperation with other LDBs. BLDB tools
will therefore contain high quality data, which will have the
confidence of their users.

3. Potential Users of a BLDB

     These fell into several major groups, the largest con-
sisting of mono- and multilingual communication mediators.
Where in the past it was primarily the translator who mediated
in the process of interlingual transfer, today many different
kinds of profession may be seen as involving interlingual
transfer. This was one of the fundamental observations made
during the study. Other mediators, whose work is becoming increasingly important, include technical writers, journalists,
and abstractors. Thus many types of people participate in the
process of interlingual transfer; the translator is but one of
many. These are all professional communicators working largely
on behalf of others to convey and mediate linguistic messages
which might otherwise not be understood. It has been recognised, for example, that product documentation is as important
as the product itself, and that in order to exploit a foreign
market successfully, or to communicate with foreign partners

or subsidiaries, documentation is needed in the language of
the countries concerned. Technical writers are then closely
involved in this process.

On-line packages preferred by this group are: term-translation equivalent-source; term-translation equivalent-source-
definition; term-translation equivalent-synonym-quality code.
Graduated information would be required in the following preferred order: term and translation equivalent, definition,
usage note or context, quality code, synonym, source, subject
code. Off-line, demand is heaviest for alphabetic or systematic mono/bilingual glossaries of term plus definition; bilingual text-oriented glossaries; phraseological glossaries
and term in context lists.

Special language lexicographers and terminologists serve
all other groups and will be able to do so more effectively
with the aid of a LDB. Their most frequent need will be for
terminological relations, which will enable the systematic
verification of concepts and terms.

Publishers of dictionaries and glossaries handle large
quantities of data. Microfiches are also useful for lexicographers, or for end-users themselves. The ease with which
a LDB can copy, merge, sort, check data may influence editorial techniques, as the hitherto rather cumbersome and expensive work with numerous consultants can be made simpler and
more economical. With the availability of keyword or term
extraction facilities from running text the compilation of
dictionaries can become more exhaustive, and statistical
evidence from text analysis is likely to influence the scope
of dictionaries. Beside producing dictionaries of the conventional formats and contents, publishers may wish to issue
other combinations of data such as linguistic thesauri of
special subject fields and also offer their products on microfiches or floppy discs. The distinction between the services
and products which can be provided by the LDB and by publishers
is likely to become blurred.

Another group which will benefit from automated

specialised lexicography consists of <u>applied linguists, LSP</u>
<u>teachers and researchers and language planners</u>. The import-
ance of LSP is growing, and again this discipline is closely
dependent on reliable, accurate and up-to-date terminology,
and efficient lexicographical tools. DANTERM is devoting much
effort to aiding the work of LSP teaching and research. Included in this group also are researchers into machine translation, which has known an upsurge in recent years. The most
advanced research is taking place here in Europe under the
aegis of the CEC, in the context of the Eurotra project. MT
systems are dependent on large, detailed, accurate dictionaries.
While these dictionaries require different associated information, there is still a need for terms themselves, their
synonyms, translation equivalents, etc. A BLDB will be a
valuable quarry for the purposes of constructing a MT dictionary. MT systems are commonly enhanced by implementing frequency lists, stop lists and so on. Again information for
these may be gained from a LDB, through statistics of usage,
for example. Statistical data on terms will also help other
applied linguists.

Efficient language planning depends on the immediate
availability of control mechanisms and the rapid dissemination
of new forms. Given the potential impact of LDBs abroad, the
uncontrolled dissemination of variants of English can, in the
long term, lead to a weakening of the usefulness of English as
an international language and to the creation of semi-
artificial languages deprived of an intimate link with a
general language, which alone can vitalise special languages.
Language planning on this scale requires a central, coordinating body able to collect, control, disseminate, even impose
terminology. This whole field of activity has not been provided for by conventional lexicographic techniques, conventional dictionaries and their associated production methods.

The case of bilingual Canada, for example, is well known:
automated techniques were employed to aid the government
language planning policy, and indeed were seen by many as indispensable to the success of this policy. This group requires

mainly batch printout of e.g. alphabetic or frequency listings
of words in texts, sequential text-oriented lists of words,
reverse alphabetical lists, etc.

Another group identified as having need of advanced
special lexicographical techniques consists of standardization experts. Standards institutes, although active for many
years in the production of small glossaries of terms contained
in standards documents, have comparatively recently begun to
extend work in this area, due to two factors: a) the recognition that standardization of objects is only possible given
a concomitant strict control over the designation of such
objects; b) the greater amount of standardizing work being done
in an ever-widening range of human activities. AFNOR, DIN and
GOSSTANDART have set up term banks linked directly to their
standards document banks. Others, such as BSI, have begun to
automate certain aspects of their terminological work e.g. the
production of machine readable thesauri for indexing and
retrieval purposes. Combining LDB work with standardization
will ensure a higher quality of standards, and a wider use of
the terminology contained in them.

A last, large group which will benefit from a British LDB
consists of mono- and multilingual information and documentation mediators, such as information scientists and brokers,
indexers, librarians, etc., who require information about
existing terminology for the reliable identification of documents. As well-founded artificial languages of indexing and
classification should be systematically related to the natural
language from which they are derived and to which they refer,
various types of specialised lexicographical tools have been
found increasingly necessary in this area. Much work has been
expended on document storage, indexing and retrieval systems.
These problems have been magnified to a great extent due to
the tremendous increase in published documents, and also to the
move towards interdisciplinary subject areas. Only recently
has it been realised that terminology and special lexicography
go hand in hand with information science. Documents are, after
all, collections of terms. These terms may be used, in an

ideal system, to index, classify and retrieve documents, thus
overcoming the limitations of documentation thesauri. LDB-
supplied linguistic thesauri, whether on-line or published,
whether mono- or multilingual, will help not just the indexer,
but also the searcher, especially the non-specialist searching
multilingual data bases. On-line tools potentially useful by
this group included packages giving: term-definition-source;
term-synonym-broad term-specific term; term-broad term-
specific term-translation equivalent; term plus complete
systematic display. Graduated information would be needed
thus: term-definition-source, synonym, broad and specific
terms, translation equivalent. Regular off-line listings
needed would be systematic and alphabetic lists of terms by
subject field, lists of definitions, sources and synonyms. A
need was also expressed for routines to aid keyword extraction,
indexing and classification. Also, it should be noted that the
needs of this group are similar at times to interlingual
mediators.

In addition, a substantial number of users of diverse
background exists who would use a LDB intermittently. They
would often use it monolingually to check the existence,
spelling or definition of a term or expression. They may wish
to understand terms in a foreign language text they can otherwise read without difficulty. They may need a specially compiled glossary of new terms in a foreign language to help in
writing a research paper, or to enable them to attend a
symposium conducted in a foreign language they are reasonably
familiar with.

Continuous interaction between the LDB, its users and
contributors is seen as vital, to ensure not just that the
data correspond to current usage, but also that the LDB does
not become an overt language planning or directive body.
While harmonisation is desirable and necessary, steps must be
taken to prevent imposition of norms from above. Harmonisation should grow out of interaction with users, who in the
end are the only ones qualified to endorse terminology. Interaction should take place on several levels and in several

modes, again in order to maintain the greatest degree of
flexibility. It has been proposed, for example, that users be
represented on the data policy advisory board, so that they
could be assured that the LDB would process terminology of
relevance to the majority of its users. A number of core
subject fields have already been identified in consultation
with potential users.

Many large user groups have substantial collections of
terminology, which it is in their interests to have dis-
seminated as widely as possible, or at least converted into
machine readable form and systematically processed for their
own purposes. Cooperation can therefore occur on the level of
users trading terminology, as it were, in return for e.g. free
processing, credit for the use of the LDB for a certain period,
validation or completion of their term records, the production
of glossaries, etc. A partnership system such as that of
Siemens or TNC should be instituted. This will encourage
partners to record terminology as it is created in the field,
and will greatly alleviate the task of the LDB. Benefits to
partners would include the processing of any terminology they
record, and access to the whole LDB, including the terminology
of other partners. Should a widespread network of partners be
set up, this will have implications for the process of harmonisation of terminology. Voluntary acceptance of terms will
serve to confirm their validity. Such a network may also
resolve some of the thorny problems of copyright.

There should also be facilities available to monitor
feedback from users, so that a user may e.g. note any terminological gaps, or missing foreign language equivalents, or
comment on the appropriateness of a term.

All users and producers of specialised mono- and multilingual dictionaries and glossaries are potential users of a
LDB as described above. They will consult a LDB if it can
offer a more reliable and quicker service than existing tools,
or if it can be used to produce lexicographic tools of a
different, new nature, responding to users' needs. The
functions of the future BLDB will be much wider than that of

traditional reference tools, and its scope will be that of an entire library of specialised lexicographical works. It will serve as a model for all future such developments in special-ised lexicography.

R E F E R E N C E S

1.   Sager, J.C. & McNaught J. (1981) - Selective Survey of Linguistic Data Banks in Europe. Report submitted to the British Library. Published by CCL/UMIST, Manchester.

2.   Sager, J.C. & McNaught J. (1981) - Specifications of a Linguistic Data Bank for the UK. Report submitted to the British Library. Published by CCL/UMIST, Manchester.

3.   Sager, J.C. & McNaught J. (1981) - Feasibility Study of the Establishment of a Terminological Data Bank in the UK. Report submitted to the British Library. Published by CCL/UMIST, Manchester.

LEXICOGRAPHY IN THE ELECTRONIC AGE
J. Goetschalckx and L. Rolling (editors)
North-Holland Publishing Company
© ECSC, EEC, EAEC, 1982

SOFTWARE FOR TERMINOLOGY DATA BANKS

A. E. NEGUS

Consultant in Information
Systems and Services
Bedfordshire, UK

Abstract

Terminology data banks can be used in a number of ways,
but the method which is likely to become increasingly
attractive in the elecronic age is on-line access by the end-
user - in effect the translator.

On-line retrieval facilities are provided with a number of
existing term banks; indeed in some cases on-line interrogation
is the prime means of access.

However, in the electronic age it will no longer be
reasonable to regard on-line term banks in isolation. Not only
will there be the oft-quoted coming together of technologies to
enable the provision of new services; the emergence of new and
more versatile equipment will permit and even encourage a
blurring of the boundaries between what might today be regarded
as quite distinct services.

One of the implications of this coming together of
services is that the software used with term banks must, if the
potential benefits are to be fully realised, offer the greatest
possible flexibility.

As in all other fields, packages will become more and more
attractive as the costs of producing and maintaining software
continue to rise and as new devices appear to offer cost
reduction, improvements in performance and the opportunity to
modify and interlink services.

1. INTRODUCTION

Terminology data banks can be, and have been, created for a number of reasons, and in many areas it is clear that the electronic age, and all it offers, is likely to have little influence on the methods chosen, or on the motivation for providing a term bank. However, there is one area where there can be no doubt that the coming of the electronic age will have profound effects on the providers of term banks, on the users, and on the type and scale of the usage that could develop.

On-line access to terminology data banks by translators is not new, but really there is very little experience of the ways in which such systems can be used for the greatest benefit of translators, or, indeed, any concerned with the promotion and exchange of information between nations. This is an area where the greatest opportunities exist, yet, because of the many varied, and perhaps unforeseen, developments which will appear in the coming years, it is also the area where the greatest number of opportunities can be missed.

Notwithstanding all the uncertainties which must exist, it is evident that increasingly severe demands will be made on the software used with on-line term banks, if anything approaching the full potential is to be realised. To see what the effects of these demands might be it is necessary, first, to look at the present situation, and then to examine some of the changes that are likely to come about, so that the implications for software development can be considered.

2. THE PRESENT SITUATION

There are a number of multilingual terminology data banks in operation today, yet although the possibility of searching on-line is common, on-line access is not the prefered method of access in all cases. Amongst the more well known systems -

by the Commission of the European Communities, Siemens AG, the Secretary of State Department in Canada and the Bundes- sprachenamt - this variety exists, as might be expected. So while the prime motivation for providing a terminology data bank - and the costs of doing so are never insignificant - is basically the same in all cases, that is to assist trans- lators in their work, the methods chosen can be quite diff- erent. Anyone familiar with developments in the computer world would, perhaps, assume that the differences in approach reflect to some extent the environment, considering costs, available techniques etc., which existed during the formative years of the service. But there are other differences concerning the way in which data is stored, and the way in which it may be searched, which can surely not have been determined by the capabilities of the available technology.

Observing these differences in approach, it is not surprising that the features offered by the software used by several services differ considerably, at least at first sight, nor is it surprising that in many cases the software is purpose built.

The reasons why this diversity exists are manifold, and some possible reasons could be a cause for considerable concern. However, the fundamental reason is probably that different circumstances have required different solutions.

So whatever the rights and the wrongs of the different approaches evidenced today, be they concerned with the value of on-line access, with the form that terminological entries should take, with the point at which human editing should come into the data collection activities, or the emphasis to be placed on different retrieval methods, what is quite clear is that there is no software in use today, certainly none with any significant real life operational experience attached to it, which is suited to accepting the challenges to be issued in the electronic age.

3. DEVELOPMENTS IN THE ELECTRONIC AGE

The theme of convergence of technologies has become
familiar in recent years and statements such as 'the computer
industry died on 31 December 1979 to be replaced by the
information technology industry' are becoming commonplace -
although there might be disagreement about the precise date
on which this miracle occured! The information technology
industry is often regarded as a bringing together of three
major industries - telecommunications, computers and advanced
office products - and a number of activities in the business
world are moving in this direction, so that it will be
possible really identify the new industry as a coherent whole.

But a merging of industries, given that new and exciting
technologically advanced products will emerge, is not all that
will emerge: not only will there be a convergence of separate
tecnologies, there will also be a convergence of the products
and services provided using advanced techniques.

To see where terminology data banks will fit into the
overall scene it is necessary to look at the separate developments which are likely to have an impact on the work of a
translator, and to consider what the interactions between
those developments might be.

The most dramatic development is likely to be the increased
power of automatic machine translation systems - although there
are those who would argue that satisfactory systems will never
be developed, in spite of increasing evidence to the contrary.
Be that as it may, the reality is that even though machine
translation is likely to be used more and more widely in the
future, it will not have a particularly dramatic impact on the
life of the typical translator. There will always be areas
where there is some doubt as to which method to choose, but
usually the distinction will be quite clear cut, with little
or no interplay between machine and human translation.

Other developments which will be far more widely used in the electronic age, simply because the technology will be more widely available, are registers of translators, showing their expertise, and possibly availability, and databases showing the availability, indeed existence, of translations. However, both of these are, to an extent, peripheral, assisting as they do at an administrative level, rather than at the level of translating itself.

The areas where developments will have significant impact on the work of a translator are in the use of word processors, the possibility of searching local information stores, and access to remote term banks facilitated by improved communication facilities.

One product of the electronic age which will be used by almost all translators in time is the word processor. Already some are making use of what is still a relatively expensive device, although the rapid reduction in costs is bringing them within the reach of more and more organisations and individuals. When the word processor is considered alone, the only real impact will be that it will bring the conventional benefits of ease of revision of typescripts, and where there is the posssibility to transfer data between work stations, using floppy disks or with a shared logic system for example, there will be additional benefits such as the ease with which a consolidated text can be produced when several translators share the translation of a large document.

However, some word processors can provide much more than this. If the machine is equipped with a standard commun- ications interface (e.g. V24) it may be possible to use the word processor as an on-line terminal - although this is not always the case. With some devices communication is only possible between the backing store of the word processor and a remote device and messages cannot be transmitted directly from the keyboard or received directly on the screen. When a

machine can be used as a remote terminal, it may be that it
can only be used in a simple mode, as a 'glass teletype', but
often, and this facility is more likely to be available with
the cheaper devices available, it is possible to make use of
the processing power available in the word processor. In
fact, particularly at the lower end of the market, there is
little difference between an intelligent terminal and a word
processor -often the physical device is the same, only the
software provided and the name under which it is marketed
differing.

It is therefore likely that many translators will, in time
be equipped with devices which allow them to use whatever
on-line terminology data banks might be available to them. And
what is more, in many cases it will be possible, at least in
theory, to use the local processing power of the terminal to
overcome the difficulties caused by having to deal with
systems which can be quite different as far as the demands
placed on the user are concerned. In practice, this is not
quite so easy. Suitable software to convert the input and
output of an on-line system into a form desired by the user is
not easy to provide, and it is also vulnerable to any changes
the operator of the system might choose to make. And the
difficulties are compounded where it is desired to access
more than one system.

There are other uses that can be made of equipment whose
aquisition is justified initially for word processing. Many
devices can be equipped with backing store large enough and
cheap enough to justify the creation and storage of local
term banks - the equivalent of the individuals card file -
and this will be an attractive feature for many. Where this
facility is used, the benefits of using local intelligence to
improve the connection to remote term banks are obviously
greater. Local stores are even more attractive when they are
created by or for a group of translators working on the same
equipment.

Another development which has been heralded for some time now, although use has only been at the experimental stage so far, is the videodisc. The potential offered by videodisc and particularly digital optical discs is tremendous. Depending on storage techniques, the capacity of a single disc can be the equivalent of as many as half a million typed A4 pages, and although the cost of recording is relatively high the cost of duplication can be as low as $5 per copy (but not if digital recording is used). Already publishers are carrying out trials with videodiscs, and if these are successful, and the technology becomes established in the market place, it is quite likely that texts such as multilingual dictionaries will become available in this form, thereby providing more comprehensive local stores of terminology for the translator with appropriate equipment. Of course, such changes will not come about simply beacause the technology is available. The decision to make, for example, a dictionary available on disc will be based on many commercial and economic factors, not least the impact on hard copy sales.

Other things, too, will have an effect, given the right circumstances. Communications facilities are going to improve as telecommunications authorities make increased use of the new technologies, such as satellite transmission, fibre optics, computers for switching and error correction, and this will bring remote on-line services closer to the user.

Another development which will have an effect, but only if the opportunities are seized by the providers of services, is the appearance of new types of computer, which will make possible, in a practical sense, services which can only be provided with difficulty today. Computer architecture has remained largely unchanged over the years, being essentially one processor unit which processes instructions serially in a set order, and the tremendous improvements in power which have been witnessed over the years have come about by improvements in speed of the components of the computer, and by

devolpments in operating system software to ensure that the
available power is fully utilised. There have been several
machines developed over the years which have used a different
approach, such as content addressable file stores and array
processors, and some of thes have gone into prodution. Until
recently, the costs of such devices have tended to be
prohibitive, so they have not been widely used. But modern
production techniques mean that they can soon - using the
ubiquitous silicon chip - be produced at a far more compet-
ative price, once the initial design work has been completed.
This latter is in itself no mean task, but nevertheless it is
certain that new architectures will become available in the
coming years, probably in the first case in the form of
'database machines' which will be used as back-ends to
conventional computers carrying out tasks such as terminal
and peripheral handling, job scheduling and file creation and
loading.

4.   IMPLICATIONS FOR TERM BANK SOFTWARE

As indicated earlier, the main impact of the electronic
age and the developments and opportunities it will bring will
be on terminology databanks used to provide on-line searching.
For other uses the impact will, in one sense, be minimal,
although other products will probably become less and less
attractive in the future. In just the same way as there has
been a swing towards on-line working in program development
(less than 10% of development is carried out in batch mode
today) on-line working will come to dominate in this field.

What will be the precise effects of the developments
mentioned earlier is difficult to say. Nevertheless, one
thing is clear. Changes will be necessary. The chances of
realising the potential benefits offered by on-line terminology
data banks must be diminished if the software used with those
term banks is not able to meet all the demands that will be
placed on it.

The software used today with existing term banks must, by many criteria be judged as excellent. However they are, almost without exception, firmly lodged in the pre-electronic age. This is hardly surprising, considering the time it takes to develop software, and certainly cannot be condemned. It is nevertheless a fact.

It is certain that considerable modifications would be needed to the software systems used with any of the existing term banks if they are to be able to take their rightful place amongst the many developments of the electronic age, some of which were mentioned briefly earlier. But experience in other fields of computing indicates that it is almost impossible to continue to develop a large and complex software system so that it can remain comparable with the latest developments.

Inevitably, new software products will be needed. It would, of course, be possible to develop new purpose built software to provide those functions which the operator of a particular term bank judges to be important, although the wisdom of following such a course must be questioned. The electronic age will not see just one round of developments; new, probably unforeseen tools will continue to appear, and creating new software will only put a system at the forefront for a time.

Bearing in mind the apparent differences in philosophy behind the several term banks in use today, it seems that many will continue to serve a restricted market for many years to come, unless there is significant change. Yet one is tempted to question how fundamental the differences really are. Many of the differences arise because of the way in which the terminological data are handled by the software, and are differences of presentation and procedure rather than anything else.

When considering how to take the best advantage of the
opportunities about to be offered the operator of a term bank
must answer the question "are the facilities needed with a
term bank really so different from those needed elsewhere, and
are there several different ways of handling terminological
data, all of them different and incompatible?" If the answers
to both parts of this question are yes, then the costs of
entering the electronic age wholeheartedly must be recognised.

While many of the costs connected with computing continue
to fall - 25% per annum is the usual figure quoted for
processing power, and even storage is reducing in cost at an
annual rate somewhere around 10% - the cost of software
continues to rise, as indeed does the cost of data collection
and entry. With most large and complex systems, and on-line
term banks certainly fall into this category, the cost of
software accounts for at least 70% of the costs incurred at
the central site. And this trend is likely to continue, with
the effects of inflation on wage rates, and even more because
of the scarcity of personnel with the requisite skills - a
scarcity that is tending to become more noticeable as more
and more sophisticated devices come on the market.

Estimating the cost of developing new software for term
banks can not be done with any accuracy, in the absence of a
full in depth investigation of all salient factors, but
comparison with the effort needed to develop other software
products of comparable power and complexity leads to the
belief that at least thirty man-years of development would be
required.

Given these considerations, it would seem that the most
sensible course to follow would be either for term bank
operators - or at least those who wish to make their files
more widely available - to seriously consider the possibilities of collaboration, or better still to see what generally
available information retrieval or data manipulation packages

can meet their present needs, and more. It would certainly
seem to be wasteful to invest too many resources into
software creation and development when one-off development
can only serve to promulgate and perpetuate incompatibilities
which will delay, perhaps for ever, the day when translators
can truly benefit from the electronic age.

And as well as serving the user better, enabling him to
link his word processor or local term bank to remote services,
the adoption of 'standard' software packages will also put the
operator into a position where he is better able to take
advantage of new developments to provide an efficient and
cost effective service. Database machines, when they become
readily available, will come complete with retrieval software,
and, most importantly, with software to enable rapid conversion from the manufacturer's other database and text retrieval
packages. Conversion from some other system, and to an even
greater extent creation of new software, will be a monumental
task - so great that it may never be possible to make the
change.

4. <u>CONCLUSION</u>

A new attitude to the provision of software for term banks
is needed if all the opportunities to be offered in the
electronic age are to be grasped and exploited. Use should
be made of standard packages, available from the manufacturer
or other reputable, established and stable organisation, so
that providers of term banks can devote more resources to
what remains the most fundamental problem - the creation and
authentication of data in the terminology data bank.

LEXICOGRAPHY IN THE ELECTRONIC AGE
J. Goetschalckx and L. Rolling (editors)
North-Holland Publishing Company
© ECSC, EEC, EAEC, 1982

Discussion of the session III
Term banks
by P. François

Wednesday morning saw the Symposium move beyond the question of
terminological data banks and consider the practical questions raised
by certain applications and the means of making them available to their
ultimate users.

What was involved was the transmission of information from its
creator (or more accurately, originator) to its receiver. The information was transmitted very largely by means of specialist language;
accordingly while Mr Mc Naught was storing technical terminology in his
data bank, Mrs Hamonno was making a study of specialist language in
English so as to extract the underlying concepts.

The most widely-known solutions to this problem were the terminological data banks described by Mr Goetschalckx and Mr Krollman. Particular requirements could nonetheless lead to more individual solutions,
such as the educational software described by Mr Decourbe or the work of
Mr Simonesics on accessing information available only in Japanese characters.

Such solutions had at least two things in common:
1.   their first aim was to construct a tool which would help the
     user;
2.   they called on a number of disciplines. More specifically, although such applications had to be evaluated using linguistic criteria,
as Mr Goffels explained, they also had to be designed bearing in mind
data-processing (the questions of software discussed by Mr Negus) organization - supplying the information at the right time and to the
right place - and, as was stressed by another speaker, more general
extra-linguistic parameters.

Apparently, then, the creation of lexicographical, terminological or any other multilingual tools involved designing and constructing complete systems using disciplines which included not only the obvious lexicography and terminology, but also data processing, organization, psychology etc.

This, however, raised a number of questions:

1. As pointed out by Mr Galinski, if a number of similar solutions were being implemented, there immediately arose the problem of standardization and coopération between promoters.

2. The scale of investment required by computer-based systems raised the question of avoiding duplication of effort; Mr Engel asked what the situation was with regard to the overlap between dictionaries and terminological data banks.

3. Lastly, the cost and the value of such tools made it imperative that they should be open to wider circles than at their inception, both by accepting data from external terminology services, however small, and by making output available over the networks.

SESSION IV
PUBLISHING AND THE FUTURE USE
OF LEXICONS

The Longman-Liege Project
    A. MICHIELS, J. MULLENDERS and
    J. NOËL

Commercial Lexicography on the Threshold
of the Electronic Age
    O. NORLING-CHRISTENSEN

A New Van Dale Project: Bilingual
Dictionaries on one and the same Monolingual
Basis
    P. VAN STERKENBURG, W. MARTIN
    and B. AL

Copyright Problems and Use of Computers
    A.H. OLSSON

LEXICOGRAPHY IN THE ELECTRONIC AGE
J. Goetschalckx and L. Rolling (editors)
North-Holland Publishing Company
© ECSC, EEC, EAEC, 1982

THE LONGMAN-LIEGE PROJECT

A. MICHIELS, J. MULLENDERS, J. NOËL

University of Liège

Summary

We begin with a brief description of the organization as a data bank of the
two English dictionaries which we are using in our project (general English
dictionary and dictionary of idioms). We then explain the lexical approach
on which our development of a syntactico-semantic analyzer of English is
based, and we illustrate the basic mechanisms of this analyzer. We place
great emphasis on the richness, the formalization and the accessibility of
the data, believing these to be key elements in the compilation of any automatic dictionary. As we see it, the success of any venture involving the
processing of linguistic data, be it documentary research, translation or
language teaching, depends on the ability to perform fine analysis at different levels (syntactic, semantic and pragmatic). One aspect of such analysis which we wish to develop here, and which will considerably enrich our
data base, is the annotation, by an interactive process, of the corpus of
definitions in our dictionaries. The definitions are written in a controlled
vocabulary which permits corrections to be established between linguistic
expressions on the one hand and semantico-pragmatic relationships on the
other. We suggest that preliminary processing of the corpus of definitions
with the aid of the information retrieval systems STAIRS (using the items
of the defining vocabulary as search keys) would make this corpus considerably easier to use.

0. PREAMBLE

We would like to begin by describing the general context within which our
current work is being carried out. Future systems of aids to translation
are based on a three-phase process : analysis of the source language, transfer from the source language to the target language, and synthesis of the
target language.

The first and third phases of this process involve only the language under
consideration; only in the second phase (transfer phase) are both languages
involved.

At present we are working on the analysis phase for English, and we are
looking for partners willing to use our system to study the transfer from
and/or to the language with which they are concerned.

A start has already been made by Prof. Nagao's team, which will be joined
by a member of our team for a period of six months.

However, we believe that a supranational body should be responsible for
coordinating the various activities in this domain to ensure that the work
done on each language can be used to maximum advantage when designing translation systems. Standardization of grammatical and semantic data in future
dictionaries would greatly reduce the problems involved in crossing linguistic barriers.

1. DESCRIPTION OF THE DATA BASE

By contract with the firm LONGMAN Ltd we have obtained the magnetic tapes
of two dictionaries produced by that company : the Longman Dictionary of
Contemporary English (LDOCE) - a general English dictionary with approximately 60 000 entries (17 Mbytes) and the Longman Dictionary of English
Idioms (LDOEI) - a dictionary of English idiomatic expressions (approx.
3 Mbytes). These are not simply dictionaries which can be read by computer.
They represent blueprints for genuine computerized dictionaries where data
are, as far as possible, formalized and consequently accessible for automatic use. Computers were involved right from the outset. The controlled
defining vocabulary used throughout the two dictionaries was machine-

checked and the printed versions of the dictionaries were produced from two magnetic tapes by computerized typesetting. However, for the purposes of our project – the development of an analyser of general English – the most important factor is the formalization of the data containde in the dictionaries.

The logical structure of an LDOCE entry (Fig. 1) reveals a number of fields where information is formalized. We shall consider three of these fields only : grammatical field, semantic codes, subject codes and registers.

(1) Grammatical field

This is made up of several grammatical codes, which primarily indicate the syntactic potential either of an entire lexical entry (path A) or of a lexical entry taken in a particular sense (path B), where the grammatical field is associated with a definition. By syntactis potential we mean the entire range of syntactic situations within which an item might fit. For example, the noun 'claim' will be coded [C 5] in the sentence 'The Government's claim that war was necessary was clearly mistaken'. [C] indicates that 'claim' is countable and [5] that it governs a clause introduced by 'that'. In contrast, in the sentence : 'His claim to know the answer was not be-- lieved', it will be coded [C 3] : countable + governs an infinitive with 'to'. An inherent feature of the LDOCE coding system is that letters (such as C) and numbers (such as 5) always mean the same thing. The transitive verb governing a clause introduced by 'that' is coded [T 5], monotransitive plus 'that'.

(2) Semantic codes

These are essentially semantic characteristics (1). Linked to a noun, they place it within a semantic hierarchy where cross-classifications are possible; T = [+ Astract], B = [+ Animal AND + Female]. Linked to a verb or an adjective, they are no longer inherent but contextual : they impose semantic restrictions on the subject, object or complement of a verb and on the noun which may be modified by an adjective. For example, within the particular context of the Stock Exchange, 'hammer' is coded U for the suject (+ collective) and H (+ human) for the object. In the sporting context, 'hammer' is coded H (+ human) for both subject and object. It should be

Fig. 1 : Logical structure of a lexical entry in the LDOCE

Conventions:

▯ = the field is a) empty

or b) it comprises a single item of data of the type invisaged

or c) it comprises several such items of data

▯ = the field comprises a single item of data of the type invisaged

▯ = the field comprises one or more items of data of the type envisaged

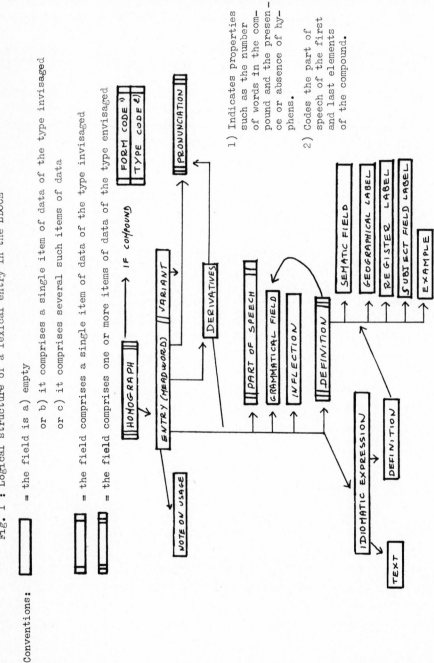

1) Indicates properties such as the number of words in the compound and the presence or absence of hyphens.

2) Codes the part of speech of the first and last elements of the compound.

noted that the semantic codes appear only on the magnetic tape version of
the LDOCE and not in the printed version.

(3) Subject codes and registers

Here too the magnetic tape version of the LDOCE gives considerably more
detail than the printed version. Although the latter does give indications
of subject (med(icine), tech(nique)) or of register (obs(olete), taboo),
the subject.dodes of the tape version are much more precise. The editors
of the LDOCE selected various of the MERRIAM codes and refined them with
sub-codes. For example, the Stock Exchange meaning of 'hammer' receives
the Merriam code EC (Economy) and the sub-code S (Stock Exchange).

A further innovation in the LDOCE (and the LDOCEl) is the attempt to form
malize definitions by using a controlled vocabulary of approximately 2000
words, not including morphological, inflectional and derivational variants.
The importance of this controlled vocabulary for our project is made clear
later in the paper.

It is not possible for us to give a detailed edscription of the LDOEl here.
Fig. 2 shows the logical structure of an entry in this dictionary.

We should simply explain that the "alpha-word' is the word under which the
idiom is found and that the annotated text indicates the morphological and
syntactical variations which the expression can undergo without losing its
idiomatic character.

Despite the great attention to formalization in the LDOCE, it will have
taken us 2 years to produce an organized data base revealing the logical
relationships between the types of information in the dictionary which are
shown at Fig. 1 (2). We are at present engaged in breaking down the grammatical fields, that is to say converting them into chains of codes, where
each code is accesible separately. The conversion of the field [T1,2] into
[T1,T2] is as simple example.

Fig. 2 : Logical structure of a lexical entry int the LDOE1

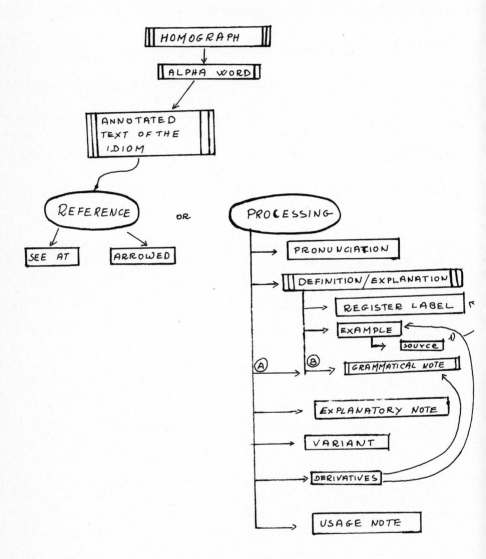

1) For examples which have not been invented
   - they may contain lexemes not included in
     the defining vocabulary.

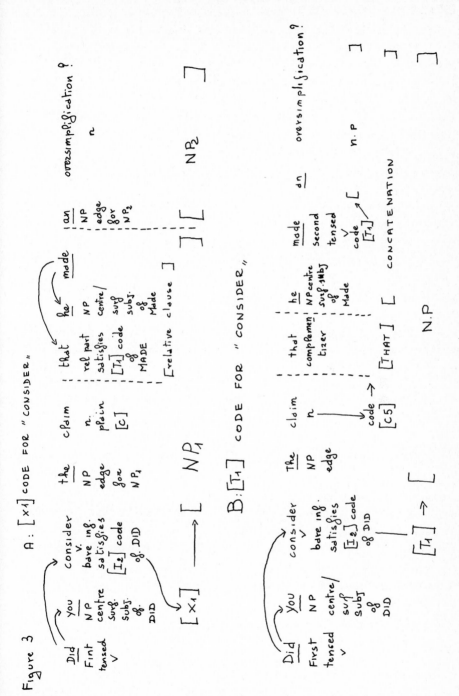

Figure 3

2. PRINCIPLES OF OUR SYNTACTICO-SEMANTIC ANALYSER OF GENERAL ENGLISH

The existence of accessible English descriptions in our two computerized
dictionaries led us to adopt a new approach to the development of analysis
modules, a so-called "lexical approach" (3,4). In contrast to general systems and microcosm systems, both of which centralize decision procedures
into their grammatical components outside the lexicon, this approach leaves
a maximum of decisions to the lexical entry : it is the lexical unit, together with all the associated relevant data, which triggers and conducts
the analysis. To begin with, the grammatical codes of the item activate
scanning procedures aimed at satisfying the forecasts emitted by the codes
concerning the syntactical environment of the item. This mechanism is illustrated in Fig. 3. The codes [T 1] and [X 1] of 'consider' are satisfied by
the same chain, but on the basis of completely different analyses. The code
[T 1] is satisfied by a single noun syntagm, the centre of which is the
word 'claim', which in turn is a statement introduced by 'that' : 'Did you
consider the claim that he made an oversimplification?' = 'Did you consider
the claim alleging that he made ... ?' The code [X 1] is satisfied by a
chain of two noun syntagms (1 : the claim that he made, and 2 : an oversimplification), which leads to a different interpretation in which 'that'
introduces a relative clause : 'Did you consider that the claim that he
made was an oversimplification?'

3. ANNOTATION OF THE CORPUS OF DEFINITIONS

The use of a controlled defining vocabulary by the lexicographers of the
LDOCE was only a first step in the formalization of definitions. We intend
to take this further by labelling each of the items which appear in a definition by means of the following annotations, which themselves refer back
to our data base :

(1) homograph number in the LDOCE

(2) definition number

(3) grammatical code selected

(4) labelled bracketing indicating how the code is satisfied by its context.

In addition, the annotated definition may indicate the anaphoric relationships and the scope of the operators. It is this latter type of information

in particular which requires human involvement and necessitates an interactive annotation procedure.

Fig. 4 gives an example of partial annotation : the definition of 'microscope'.

It will doubtless be impossible to determine the scope of the operator
'and' and the referent of 'them' by computer analysis. However, our analyser will be capable of associating code [V 2] with 'makes' on the basis of
the context : 'very small near objects' (NS : noun syntagm) + 'seem larger'
(infinitive without "to"), and on the basis of this association 20 of the
22 definitions of the first homograph "make" in the LDOCE can be excluded.

Moreover, the identification of the chain 'instrument ... used for examining
... ' will enable the word 'microscope' to be associated with the word
'examine' in the instrument-action relationship. This is an example of the
link between linguistic expression and semantic-pragmatic relationship which
can be established in the corpus of definitions, since the use of a controlled vocabulary ensures the recurrence of a restricted number of lexico-
syntactical arrangements to express certain relationships without which the
definitions could not be articulated (5).

There is no doubt that the annotation of definitions and the establishment
of such lexico-syntactic arrangements involves an enormous amount of work.
However, we believe that the IBM-STAIRS information retrieval system should
help to guide and speed up this work by revealing the most promising co-
occurences. To begin with, basic items of the defining vocabulary, such as
'instrument' and 'use', could be used as search keys.

BIBLIOGRAPHY

LDOCE = LONGMAN DICTIONARY OF CONTEMPORARY ENGLISH, Longman, 1970
          (editor-in-chief : Paul Procter)
LDOEI = LONGMAN DICTIONARY OF ENGLISH IDIOMS, Longman, 1979
          (editor : Thomas Hill Long)
(1)   = Katz, J.J. et Fodor, J., The structure of a semantic theory,
          LANGUAGE, vol. 39, 1963, p. 170-210
(3)   = Nagao, M., Tsujii, J., Mitamura, K., Hirokawa, H., Kume, M.,
          A machine translation system from Japanese into English,
          in COLING 80, Tokyo, 1980, p. 414 à 423
(4)   = Rieger, C., Five aspects of a Full-Scale Story Comprehension Model,
          in Findler, N.V. (ed), ASSOCIATIVE NETWORK Academic Press,
          New York, 1979, p. 425-462
(5)   = Clark, E.V. and Clark, H.H., When nouns surface as verbs,
          LANGUAGE, vol. 55, Nr 4, 1979, p. 767-811

LEXICOGRAPHY IN THE ELECTRONIC AGE
J. Goetschalckx and L. Rolling (editors)
North-Holland Publishing Company
© ECSC, EEC, EAEC, 1982

COMMERCIAL LEXICOGRAPHY ON THE THRESHOLD OF THE ELECTRONIC AGE

by

Ole Norling-Christensen

I am neither a linguist nor a terminologist, but a publisher, and my original intention in attending this symposium had merely been to listen and learn. However, since our publishing house in fact also uses data processing - albeit at fairly primitive level - in producing dictionaries, and since we plan to extend the use of these techniques, I have been asked to present a paper.

Our publishing house, i.e. Gyldendal, Denmark, publishes general dictionaries - particularly bilingual dictionaries - of the kind used in all schools and in most offices and homes. We also publish lexicons (general and specialized encyclopaedias).

One of our lexicons is to be used in the Danish viewdata experiment (Tele-data), which is scheduled to begin on 1 january 1982. However, apart from this, none of our dictionaries of lexicons has so far been accessible via the electronic media. They are still 'simply' books.

However, books, including dictionaries, are increasingly being produced, by our publishing house and others - by electronic means, i.e. by EDP. I am not qualified to give a comprehensive account of the use of electronic aids by European dictionary publishers for lexicographical purposes. I can, however, give a general outline of the situation of (dictionary) publishers on the threshold of the electronic age and describe both our own experiences and plans and certain other projects - particularly Scandinavian ones - which I am familiar with.

As regards my own firm, I can tell you quite briefly that Gyldendal, Copenhagen, is a traditional all-round publishing house, of medium size by European standards and amongst the biggest in Denmark. We produce a large number of textbooks and have a virtual monopoly in bilingual dictionaries.

211

Most of the projects under discussion at this symposium are being carried
out by public or semi-public institutions and do not have to be paying
propositions in the strict economic sense. However, the commercial
publisher must consider the question of profitability, and it is characteristic that it has so far been specialized published houses, in particular, who have enthusiastically adopted the computer, particularly the
integrated EDP (data base) for use in editing work. The input in question
is typical data which is also used in other contexts, and the output does
not only consist of printed matter such as books.

Telephone companies, which were among the pioneers in this field, provide
a typical example: every change of telephone number, name or address is
entered into the company's data base once and once only. This single data
base can then be used to produce a telephone directory covering either
the entire country or a particular town, as required. In addition, the
entries can be arranged by name, number or sector. Only when a directory
is to be printed is the relevant information - subject to last-minute
updating - retrieved in the desired order and given the typographical
form required. The same data base is used as an address file for making
out bills and for direct reference, not only by the directory enquiries
services but also -in certain places in France - directly by subscribers
via their domestic terminals. Ultimately this could do away with the need
for a book, i.e. a telephone directory, as such.

Catalogues and trade and other directories etc. are produced in a similar
way, as are laws, the debates of the Danish Folketing and increasingly
large sections of the newspapers. Thus, it is presumably merely a question of time before the publishers of dictionaries feel obliged to adopt
the same method.

The general, non-specialist publishing houses, i.e. those who publish a
mixture of novels, poetry, schoolbooks, dictionaries or popular reference
works etc., have - like all other business - already been using computers
for administrative purposes for some time. Gyldendal has also developed
an on-line system which permits booksellers throughout Denmark to see via
their terminals whether a book is in stock and what it costs, after which
they can order it directly via the same terminals.

However, unlike the specialist publishers and certain university institutes, the new technology has not so far caused any great changes in the
way we or out authors carry out editing work. So far, very few data
terminals are used in this area, and manuscripts are still written on
paper.

Certain compilers and editors of dictionaries, however, would now appear
to be ready to take the plunge and adopt the new technology. A Russian-
Danish dictionary has been published in Copenhagen which was entered
directly by the author and his assistants into the system at the EDP
Centre of Copenhagen University (RECKU), and subsequently using the
centre-s photocomposition unit. The publishing house had only to see to
the printing and marketing. Attempts are being made to produce other,
more research-oriented publications in a similar way, for example an Old
Danish dictionary (by Det Danske Sprog- og Litteraturselskab), and I will
not deny that we publishers are a little anxious about this form of
competition.

However, we are also convinced that we have a know-how which will enable
us to continue producing most books, even in the electronic age.

In both the above cases, typographical coding was used where a non-media-
dependent structuring of the text would presumably have been more appropriate.

Thus, when I said in my introduction that most books are produced with
the aid of EDP, this has nothing to do with advanced editing systems.
However, computer composition systems have become almost universal among
our suppliers and printers.

This means, inter alia, that at some point in production - at the composing and proofreading stage - practically all books and other printed
texts will have been stored in a machine-readable form, e.g. on punched
tape, magnetic tape or disc. Texts can be stored in this form, which is
easier and cheaper to correct and update than traditional media, i.e.
lead or photographic film.

This means that it is possible - at least in theory - to make use of the texts in forms or contexts other than those originally intended.

However, so far this possibility has only been used to a limited extent in practice. This is not so much out of lack of imagination but rather because of traditional demarcations between disciplines, the lack of standards or the inappropriateness of existing standards, and doubts regarding the profitability of the development work required. On the other hand, in the graphics sector EDP systems have clearly proved themselves to be economically viable for composing, proofreading and making up, and suppliers of typographical composition systems offer an ever increasing number of programmes for the integration of editing, typographical and adminstrative processes. However, the majority of these programmes are aimed particularly at the newspaper market and could not simply be taken over as they stand for use in producing a dictionary or lexicon.

Nevertheless, the new technology has radically changed the way in which we produce dictionaries and lexicons (encyclopaedias) by enabling corrections in the texts to be made more cheaply, more easily and more quickly.

In the past, our dictionaries were revised every 20 or 30 years. More frequent revisions were impossible from the economic point of view, since all the composing and proofreading etc. had to be done afresh each time. Nowadays, we can issue revised additions of the best-selling dictionaries (English, German, French) every two or three years.

Similarly, we have bee able to publish a ten-volume lexicon over a period of 13 months, with every volume updated to within a few months before publication. In the past, one had to think in terms of a maximum of two or three volumes per year in the case of works of this kind.

Most of the dictionaries and lexicons for which I am responsible are typeset in our own photocomposing room. An intermediate product is a magnetic tape which can be processed using theEDP system belonging to the administration department of the publishing house. Thus, unlike many publishing houses which haveno composing room of their own, we have free access to the machine-readable text, which means we can perform various functions, such as the following, on our text files:

1. Each article in our encyclopaedias bears one of a total of approximately 200 subject codes, inthe form of a number indicating, for example, organic chemistry, French literature, mammals, etc.Thus, we have been able to use the computer to obtain current statistics regarding the volume oftext, i.e. the number of lines, under each subject code and each letter of the alphabet. In addition, we have been able to use the computer to sort all the articles by subject group, so that each subject area could be sent to an expert for revision, after which the text was resorted alphabetically.

2. In thedictionaries we have modernized the phonetic transcription and standardized our system of abbreviations by instructing the computer to carry out a series of precisely-defined general corrections along the following lines 'replace the string '...aaa...' with '...bbb...

3. For the purposes of a thorough revision of our big Danish-English dictionary (approximately 2 000 pages) we sorted out the lines containing special strings of characters, i.e. usage labels such as 'econ., jur., chem., etc.' so that experts in the field in question could go through the words and expressions thus marked together with their translations.

4. At this very moment we are planning to use the computer to separate out the Danish section of our Danish-French dictionary in such a way that a new target language can be inserted, i.e. Italian. This will save a lot of work on the production of a Danish-Italian Dictionary. None of this, however, is carried out on-line but rather in batch runs, often with ad hoc programs, on the administration's EDP system, and the input and output files are typographically structured. However, I do not regard these machine-readable dictionary texts as particularly suitable for further editing purposes, since they are coded not according to the internal structure of the dictionary, but according to the typographical appearance of the finished book.

A (bilingual) dictionary consists of a series of articles in alphabetical order. Each article contains, in a particular order, information about the headword, such as class, conjugation, pronunciation, translation(s), usage labels for subject area (e.g. law, chemistry, zoology, etc.) or stylistic level (formal, slang, vulgar), examples of the use of the word in conjunction with other words, translations ofthe examples, compounds, derivatives etc. - i.e. every word is accompanied by a long series of functions. The typographical codes do not divide the text up according to these categories, but rather into sections with the same typeface (e.g. semi-bold, italic, continental pica, capitals) and into lines of equal length (justification); this information is required by the composing machine which has to translate the data into type, but it is not particularly useful for rational dictionary editing. For this purpose, coding on the basis of the function of the word in the dictionary would be far more useful, and this coding could easily be translated into typographical codes when the book was to be printed, since there is a direct mapping from function to typography but not vice versa.

For the revision of existing dictionaries, which is our main activity as a publisher of dictionaries, a most useful facility would be the ability to carry out a usage labels search. To give just one example, words and expressions which were described as 'slang' ten years ago will nowadays presumably have become part of everyday speech or will have disappeared from the language. It should therefore be possible to locate and inspect these words.

Naturally, new dictionaries can be structured in this way at the manuscript stage - roughly speaking according to the categories used in the BONNLEX system, as we saw yesterday. However, what about existing dictionaries which we as publishers make our living from by publishing revised editions of them?

I should like to refer in this connection to an interesting Swedish project, i.e. the English-Swedish dictionary published by Essette Studium last year. The manuscript, which was written in the traditional manner and included typographical codes, was nearly finished when it was decided to apply a structured EDP solution. It was decided to key-in the manuscript as it stood and then to analyse each word by means of a computer program which related the typographical codes to the position of the word in the dictionary article. In this way, it was possible to determine the function of the word with a high degree of probability.

In the following years, the editors continued in the same way with the structured text.

This was an expensive process, however, in spite of the fact that the text was divided into only seven categories, i.e. seven differnet functions, which is still a fairly small number.

One of the aims in this Swedish project was to be able to sell a 'skeleton' English dictionary with unspecified target language to other countries requiring a large English dictionary. Another objective was to be able to use parts of the material for other purposes, such as smaller dictionaries.

This work is currently in full swing. A third possibility, which I have seen used by Chambers in Scotland, is to publish several editions of the same dictionary, each with its own system of phonetics.

Our publishing house is currently conducting a different experiment along the same sort of lines, but with a unilingual dictionary, i.e. 'Ny Ord: Dansk 1955-75' (New Words in Danish, 1955-1975), which is being produced by the Dansk Sprog.... (Danish language Board).

The text is structured at the deying-in stage. This project has already been presented at the Workshop in Pisa on 20 - 22 May and I will therefore not go into details.

In our countries, all bilingual dictionaries tend to be very similar and are essentially on the same tradition. If a number of publishers within and outside the Communitycould agree on a common standard, i.e. a common format, for the internal structuring of their dictionaries, this would increase the possibilities for exchange of dictionary material and for re-organizing existing material to produce new dictionaries which have

have hitherto not been economically viable. proposition. This would be
particularly important for the minor languages - not least for the
languages spoken by our migrant workers. Standardization of this kind
will also presumably be necessary if commercial dictionaries are to be
included in a European Lexical Data bank, such as Mr. Roland haas of the
Commission prepared us for 18 months ago by sending questionnaires to a
large number of publishers.

We plan to carry out structuring of this kind with our own dictionaries
and to invite our colleagues in other countries to take join us in this
project. We have not set our sights nearly as high as the linguists
present here today but we are also keen to learn from them.

The next step, after the bilingual dictionaries have been structured,
will be to bring together dictionaries with common elements in one data
base - a typical example for us would be all the dictionaries with Danish
as their source language. This would make it far simpler to update the
Danish word list and to produce dictionaries from Danish into new target
languages.

I was also intending to say a few words on copyright, but since I have
discovered that Mr. Olsson from Sweden intends to deal with this subject
- and knows much more about it than I do - I shall be very brief. I would
merely like to raise the following - perhaps provocative - question:
Should the dictionaries of the future be protected by individual copyright at all?

Copyright legislation is, in principle, aimed at protecting the individual; collective copyright is a very troublesome exception from the
general rules, when two or three co-authors are involved, but becomes an
impossibility when it is a question of 20 or 30 people whose individual
efforts cannot be distinguished in the finished book.

An encyclopaedia today is not the work of a single person - and the same
will be true of the dictionaries of the future. It should rather be
likened to a film where the director, actors and cameramen, etc. all have
their part to play in producing the finished product and receive a

single payment from the producer (or publisher) for doing a certain job. It is impossible to distingbuish the object or extent of individual copyright.

Even today - when dictionaries are still the work of an individual - there are major injustices, because of the inter-relationship of copyright and payment of royalties. The author who painstakingly revises and updates a work is paid the same as the one who merely has his old dictionaries reprinted and, in Denmark, those who produce English dictionaries get more for their work than those who produce German dictionaries, because English dictionaries are the ones which sell most. The producers of French dictionaries cannot make a living from this work, and the people who produce Spanish and Italian dictionaries would starve to death in Denmark, if they did not have a steady job and work on dictionaries as a hobby. The work involved is the same, but the demande is different.

In conclusion, I should like to say a few words about the situation of the publisher in the electronic age, a subject which is already being studied both in the individual countries, European Community Publishers' Association and the International Publishers' Association.

The publishers who survive will not only publish books, but will be production companies, in the widest sense of the term, which buy, process and resell information.

Thus, the raw material in the future might still be an author's manuscript, but it might also be, for example, data taken from the many data bases in Euronet-Diane, Lockheed etc., and while the product in the future might still be a book, it might just as well be a magnetic tape, a diskette, a chip (Read Only Memory) or even an on-line link with the customer.

LEXICOGRAPHY IN THE ELECTRONIC AGE
J. Goetschalckx and L. Rolling (editors)
North-Holland Publishing Company
© ECSC, EEC, EAEC, 1982

A NEW VAN DALE PROJECT:

BILINGUAL DICTIONARIES ON ONE AND THE SAME MONOLINGUAL BASIS

P. VAN STERKENBURG, Dutch Lexicological Institute, Leyden

W. MARTIN, University of Louvain and Antwerp

B. AL, Free University of Amsterdam

Abstract

The Nieuw Woordenboek der Nederlandsche Taal (New Dictionary of the Dutch
Language) was first issued in 1872 under the name of Van Dale.

Since then reprints and new editions have followed each other with some
regularitiy. To the general public Van Dale became the outstanding
authority on language matters. In 1976 the Van Dale publishing firm
decided to expand this monolingual Van Dale by a new series of bilingual
dictionaries, comparable with each other and based, as far as the volumes
Dutch-foreign language are concerned, on one and the same synchronic
basis. The latter itself would, as a synchronic dictionary, form part of
the new series. In the present article the most important features of the
new products will be set out, their interrelation (comparability) will be
demonstrated, and the role of the computer within the whole enterprise
will be outlined.

1. Introduction

Within the tradition of Dutch lexicography the monolingual dictionary
of Johan Hendrik Van Dale [1], better known under the name of the
'Dikke Van Dale' ('Van Dale, Unabridged'), has, ever since 1872, been
a tool desired by many for its linguistic authority, and/or a vade-
mecum regularly consulted on the most diverse matters (ranging from
judicial decisions to cryptograms). To the general public Van Dale is
the largest and best in the field of the Dutch language.

The scientific basis for Van Dale is the famous Woordenboek der
Nederlandsche Taal (WNT) ("Dictionary of the Dutch Language") which
was started in 1851 and which at present has arrived at the "tail-let-
ters" of the alphabet [2]. However, since the WNT describes material
from the period 1500-1920, this means that the description in Van Dale
from 1920 onwards solely rests upon the personal qualities of the
present editors. Van Dale is produced and published by Martinus
Nijhoff in The Hague, a daughter company of Kluwer. It is not our
intention to evaluate the existing Dutch monolingual dictionaries. We
would like to draw attention to the movement that can be observed in
the ranks of the makers and users of bilingual dictionaries with Dutch
as a target or as a source-language. There is criticism and concern.

Quite recently (NRC Handelsblad, June 5th, 1981) Jisk Knijpstra, in a
discussion with Ieme van der Poel, has aired his very severe criticism
of the existing French desk dictionaries as follows: "The existing
dictionaries are hopelessly out of date, they contain too many inac-
curacies and often present doubtful coinages instead of living material taken from spoken French. The modern use of language, as one
finds it reflected in newspapers and magazines, in fact is hardly
considered. This is the more surprising and disastrous as, for example,
schoolexaminations very often draw on texts from Le Monde and the
Nouvel Observateur". (Report on the Colloquium on dictionaries organized by Maison Descartes, Amsterdam, April 1981).

In the leading article of the monthly Onze Taal ("Our Language")
(August 1979, p.45) the Dutch translator with the European Community,
A. Rohaert, asks the question: "Is the passing bell tolling over our
dictionaries?".

Rohaert's greatest concern is that possibly in the near future no longer a publisher will be found willing to publish a bilingual Dutch dictionary. That his pessimism is not shared by everyone, already became clear a.o. from the reaction of E. Cohen, ex-publisher, in the same periodical in October 1979. It may appear from what follows here as well.

2. Van Dale Projectontwikkeling B.V.

("Van Dale Project Development Ltd.")
In the Kluwer concern various reorganizations took place in 1975. As a direct consequence a new daughter company, viz. Van Dale Projectontwikkeling B.V. ("Van Dale Project Development Ltd.") was founded. In 1976, Pieter Hagers, being charged with the organization of the new company, contacted various linguists in the Netherlands and Belgium, in order to get an answer to his question of how to set up a new dictionary undertaking that was to distinguish itself as substantially as possible from all competitors.

In the course of 1976 the late Jan-Peter Ponten composed his Overwegingen met betrekking tot een programma voor een verklarend voordenboek van het Nederlands ("Reflections on a programme for an explanatory dictionary of Dutch") [3]. This theoretical programme would lead to a scientific investigation into the methods of lexicography, but contained too few concrete points of departure for a concern that was indeed willing both to investigate and to invest, yet at the same time wanted to bring, within a reasonable lapse of time, a new product on the market.

One of Ponten's basic tenets however was that to make the new dictionary project a successful undertaking an inventory of present-day Dutch should be made containing explanations, definitions, synonyms and usage information. This inventory should then form the basis for bilingual dictionaries, providing the latter with a common denominator.

3. An inventory of present-day Dutch

In the autumn of 1976 at the request of P.Hagers, Ponten's theoretical points of departure were translated into a practical set-up by Van Sterkenburg as follows:

3.1 The creation of an <u>inventory of present-day Dutch</u> based on an extremely large text-corpus, compiled according to carefully formulated criteria, as was advocated initially, was not feasible within the time period fixed by the publisher. The corpus leading to an inventory of present-day Dutch therefore, had to remain mainly based on traditional compilation work, in this case the "Dikke Van Dale". Next to this, a mini-corpus consisting of "ordinary" reading-matter was built up and put on magnetic tape. That is all sorts of periodicals and magazines having a regular house-to-house delivery, were added to the original material, for example: <u>Wat iedereen over drugs zou moeten weten</u> ("What everyone should know about drugs"); <u>Drukwerk helpt de wereld draaien</u> ("Printed matter helps the world go round"); <u>De Stadskrant</u> ("The City Newspaper"); <u>De Geheelonthouder</u> ("The Teetotaller"); <u>Muziek deze Maand</u> ("Music this Month"); <u>de Microgids</u> (small weekly for radio and television programmes); <u>Fundamenteel beleggen</u> ("Investing Money from A to Z"); <u>Uitleg</u> (a fortnightly magazine issued by the Dutch Education Office); <u>Auto-Kampioen</u> issued by the ANWB (a monthly for motorists); <u>Mensen van Nu</u> (popular magazine on all sorts of actual problems concerning daily life); <u>Stripschrift</u> (magazine on stripcartoons); <u>Intermediair</u> (a weekly on accountancy, anthropology, economics, econometrics, information theory, (ortho)pedagogics, planning and urbanization, political science, psychology, etc.), and many others.

At the same time a small group of informants was asked to take notice of new words and new uses of already existing words taken from many texts in the field of astronautics, electronics, women's lib., economy, medical care, environment, education, trade unions, to mention only a few of them.

3.2 The approximately 220,000 entries from the "Dikke Van Dale" had to be reduced to 80 à 90,000 lemmata, both for scientific (synchronic) and for extra-scientific (economical) reasons. To facilitate this selection the tenth edition of <u>Van Dale</u> was transferred to magnetic tape in its entity. Independently of each other three Dutch-speaking lexicographers then provided every entry and every meaning with a "synchrony-code", i.e. they specified with figures ranging from 0 up to 5 whether a word and/or a meaning should be taken up in a new dictionary of the desired size or not. The computer then split off those words that had received the label "appropriate" respectively "inappropriate" or "obsolete" (for example, many proper names and sailing-vessel terms, regional vocabulary, terminology of the colonial past, transparent derivations and compounds etc.).

3.3 Since there was no contemporary dictionary of Dutch synonyms available, an encoding system was developed to obtain a raw corpus of synonyms from the existing definitions of the "Dikke Van Dale" (4).

3.4 Despite the qualities of such lists as Woordfrequenties in geschreven en gesproken Nederlands ("Wordfrequencies in written and spoken Dutch") (Utrecht 1975) by P.C. Uit den Boogaart, and Eveline de Jong's Spreektaal. Woordfrequenties in gesproken Nederlands ("Spoken Language- Wordfrequencies in spoken Dutch") (Utrecht 1979), there is no frequency-list of present-day Dutch based on an extensive corpus available. The criteria used then to indicate high-frequency words and to fix the order of the meanings within a polysemous word will mainly be valency and experience (subjective frequency).

3.5 A descriptive framework was developed in order to have all lemmata dealt with in a uniform way and to enable the computer to process the material so that some sort of database would originate, making the derivation of byproducts and reprints economically justified.
The main features of an entry are:
1. technical information: word, variant forms if any, references and pronunciation, frequency information, grammatical information, labels which obtain for all meanings, references to a register containing proverbs;
2. meaning descriptions with possible applications and synonyms;
3. examples of the grammatical-syntactic combinatory possibilities of the word in its various meanings.

Voorbeeld: market ("market")

<u>Markt</u>   <f > <14; -en > <→ spr. 153, 376 >

<u>0.1</u>   openbare verkoop en koop op een daarvoor bestemde plaats in de open
       lucht, waar goederen aanwezig zijn

<u>0.2</u>   plaats waar markt wordt gehouden

<u>0.3</u>   de uitwisseling van allerlei producten die ergens plaats heeft

<u>0.4</u>   prijs waartegen iets ergens wordt verhandeld

<u>0.5</u>   < hand. > geneigdheid om te kopen; intensiteit van de handel

<u>2.2</u>   de <u>Grote</u> -

<u>2.3</u>   de <u>Europese</u> -

<u>2.5</u>   de - <u>was</u> <u>stil</u>

<u>3.4</u>   de - <u>bederven</u>; <u>een</u> <u>stijgende</u> -, <u>een</u> <u>dalende</u> -

<u>6.1</u>   de - op <u>het</u> Waterlooplein; <u>naar</u> <u>de</u> - <u>gaan</u>; op <u>de</u> -
       <u>kopen</u>, <u>ter</u> - <u>gaan</u> <u>bij</u> <u>iemand</u> a) bij hem kopen
       b) bij hem voorlichting, hulp enz. zoeken;
       <u>in</u> <u>de</u> - <u>zijn</u> <u>voor</u>, gegadigde zijn voor; <u>aan</u> <u>de</u>
       - <u>komen</u>, aanbieden; <u>van</u> <u>alle</u> <u>-en</u> <u>thuis</u> <u>zijn</u>,
       overal raad op weten

<u>6.4</u>   de - <u>van</u> <u>eieren</u>; <u>goed</u> <u>in</u> <u>de</u> - <u>liggen</u> a) gevraagd
       zijn   b) <fig. >een goede naam hebben;

<u>¶.1</u>   <u>bij</u> <u>het</u> <u>scheiden</u> <u>van</u> <u>de</u> -, <u>leert</u> <u>men</u> <u>de</u> <u>kooplui</u> <u>kennen</u>,
       iemands ware karakter blijkt pas als het erop aankomt

Explanation of the codes used

1   noun (11 masc., 12 fem., 13 neut., 14 masc. and fem.)

2   adjective

3   verb (31 intransitive, 32 transitive, 33 reflexive)

4   pronoun

5   adverb

6   preposition

7   article

8   conjunction

9   interjection

¶   special case

For the explanation of the double digit code after the black diamond see
below (English example: <u>distant</u>).

After the theoretical aspects had been translated into practice, a time schedule was drawn up that should lead to the production of 21 dictionaries, divided into three series of seven. Planned are:

1. a series containing large editions of Dutch-Dutch, French-Dutch, Dutch-French, German-Dutch, Dutch-German, English-Dutch and Dutch-English dictionaries;
2. a school edition of the above dictionaries;
3. a paperback edition of these dictionaries.

These new products do not owe their <u>raison d'être</u> to what G.J. Forgue [5] calls "the probable needs of the mythical creature known as the average or typical user" (1979:127), but instead are based on a market-analysis carried out in 1979 of, among other things, the needs of those users [6]. Almost everybody holds the view that a Dutch-Dutch dictionary should in any case give information about:

1. the correct spelling of words;
2. the meaning of words.

Apart from this, people think that a dictionary should also take up old-fashioned words and words with related meanings. There is less interest in etymology, taboo-words, antonyms and regional words. Foreign language dictionaries should, according to the informants, of all things, provide information on: spelling (62%), pronunciation (55%), various translation equivalents (45%) and plural forms (43%).

Inquiries such as these however should be relativized. The fact is that people do not always know what to expect from a dictionary and what not. Nevertheless, it is encouraging that attempts are being made to get dictionaries more "user-minded". Also in what follows the needs of those users have been seriously considered.

4. <u>The bilingual dictionaries</u>

As it was stated before, the new Van Dale project should not only lead to a new synchronic monolingual Dutch dictionary, but to a series of bilingual dictionaries as well. English, French and German were taken up as L2's. This series was meant for a Dutch speaking public and should, to user the publisher's words, "be marked off both by its originality and by its usefulness". Moreover all of it should be published within "a reasonable lapse of time" (two to three years' production time for the large volumes e.g.).

In order to realize this, at first sight presumptuous, but so challenging a programme, a <u>Mono- Bilingual Management Team</u> was formed consisting of the Publisher (P.Hagers) and of the respective dictionary editors (P. van Sterkenburg (chairman) and W.Pijnenburg for Dutch, W.Martin and G.Tops for English, B.Al for French, the late J.P.Ponten and H.Cox for German).

Based partly upon Ponten's proposals for a Dutch monolingual dictionary, partly upon the specific needs of bilingual dictionaries the following was decided upon:

4.1 First of all, as the dictionaries were meant for a Dutch speaking public, what we needed to begin with, was indeed an <u>inventory of modern Dutch</u> as advocated by J.P.Ponten, containing explanations, definitions, information concerning semantic and syntactic usage, and a set of synonyms or pseudo-synonymous paradigms; this Dutch monolingual data-bank could then serve:

a) as a common information source for the microstructure of the translation dictionaries with Dutch as a target-language (E-D; F-D; G-D);

b) as a common starting-point for the macro-structure of the translation dictionaries with Dutch as a source language; the D-E, D-F, D-G translation dictionaries, but for language specific items, would then have a common basis, viz. the world view of the Dutch language user.

4.2 A second requirement which was thought to be essential had to do with recent developments in linguistics: we thought that <u>grammar and lexicon should no longer be kept apart</u>: being confronted with texts in communication, it is rather unnatural to keep the several components playing a role in the understanding and/or production of these texts, apart. Therefore it was decided that a <u>contrastive grammar</u> should be included <u>in the form of a lexicon</u> and that the dictionary or better, the lemmata of the dictionary should refer to the grammar.

4.3. This new series of dictionaries should not only be modern and innovative, it also should be user-oriented, therefore a.o. the dictionaries should be <u>mutually comparable</u> in aim, scope, and method. The user then should not have to learn for each language a different method. The clearest example of this user-oriented treatment is the way <u>idioms</u> and <u>non-idioms</u> are dealt with. As is well-known an idiom is a complex lexical unit the meaning of which is not deducible from the meaning of its component parts [7]. Therefore <u>idiomatic expressions</u> are taken up in the micro-structure <u>together with non-idiomatic expressions</u>, as the former differ from the latter only because of semantic reasons. As the dictionary-user uses a dictionary a.o. precisely because of his lack of semantic knowledge one can not rely upon this non-existing knowledge to structure the information the dictionary contains, instead one should <u>rely upon the combinatory (and so syntactic) possibilities to structure the example phrases and expressions, including the idiomatic ones</u> (for examples see below).

4.4 A fourth and last, but not least, requirement for a lexicographical product to be successful in the 80's was, so it seemed, its <u>computability</u>. What we wanted was not only a traditional product in the form of a book, but a powerful database which could give rise to all kinds of interesting derivatives and by-products. To mention only some of these: a well-structured computerized Dutch monolingual dictionary should generate a dictionary of synonyms or pseudo-synonyms, dictionaries such as conceived of here, containing context-sensitive data, should be a help in disambiguating words, as it is a well-known fact that language in context is not so ambiguous, or it should be possible to generate from our E-D dictionary e.g. a list of English idioms showing a particular syntactic pattern (A+N e.g.), or a list of temperature adjectives with their habitual and/or idiomatic nominal collocations, or a list of English collective nouns in combination with verbs, etc.etc.

It shall have become clear from all this that this fourth requirement
was one for formalized, accessible and structured information.

Apart from all this the dictionaries should show the richness and
reliability former, good, dictionaries always have shown: presenting
information lying on all levels, ranging from orthography over
phonetics, morphology, syntax, semantics, to usage, In the same way
the dictionaries should stand a crucial test, viz. that of up-to-
dateness, such as they should be able to cope with language variety.
Of course it is rather obvious indeed that such characteristics
should be taken into account, however perhaps less evident was
that we wanted to take into account <u>frequency</u> as well. Marking the
most (some 10,000) frequent items as such, we could give users having
difficulites with these items a hint for them to pay some more
attention to the items in question.

5. Examples

After having dealt with "bilingual" intentions and requirements one
may wonder what this "bilingual" pudding now really tastes like. To
make the preceding more concrete therefore, some examples will be
given taken from the English-Dutch (5.1), the French-Dutch (5.2) and
Dutch-French Volume (5.3). Most probably the French-Dutch dictionary
will appear first (the editing will be finished by the end of 1981),
shortly thereafter followed by the German-Dutch and the English-Dutch
dictionary. The L1-L2 series will be started in 1982 (making use a.o.
of the reversal of the L2-L1 part). For the sake of convenience only
the English-Dutch example will be commented upon (5.4).

5.1 English-Dutch example

$ 111100 <u>dis.tant</u> [dɪstənt] <f> <2 ; -ly>

I   <21>

0.1   <u>ver</u> ⇒ afgelegen, verwijderd, langgeleden

0.2   <u>afstandelijk</u> ⇒ <u>gereserveerd, op een afstand</u>, koel, terughoudend

0.3   <u>zwak</u> ⇒ <u>gering, flauw</u>

◆

1.1   in the -- future <u>in de verre toekomst</u>; the town was two hours
       -- <u>de stad lag op twee uur afstand</u>;
       the -- sound of thunder <u>het in de verte rommelend onweer</u>;

-- times <u>langvervlogen tijden</u>

<u>1.3</u> a -- connection <u>een zwak/flauw verband</u>

<u>3.1</u> a ship --ly seen <u>een schip dat in de verte te zien</u>
<u>was</u>

<u>6.1</u> a town 50 miles -- <u>from</u> London <u>een stad op 50 mijl</u>
<u>van Londen</u>

<u>6.2</u> she is always very -- <u>to</u> me <u>ze doet altijd erg</u>
<u>afstandelijk tegen mij</u>;

<u>II</u> <22>

<u>0.1</u> ver⇒<u>over een grote afstand</u>

<u>0.2</u> ver⇒<u>niet nauw verwant</u>

◆

<u>1.1</u> a -- journey <u>een verre reis</u>

a -- look <u>een starende/verre blik</u>

<u>1.2</u> -- relations <u>verre familie</u>

<u>1.¶</u> <spoorwegen> -- signal <u>voorsein</u>; -
- early warning (system)
<u>radarsysteem ter waarschuwing voor een</u>
<u>raketaanval</u>.

5.2 <u>French-Dutch example</u>

<u>poche</u> [pɔʃ] <f> <l>

<u>I</u> <11> inf. <u>0.1</u> <u>pocket</u>;

<u>II</u> <12>

<u>0.1</u> <u>zak</u> <in kleding>

<u>0.2</u> <u>uitgezakte plooi</u> ⇒ bobbel;

<u>0.3</u> <u>zak</u> <verpakking >;

<u>0.4</u> <u>vak</u> <in tas, portefeuille >;

<u>0.5</u> <u>(vang)net</u>⇒sleepnet;

<u>0.6</u> <geol.> <u>holte</u> ⇒put, laag;

<u>0.7</u> <biol.> <u>buidel</u>⇒krop;

<u>0.8</u> <fig.> <u>haard</u>⇒punt;

◆

<u>1.1</u> argent de -- <u>zakgeld</u>;

lampe de -- <u>zaklantaarn</u>;

livre de -- <u>pocket</u>;

les mains dans les poches <u>moeiteloos, zonder een</u>

<u>poot uit te steken</u>;

théâtre de -- <u>vestzaktheater</u>;

<u>1.6</u> -- de gaz <u>gasbel</u>;

-- de pétrole <u>olielaag</u>;

<u>1.8</u> -- de résistance <u>verzetshaard</u>;

<u>3.1</u> acheter, vendre chat en -- <u>een kat in de zak kopen,</u>

<u>verkopen</u>;

      <inf.>   n'avoir pas sa langue dans sa -- <u>niet</u>

                 <u>op z'n mondje gevallen zijn</u>;

                 n'avoir pas les yeux dans sa -- <u>z'n</u>

                 <u>ogen niet in z'n zak hebben</u>;

                 faire les poches à qn. <u>iemands zakken</u>

                 <u>doorzoeken, leeghalen, rollen</u>;

                 mettre qn. dans sa -- <u>iemand in z'n zak steken</u>;

<u>3.2</u> elle avait des poches sous les yeux <u>zij had wallen</u>

<u>onder haar ogen</u>;

ton pantalon fait des poches aux genoux <u>er zitten</u>

<u>knieën in je pantalon</u>;

<u>6.1</u>   <inf.>   l'affaire est <u>dans</u> la -- <u>de zaak is</u>

<u>rond, bekeken</u>;.

payer <u>de</u> sa -- <u>uit eigen zak betalen</u>;

      <inf.>   en être <u>de</u> sa -- <u>er (geld) bij in-</u>

<u>schieten</u>;

il a 100 F <u>en</u> -- <u>hij heeft 100 F op zak</u>;

<u>8.1</u> je le connais comme ma -- <u>ik ken hem door en door</u>.

5.3 Dutch-French example

<u>lucht</u>   <14>

<u>0.1</u>   <gasmengsel om aarde ><u>air</u> <u>m</u>;

<u>0.2</u>   <dampkring> <u>atmosphère</u> <u>v</u>, <u>air</u> <u>m</u>;

<u>0.3</u>   <adem > <u>air</u> <u>m</u>, <u>haleine</u> <u>v</u>;

<u>0.4</u>   <buitenlucht> <u>air</u>   <u>m</u>;

<u>0.5</u>   <hemel> <u>ciel</u> <u>m</u> ⌐ les ⌐ <u>airs</u>   <u>m</u>;

<u>0.6</u>   <wolken> <u>ciel</u> <u>m</u>;

<u>0.7</u>   <zonder waarde> ≠ <u>quantité</u> <u>v</u> <u>négligeable</u>;

<u>0.8</u>   <geur> <u>odeur</u> <u>v</u> ⟹ relent <u>m</u>;

◆

2.1 warme, polaire, bedorven -- (courant m) d'air
chaud, polaire, vicié;

2.4 in de open -- en plein air;

2.5 een bewolkte, betrokken, heldere -- un ciel
nuageux, couvert, clair;

2.6 er komt een lelijke -- opzetten un ciel menaçant
s'amène;

2.8 een akelige -- une mauvaise odeur;

3.1 -- inademen respirer (de) l'air;

3.3 -- krijgen prendre haleine;
-- geven aan iets donner libre cours à qc.;

3.4 een --je scheppen prendre l'air;

3.7. doen of iemand -- is ignorer qn;

3.8 de -- van iets krijgen avoir vent de qc.;

6.2 de vogel vliegt in de -- l'oiseau vole dans les airs;
(van blijdschap) een gat in de -- springen bondir
(de joie);
iets in de -- laten vliegen faire sauter qc.;
vlieg in de --! (allez) au diable!;
dat hangt in de -- ce sont des paroles en l'air;
in de -- zweven planer dans les airs;
in de -- zijn ⟨radio, tv⟩ émettre, diffuser;
die bewering is uit de -- gegrepen cette affir-
mation est inventée de toutes pièces;
uit de -- komen vallen tomber du ciel, des nues;
er is geen vuiltje (wolkje) aan de -- aucune
menace ne se profile à l'horizon;

6.5 de --en van Ruysdael les ciels de Ruysdael;
het onweer is niet van de -- l'orage continue
sans cesse

5.4 Comment

Taking the English-Dutch example distant as a case in point the
following should be stated:

1. First of all there is a code (after the dollar-sign) which is helpful
    in generating by-products such as desk editions, school editions, paper-
    back editions and the like.

2. Next there follows the item in question (+ hyphenation, + possible
    spelling variants, + phonetic information, + frequency information, +
    grammatical information; where needed one also finds field labels,
    stylistic labels, references to a list of proverbs etc.).

3. The lemma distant is subdivided into two parts: the first part
    contains those meanings that can be used both attributively and
    predicatively (=21), the second part (=22) contains the meanings
    which can be used attributively only (one will have understood that
    in the code just mentioned 21 and 22 are subdivisions of class 2
    which stands for adjectives such as 1 stands for nouns, 3 for verbs,
    6 for prepositions etc.; it will also have become clear hereby that
    the L2-L1 dictionary is not only a dictionary meant for understand-
    ing, but for production as well).

4. The semantics of the item in question, i.e. the translation equival-
    ents and the translation of the examples, are organized as follows:
    - First there is a "translation profile" (what one finds before the
    black diamond) containing basic translation equivalents (to be found
    before the double arrow), after the arrow one finds variants (syn-
    onyms, pseudo-synonyms, contextual variants etc.). It will be clear
    that we rely upon the (Dutch) native speaker's competence to make a
    choice here (remember that the dictionaries are meant for a Dutch
    speaking public). The translation profile serves as a kind of short
    cut to the semantics of the item in question.
    - After the black diamond one finds the so-called contextualized
    equivalents. The double digit code refers to the following:
      - the first digit indicates the grammatical category of the combi-
        nation word,
      - the second digit refers to the meaning number as described in the
        translation profile.

    Someone who does not know, after having read the translation profile,
    how to translate distant times e.g., should look it up under a code
    starting with 1 (=noun). Someone who does not know how to translate
    distant signal e.g., should look it up under the codes starting with
    1 as well, it will then be observed that distant in this wordgroup is
    a kind of unique alloseme not being covered by the meanings indicated

in the translation profile. Instead of a meaning number a paragraph sign is used therefore, marking this way, idiomatic expressions.

6. Conclusions

By way of conclusion then we could state that although we know all too well that like a woman's a lexicographer's task is never done, we thought we had to give an impetus to the extension and the further exploration of this challenging, difficult but so fascinating a task. This then lead to the set up of a new series of Van Dale dictionaries which are mutually comparable because of

- identical contents, viz.:

  ✘ a preface with user's guide

  ✘ a grammar in the form of an alphabetical lexicon

  ✘ entries in alphabetical order

  ✘ an alphabetical list of current proverbs

- identical form (a.o. same printing conventions and structure of information),

- the same underlying lexicographical principles leading to a systematic description of the lemmata. This description can be split up into three main parts:

  ✘ non-semantic information (spelling, pronunciation, frequency information, grammatical information, references to list of proverbs, usage-labels)

  ✘ semantic information (semantic profile): definitions and explanations resp. translation equivalents (if needed with labels), synonnyms or semantic variants

  ✘ semantico-syntactic information (contextualized equivalents) treating both idioms and non-idioms, the latter consisting of both free and habitual collocations

- a common basis (the new synchronic Dutch dictionary) serving as a microstructural (in the case of the L2-L1 dictionaries), resp. a macrostructural (in the case of the L1-L2 dictionaries) common source.

All in all the new series hopefully will be marked off (in comparison to similar dictionaries) by

- a more intensive microstructure having a clear, systematic and elaborate semantic part containing a.o. synonyms and contextualized variants

- an alphabetical grammatical lexicon
- a separate alphabetical list of current proverbs (the latter two
  features serving a.o. to relieve somewhat the "lexicon's burden")
- frequency information
- a conscious user-orientation.

If the dictionaries however really are like they claim to be it is up
for the users to find out.

Anyway this new project has tried at leat to give lexicographical
theory and practice a new impetus. It is to be hoped that it was as
impetus in the right direction.

7. References

(1) See P.G.J. van Sterkenburg, Johan Hendrik van Dale en zijn
    Woordenboek, Martinus Nijhoff, 's-Gravenhage (in press).

(2) Matthias de Vries, L.A. te Winkel e.a., Woordenboek der Nederlandsche
    Taal, 's-Gravenhage 1864.

(3) See also Ponten's other publications on this subject:
    Krontrastive Semantik und bilinguale Lexikographie.
    In: Grundfragen der Methodik des Deutschunterrichts
    und ihre praktischen Verfahren, 210-217, München 1975.
    Zum Programm eines bilingualen Wörterbuchs. Ein Beitrag
    zur niederländisch-deutschen Lexikographie.
    In: Deutsche Sprache 3, 131-146, 1975
    Das Ubersetzungwörterbuch und seine linguistischen
    Implikationen. In: Probleme der Lexikologie und Lexi-
    kographie. Jahrbuch 1975 des Instituts für deutsche
    Sprache, IDS 39, 200-211, Düsseldorf, 1976.

(4) For a demonstration of the possible uses of such a corpus we refer to
    W. Martin, B.Al, P.van Sterkenburg, From textual data to lexicogra-
    phical information.In: Dictionaries in Lexicography ed. R.R.K.
    Hartmann (to be published by O.U.P.).

(5) G.J.Forgue, Neologisms in American English since 1945: Indicators of
    Cultural Change. In: R.R.K.Hartmann, Dictionaries and their users.

Papers from the 1978 B.A.A.L. Seminar on Lexicography, ITL 45-46, 127-134, 1979.

(6) Investigation done by NIPO (Nederlandse Instelling voor Psychologisch Onderzoek) based on a sample of 20,422 Dutch families.

(7) See a.o. A. Healy, English Idioms. In: Kivung, vol.1, 71-108, 1968.

LEXICOGRAPHY IN THE ELECTRONIC AGE
J. Goetschalckx and L. Rolling (editors)
North-Holland Publishing Company
© ECSC, EEC, EAEC, 1982

COPYRIGHT PROBLEMS AND USE OF COMPUTERS

A. HENRY OLSSON

MINISTRY OF JUSTICE

SWEDEN

Summary

The main aim of copyright is to promote intellectual creativity
by granting legal protection to authors and other creators of literary,
artistic and musical works. This is done mainly by granting the bene-
ficiaries rights in the works, i.a. the right to make copies of the
works, to perform them publicly etc. The copyright protection is granted
in national laws on copyright. Copyright is, however, also protected by
international conventions to which the majority of the states of the
world are parties.

Copyright is to some extent challenged by the advent of new means
for dissemination of works, i.a. computers. The new media have implied
an increased demand for protected works but at the same time to a considerable extent diminished the authors' possibilities to control the
use which is made of their works. It is important to protect the legitimate interests of the authors and at the same time not hamper the
development of the new and important computer technology.

For the reasons now mentioned it has become necessary to establish
some sort of international legislative framework to settle the relations between copyright and the use of computers. These problems are
currently under study in the international intergovernmental organizations, WIPO (World Intellectual Property Organization) and UNESCO.
Efforts are undertaken to draft international recommendations for
settlement of copyright problems arising from the use of computers.

1. INTRODUCTION

Copyright is an important tool for the economic, social and cultural
development of society. The main aim of copyright is to give certain exclusive rights to authors, composers, artists and other creators of literary and artistic works in order to stimulate intellectual creativity and
thus the development of society in a wider sense. Copyright also serves
as an important safeguard for producers of e.g. books, phonograms and motion pictures by safeguarding the investments made for publication of
such works.

The basic exclusive rights granted to authors and other creators are
a) the right to reproduce (=make copies) of the work
b) the right to communicate the work to the public
c) the right to make translations or adaptations of the work
d) certain other rights, which may be differently shaped in diffe-
    rent countries, e.g. the right to control the distribution of
    copies.

The rights now mentioned are exclusive which means that nobody may
without the permission of the author undertake any of the acts now mentioned.

To these essentially economic exclusive rights comes also a set of
rights called "the moral rights". These imply essentially that the author
has a right to claim his or her name to be stated when the work is made
available to the public and to oppose acts which involve a multilation or
distortion of the work.

The rights now mentioned are not eternal but subsist for a certain
period. This can be different in different countries but comprises in most
cases the lifetime of the author and 50 years from his death.

In most legislations there are certain limitations on the exclusive
rights of the authors. These limitations vary in different countries both
as regards the purpose and the drafting. In the Anglo-Saxon   legal tra-
tition an important legal concept in this context is the provisions on
"fair use" or "fair dealing". In the continental legal tradition these
limitations are usually drafted so as to aim at specific situations. So
is e.g. in many legislations the making of single copies for private use
allowed. Other limitations on copyright are e.g. the right to make quotations, a certain right to make recordings for educational purposes and a

right to "free" public performance under certain conditions.

The rights granted to authors under copyright legislation are usually safeguarded by sanctions for those who utilize a work without proper
authorization by the right-owner. These sanctions could be civil (compen-
sation for damages, seizure, etc.) or criminal (penalty in the form of
fines or imprisonment).

National copyright provisions are usually embodied in Copyright
Acts. There is, however, since the end of the 19th century an international system for the protection of copyright. The reason is that intellectual creativity does not know national frontiers and that the dissemination of works is an international phenomenon. The international copyright system is based on two conventions. One is the Berne Convention for
the Protection of Literary and Artistic Works of 1886. The second one is
the Universal Copyright Convention of 1952 (UCC). Both conventions are
based on the same principles, viz. a) national treatment, meaning that a
country which is party to the convention shall grant nationals from other
contracting countries the same protection as it grants its own nationals,
and, b) minimum protection, meaning that the protection must not be below
a certain level. The difference between the conventions is basically that
the minimum level of protection is lower under the UCC than under the
Berne Convention and that under the Berne Convention copyright protection shall be granted without any formalities whereas under the UCC
certain formalities are allowed. Around 70 countries are members of each
one of the Conventions. Most European countries are members of both conventions. The United States and the Soviet Union are members of the UCC
but not the Berne Convention.

The international protection of copyright - which implies basically
an obligation to protect works from other countries in the same way as
one protects one's own - is of fundamental importance for the international exchange of cultural goods. At the national level copyright protection is a very important factor not only as an element of cultural
policy but also in strictly economical terms. A recent survey in Sweden
shows that the copyright industries (= i.e. those industries which base
their activities on copyright-protected material) account for 4,3 % of
the Gross National Product. There are reasons to believe that roughly the
same figures are valid for other industrialized countries.

2. COPYRIGHT AND NEW TECHNOLOGY

When the concepts of modern copyright developed during the second
half of the 19th century the main means for dissemination of works was
printing and public performance. During the 20th century new such means
have developed such as broadcasting, sound recordings and motion pictures
(cinema films). The last decades have witnessed the advent of new and even
more powerful devices such as television (by means of Herzian waves or
cable) photocopying machines, communication satellites and videograms.
Another such device is the computer. Computer technique can be used for
storage and retrieval of protected works and also for creation of works.

The development of these new media has in many respects a far-reaching impact on the exercise of copyright and also on copyright itself.
This impact can briefly be summarized as implying two factors. One is an
enormously increased need for protected works for use in the new media
and very often a demand for a rapid access to the works. The other factor
implies what is called a fragmentarization of copyright in the sense that
the increased number of users has made it difficult for the copyright
owners to control the use made of their works.

As a consequence of the technological development it has become
necessary to strike a balance between the users' needs and the legitimate
interests of the authors. On the one hand copyright protection must be
safeguarded, the reason being the important role which copyright plays
in the context of cultural and economic development of nations. On the
other hand one should not hamper the development of new means for dissemination of culture.

3. THE SPECIAL COPYRIGHT PROBLEMS IN RELATION TO COMPUTERS

As mentioned above the computer is a powerful tool for storage, retrieval and dissemination of information. The rapid development of information technology has implied the creation of computerized information
and documentation systems. Such systems have been established both at the
national level and at an international level. The development has also
implied a trend towards systems which enable a direct access from the
public to the data base. Furthermore computers are more and more largely
used both for creation of works, e.g. works of art and musical works, and

for translation and adaptation of works and for compilation of facts in computerized data bases.

Copyright implies an exclusive right for the author to control the use of his work. In principle the situation does not change because the use is made by means of a computer. The relations between copyright and computers are, however, very complex not only because most national copyright laws are not entirely clear in this respect but also because of the international character of this utilization.

4. TYPES OF MATERIAL FED INTO A COMPUTER

4.1 From a copyright point of view the material fed into a computer can roughly speaking belong to one of the following four categories.

a) single data or single pieces of information (e.g. name of the author, title, publisher, year of publication)

b) abstracts or summaries of existing works (e.g. abstracts summerizing the main features of a existing work)

c) full texts of existing works (e.g. where a scientific article or a copyright-protected compilation of information is stored in a data base)

d) collections of data or facts (e.g. tables, word lists).

4.2 In addition to what has been said now also a computerized data base itself can enjoy copyright protection.

4.3 Furthermore a thesaurus structured for exploitation of a given computerized data base can be protected by copyright

4.4 A general prerequisite for copyright protection in the cases mentioned in 4.1-4.3 is that the material is original in character and results from a creative effort by its author. This implies that single data etc. (4.1.a.) do not enjoy protection. As regards the abstracts (4.1.b.) three situations are possible, viz i) the abstract is only an enumeration of facts etc. from the preexisting work and does not enjoy copyright protection, ii) the abstract is original in character and constitutes an adaptation of the preexisting work; in this case copyright subsists in the adaptation but its use requires an authorization from the author of the

reexisting work, and iii) the abstract is original in character but is
independent from the preexisting work and does not constitute an adaptation; in this case a copyright in the adaptation exists which is not
linked to the copyright in the first work.

5. ACTS WHICH REQUIRE AUTHORIZATION BY THE COPYRIGHT OWNER

5.1 Basic rights involved

The basic rights under copyright law which are affected by use of
works in connection with computers are mainly
    a) the right to reproduce the work
    b) the right to communicate the work to the public
    c) the right to translate the work
    d) the right to adapt the work
    e) the moral right

These rights are invarious respects affected by various operations
in the computer system. What is said in the following aims at clarifying
the legal situation. The practical application is dealt with in paragraph 6.

5.2 Input

There have for a long time been discussions in interested circles
whether the consent of the author is required already at the input stage
or only at the output. One reason for the former standpoint is said to be
that the author more or less looses the control of the work once it is
fed into a computer and that the point where authorization is needed
consequently should be the input. An argument for the latter standpoint
is said to be that one does not know until the output stage if an utilization actually takes place.

The international opinion seems, however, more and more agree that
the input in computers of protected material (both in the form of cards
or tapes and in the form of a fixation in the computer's memory) constitutes a reproduction under copyright law and requires authorization by
the author or other holder of the copyright.

What has been said implies that input as just stated may take place

i) without authorization in the case mentioned in 4.1.a., but

ii) requires an authorization in all the other cases mentioned in 4.1.b.-d. provided that the criteria for copyrightability are met.

5.3 Output

The legal situation as regards output of protected works is much more complicated than as regards input. In this case the problems apply not only to preexisting works (paragraphs 4.1.b.-d.) but also to the data base itself (paragraph 4.2). Furthermore they apply also to the output of works in the form of translations or adaptations made in the computer.

As regards output one has to take into account two situations.

The first one comprises output in the form of hard copy print-outs. Such output is to be considered as a reproduction under copyright law.

The second situation is when the output is made in the form of visual images (on a screen or cathode ray tube etc.). In this case different legal concepts can be applicable in different countries e.g. public performance, public display, communication by wire, broadcasting, reproduction etc. There is not so far any internationally agreed way on how to look at these problems. The copyright problems as regards output are immensely important in a larger context. One of the main safeguards of the authors under copyright legislation is the right to control the reproduction. The use of computers implies, however, often that no copies are made at the output stage. Consequently a widespread use of computers for utilization of works may imply a challenge to the very fundaments of copyright and the socio-political, cultural and economic interests which copyright law is intended to serve. It is consequently highly desirable that States can agree on their approach to this problem.

5.4 Limitations on copyright in relation to computers

In addition to the problems of principle mentioned in paragraphs 5.2 and 5.3 there are also certain other questions to solve as regards the relations between copyright and computers. One such problem is how to apply the limitations on copyright in this context. As an example could be mentioned that generally speaking copyright legislation in most countries allows explicitly/implicitly quotations and making of copies for private use. Such quotations and copies made from material in a

computerized information system implies, however, also a utilization of
the data base itself and may imply a substantial weakening of the protection of the persons having rights in the material. It is consequently
important to find a solution to these problems.

5.5 Moral rights

In operations consisting of storage and retrieval of works in computer systems it is necessary to take into account the authors' moral
rights. These operations must consequently not imply distortion or muti-
lation of the works and must not lead to the omission of the author's
name.

6. ADMINISTRATION OF THE RIGHTS

A solution of the copyright problems in relation to computers comprises two stages. One implies a clarification of the legal situation
and this is dealt with in paragraphs 3-5. The second stage concerns feasible ways of exercising these rights so as to satisfy both the users of
the systems and the copyright owners.

As regards the exercise of copyright in relation to computers it
is - like as regards other technical means for mass utilization of protected works - necessary to rely on more or less collective solutions. It
is in many cases not realistic to expect individual negociations to take
place as regards such uses.

In principle two solutions are - at least theoretically - possible
in this respect. One implies that States in their national legislation
provide for non-voluntary licenses as regards storage and retrieval of
works in computers. In this respect one has, however, to take into account
that the international copyright conventions establish certain limits as
regards the possibilities for States to institute such licenses.

The second solution implies contractual arrangements between
authors or their organizations on the one hand and the users or their
organizations on the other hand. Sucu contractual arrangements could provide for the conditions relating not only to input but also to output,
remunerations for different forms of use etc. Because use of computers
for the purposes mentioned here is after all only in a nascent stage such
agreements at least more comprehensive ones, are still relatively few.

One could, however, expect a rapid development in this respect. Such a development is, in fact, highly desirable in order not to hamper further utilization and increase of computerized information systems.

7. SPECIAL PROBLEMS AS REGARDS LEXICOGRAPY

In principle what has been said in paragraphs 4 and 5 applies also to glossaries, dictionaries and other lexicographical tools. Also here it is necessary to clarify the legal situation and look for feasible measures as regards the exercise of the rights.

As regards lexicography some points are particularly important, viz. i.a. the following.

1. A glossary, dictionary and other compilation of facts etc. can very well constitute a work protected by copyright provided that it is structured and elaborated in such a way as to be original and the result of a creative effort of its author. Such works are in some legal systems called collective works or compilations.

2. Input of such a work into a computer requires authorization by the author.

3. Input of single data, facts (bibliographic or others) do not require authorization.

4. If the creation takes place in the computer (in the sense that the data fed into it are being structured) copyright subsists in the created work and belongs in principle to the person who has made the creative effort resulting in the work.

5. Translations and adaptations which take place in the computer require the authorization of the author in so far as they are made available to the public.

6. Output of the protected material (whole works including protected compilations, translations, adaptations and compilations etc. made in the computer) in the form of hard copy print-outs requires authorization of the author.

7. If and to what extent output of protected material in other forms (screens, tubes) requires authorization depends on the legislation in the country where the output takes place.

8) Output of single data (which have not been compiled and struc-

tured into a protected form in the computer) in original or translated form does not require authorization.

9. Basically the programmer is not to be considered as a co-author of the work which may be created by means of his programme. Such co-authorship presupposes that he has contributed to the work by a special creative effort resulting in the copyrightability of the work.

10. The right which an author can enjoy according to what has been said now may belong not to him but to e.g. his employer. If and to what extent such is the case is determined in the national legislation.

8. INTERNATIONAL WORK ON THE PROBLEMS

As everybody knows computer technology is developing very rapidly and implies i.a. the establishment of large national and international computerized information systems. It has consequently become very urgent to find a solution at an international level of the problems in connection with the use of computers. These problems concern two completely different categories of material.

One set of problems relates the protection of computer software (the programs themselves, program descriptions and so-called supporting material). In this respect WIPO (World Intellectual Property Organization; a United Nations specialized agency) has initiated a work with the ultimate aim of improving the legal protection of software (which to-day falls somewhere between the copyright conventions and the conventions in the industrial property field).

Another set of problems concerns copyright in the material processed by means of a computer, viz. the problems dealt with in paragraphs 1-7 above. Here WIPO and Unesco (United Nations Educational, Scientific and Cultural Organization) have jointly initiated a work aiming at establishing international recommendations for settlement of copyright problems arising from the use of computers. A first meeting of governmental experts on these problems was held in Paris in December 1980. It was there decided that Draft Recommendations should be established. Such a Draft is under way and will in due time be further discussed in a new meeting. It goes without saying that such recommendations will have a determining effect on the further development in this important field of information technology.

PANEL DISCUSSION

**Session IV - PUBLISHING AND THE
FUTURE USE OF LEXICONS**

Contribution to the Panel Discussion
C.R.H. INMAN

Contribution to the Panel Discussion
R.R.K. HARTMANN

Report on the Discussion in Session IV by
L. ENRIQUES

Remark made at the Symposium by
B.T. ATKINS

Summary of the Round Table Discussion by
A. REICHLING

LEXICOGRAPHY IN THE ELECTRONIC AGE
J. Goetschalckx and L. Rolling (editors)
North-Holland Publishing Company
© ECSC, EEC, EAEC, 1982

Contribution to the panel discussion

by

C.R.H. INMAN

The Primary Communications Research Centre was set up in Leicester University by the Research and Development Division of the British Library. Its task, broadly speaking, is the investigation of all aspects of the way in which research information is transmitted from originator to user. Examples of the Centre's work are the studies of legibility and of standards for documentation described by Mr. Ennis yesterday, studies of 'grey literature', of refereeing procedures in scholarly publishing and of the impact of new technologies. The Centre is much concerned with the role of the scientific journal, and the publishers and editors of such journals had indicated to us concern over the problem of scientific papers submitted by authors whose first language is not English. I am working on this particular problem.

One of yesterday's speakers mentioned the inevitable loss of information in the translation process. One of my concerns is the loss of information which occurs in the editing process. The editors of scholarly journals cannot - on both economic and practical grounds - be specialists in both the subject area of their journals and in foreign languages. They are therefore presented with particularly difficult problems by papers from authors whose English is imperfect. An exercise carried out at Primary Communication, although based on too small a sample of editors and material to give definitive answers has highlighted one aspect of the problem.

A group of twelve editors was asked to edit for publication a paper written in English by a non- English author. In the eight sentences selected for detailed analysis, the twelve decided overall that a total of some sixty items required change. However, only a quarter of these items were changed by more than half the editors. This means that three quarters of the items changed by different editors had been found unexceptionable by a majority. To coumpound this lack for the amendment of the sixty items. Moreover, none of the final versions were felt to have overcome the initial problem that the paper appeared difficult to understand on first reading.

As the editors were clearly unable to agree, we, at the Centre carried out our own sentence by sentence analysis of the text. We found a total of seven items only which were clearly unacceptable to a native English speaker. Moreover, five of the eight sentences, taken in isolation, seemed to be grammatical. On this showing, the author's 'English' in the popular sense, was really not all that bad. What then was the problem? A further examination of the material led us to the conclusion that the author had failed to structure his text properly in English. We identified fifteen occasions when he had either failed to make use of or made improper use of reference and linking devices. Involved were both back and forward reference, either overtly by means of linguistic items and repetition or by ellipsis; co-ordination and subordination were also faulty. In other words, his problem was grammatical, but not at the sentence level.

Our editors had minimal success in perceiving this problem. Perhaps two or three noted questions in the margin, but there was a marked absence of attempts at a solution of specific instances. Instead, we had a blanket correction of what did not really need it in an attempt to produce an acceptable final version.

What is the relevance of this to lexicography? It is difficult to see how lexicography can be of direct help to the editors in overcoming the problems they face with papers of this kind. However, surely some assistance can be given to the authors.

There has been a marked tendency in the symposium to discuss dictionaries and their future electronic derivations only in their role as the tools of translators. Researchers writing - or reading - in a language not their own also important, and perhaps more numerous users of dictionaries. Their needs deserve consideration. If lexicography is moving towards an era of on-line electronic systems, then the constraints of the print-on-paper medium no longer apply. This being so, do not the traditional distinctions between defining dictionaries, translating dictionaries, context dictionaries and grammars become artificial? Cannot a functioning electronic system encompass all the information contained in such works in a form which would allow the user to call up as much or as little as is needed?

If, as seems the case, it is intended to make terminology banks readily accessible on-line by individual translators, and not only those working in large concerns, then surely a much extended system of the kind I have suggested could be made available as a tool to the hard-pressed scientist trying to express himself in an unfamiliar language.

LEXICOGRAPHY IN THE ELECTRONIC AGE
J. Goetschalckx and L. Rolling (editors)
North-Holland Publishing Company
© ECSC, EEC, EAEC, 1982

Contribution to the panel discussion

by

R.K.K. HARTMANN

As one of the few contributors to this symposium who has actually compiled a real dictionary, I hope I may be allowed a few personal remarks which are meant as constructive criticism.

My first point concerns the purpose of our meeting. Our brief was (which was quite explicitly stated in the objectives) 'to assess the need and review present methods of overcoming the language barrier in a multilingual society, with particular reference to glossararies, dictionaries and other lexicographical tools'.

'Overcoming the language barrier' is always a good slogan, but in fact we haven't heard much about the role of the dictionary in a multilingual context. In what ways can dictionaries actually overcome the language barrier, and what does the barrier consist of, who experiences it, and how can we help those who do?

My second point follows on from this: have we lost sight of the dictionary and its user?

We heard, on the first day, about diacristics in Arabic and Greek, about legibility of scientific papers, and spelling problems of school children and their teachers, but not enough about the fascinating computer assisted German and Japanese dictionary projects reported on by Professors Lenderst Nagao. Today, again we heard this morning more about the problems and dreams of setting up data banks and interacting with computer systems than with the making of real dictionaries for real people. There are many different kinds of dictionaries consulted by many different kinds of users for many different dins of purposes. Most of these have had no experience of the sort of gadgets we have talked about, nor are they likely to have the opportunity in the foreseeable future to benefit from them.

My third point is a plea to producers and providers of dictionaries to look again a bit more closely at the needs of their potential users. There are precedents for this and some models we can follow.

Samnel Johnson said back in 1747 that 'it is not enough that a dictionary delights the critic, unless at the same time it instructs the learner'. Jacob Grimin's historical dictionary had not only the scholar in mind, but he wanted the whole community to benefit from it. More recently, some linguists have begun to question whether the general dictionary can fulfil all the various functions it is supposed to perform, and there has been some illuminating research on the communicative which people consult dictionaries contexts in. The EFL learner who uses the longman dictionary is only one such category of user. We now know that we have to sub-divide the undifferentiated notion of the general user into learners (beginners and advanced, mother-tongue and foreign-language), writers, librerians, secretaries, translators, experts in various disciplines, etc.

Some publishers have started to make detailed surveys to find about their various categories of consumers (e.g. Brand-stetter, some have started to issue instruction booklets for the efficient use of their products (e.g. Oxford U.P. for their student and advanced learner's dictionaries).

I do think that we must get our priorities right and move from a pro-ducer-type of lexicography (that only talks of the problems experienced by the compiler) to one that takes the consumer or user into account.

My fourth and final point is concerned with the future - what kind of framework do we need to make progress?

First of all we need some more research into the pragmatics of dictionary use, what Herbert Erust Wiegand has called a 'sociology of the dictionary user'.

We shall not make progres merely by introspectively looking at what sorts of applications we can find for our expensive toys, but we need to ask where the points of communicative conflict and deficit are - the real language barriers - but that would require a problem-solving spirit and an outward look at the real world.

LEXICOGRAPHY IN THE ELECTRONIC AGE
J. Goetschalckx and L. Rolling (editors)
North-Holland Publishing Company
© ECSC, EEC, EAEC, 1982

Report on the discussion in Session IV

by

L. ENRIQUES

Report on the discussion in Session IV (Publishing and the future use of lexicons).

1. Summary

1.1 In the course of Session IV there was a lively discussion on two main themes:

1.2 The relationship between new electronic technology and commercial publishing on monolingual and bilingual dictionaries;

1.3 Protection of copyright, with particular reference to new electronic technology and dictionaries as such.

2. Publishing and new technology

2.1 It was pointed out (R.R.K. Hartmann) that a commercial dictionary must be compiled with a view to the needs of the final user and not those of the lexicographer. In principle, this requirement was independent of the use of new electronic technology, although such technology could also be used to meet it.

2.2 It was pointed out (J. Ehlers) that many of the major European publishers of reference works had undoubtedly already begun projects for new dictionaries in which computers were used also for lexicographical purposes. Only a few of these publishers had taken part in the Symposium.

2.2 It was mentioned (L.Enriques) that the electronic revolution had already been in progress for a number of years in many publishing houses. In particular:

2.3.1 Remote video units were available, with a capability for recording on floppy-disk, on which the author could write and correct lexicographical works, using various alphabets and types (italic, roman, bold etc.).

2.3.2 Optical readers were available which were capable of recording the various characters and distinguishing among the various typefaces.

2.3.3 Programmes were available which were capable of justifying a photo-composed text sentence by sentence (and not line by line) and of making up into pages with vertical justification.

2.3.4 It was now possible to publish dictionaries of a new type, using largely automatic methods involving data banks. For example, the McGraw-Hill-Zanichelli English-Italian and Italian-English Scientific and technical Dictionary had been produced 90% automatically from the magnetic tape of an American encyclopaedic dictionary.

2.4 It was pointed (B.T. Atkins) that from the lexicographer's point of view it was not enough for the computer to perform the task of filing, ordering and checking the uniformity of lexicographical data. The computer should also help the lexicographer in the following fields:

2.4.1 Indicating lists of terms to be included in a dictionary, with selection and inclusion criteria.

2.4.2 Filing and retrieving syntactic models in various languages, sentences, idioms etc.

2.4.3 Indicating the prevalent use in practice of each term in the various languages.

2.4.4 Indicating and comparing various ways of making phonetic transcriptions.

2.4.5 Identifying the criteria for updating dictionaries.

2.4.6 Developing methods for extracting partial specialized dictionaries
from an existing dictionary.

2.5.   The essential role of the lexicographer in deciding which terms to
include in a lexicon and in attributing to each entry the various
meanings which can be extracted from a 'corpus' was confirmed (R.
Reinsma).

3.   Copyright and new technology

3.1   There was no discussion of the statement by the speaker (A.H.
Olsson) that copyright precluded the insertion into a computer
memory (or into other electronic storage systems) of protected
works. In other words, it was the input to the computer which was
forbidden unless the agreement of the holder of the rights was
obtained and not only output on other physical media.

3.2   The question was raised (J.M. McNaught, J. Ehlers) of the special
position of dictionaries and other reference works with regard to
copyright. For example, dictionaries contained lists of words
which, if considered singly, were undoubtedly public property and
therefore could not be protected by patent or copyright. However,
the objection was raised that the compilation of a lexicon, since
it was a sum or selection of lists of terms, involved creative
work. Thus, even if individual words were not protected, a collection of words was. Moreover, any literary work was a <u>collection
of words</u>.

3.3   The question was raised of the protection of software for data
processing applications (S.Yagil, P.Fleury). The answer was that
software was undoubtedly protected in principle by the laws on
copyright or on patents. However, specific laws on the matter were
lacking in all countries except the USA and Bulgaria.

3.4   It was hoped (H. Werner) that a documentation centre on copyright
problems, with particular reference to lexicography, would be set
up.

LEXICOGRAPHY IN THE ELECTRONIC AGE
J. Goetschalckx and L. Rolling (editors)
North-Holland Publishing Company
© ECSC, EEC, EAEC, 1982

Remark made at the Symposium

by

B.T. ATKINS

The general lexicographer has two main problems with specialiwed terminology:

    (1) <u>selection</u> - which items to include

    (2) <u>definition</u> (monolingual dics) or <u>translation</u> (bilinguals);

and the computer can help in the solution of both of these problems:

    (1) by providing criteria for inclusion (frequency etc)

    (2) by facilitating access to reliable information (term banks etc).

General lexicography however poses much greater problems to the computer than merely those raised by specialised terminology, which forms a relatively small part of his work. Some areas of general lexicography which might profitably be examined from this point of view include:

- establishment of headword list;
- offering headword list which may readily be reduced from say 100,000 to 80,000 to 60,000 etc items;
- criteria for headword status (compounds, phrases etc);
- storage, manipulation & retrieval of phonological, syntactical, semantic, morphological & pragmatic facts;
- consistency of style labels (register etc);
- validating of cross-references;
- cross-checking (in bilinguals) of items in source & target languages;
- control of defining vocabulary (in monolinguals);
- consistency of individuals' work in large team of compiler;
- avoidance of circular definitions (in monolinguals);

- provision of corpus of written and spoken language;
- ready reference to instances of use in corpus, by means of concordancing;
- flexibility of databank and consequent enhanced potential etc.

Unlike most other specialists, lexicographers are rarely able to discuss openly with their counterparts in other establishments such problems as those mentioned have. The marketability of their product, and consequent towards a solution of these problems tends to be duplicated many times over. Already, as papers at this symposium have shown, many publishers are committed to considerable funding of research into monolingual databases. Indeed, in the area of monolingual lexicography it is probably too late now to avoid the duplication of effort resulting from commercial demands. However, it is not yet too late to prevent such a waste of effort in the domain of bi- and multilingual databases.

Suggestion

That an attempt should be made to set up an international research institute into computerised multilingual databases.

That such a venture might be funded by publishers, multinationals, the EEC and other European organisations (if the load is spread far enough it should be considerably lightened);

That research work done in this institute should be available to all the funding bodies, and might also provide a source of revenue by being offered for sale on the open market;

That all the funding bodies should be able, additionally, to commission from the researchers one or more specific program(s) or other piece(s) of research to meet their particular needs, this research to be kept strictly secret from any other organisation; such a commission to be paid for a course; a similar facility could be offered on the open market, and the funding bodies allowed concessionary rates.

Such a research institutes would offer the possibility of collaboration to linguists, computer scientists and lexicographers of at least all the member countries of the EEC, and possibly many more; it would avoid a great deal of duplication of effort and consequent diminution of quality, and by uniting such skills should encourage and accelerate progress in the field of multilingual lexicography.

I am grateful for the interest which participants have shown in this suggestion, and particularly for Dr. Gibb's proposal that the CEC might offer a forum where the matter may be further discussed.

LEXICOGRAPHY IN THE ELECTRONIC AGE
J. Goetschalckx and L. Rolling (editors)
North-Holland Publishing Company
© ECSC, EEC, EAEC, 1982

Summary of the Round table discussion

by A. Reichling

The last day of the symposium was devoted to a Round Table, the purpose
of which was to enable all participants to draw together the threads of
the preceding sessions. To start the discussion the rapporteurs gave brief
reports on the various addresses, and the chairmen of each session were
invited to raise any points which had not been fully treated in the
ensuing debates. The background to the discussion was the observation
made by several individuals that, although the symposium had enabled the
participants to review what had been done or was currently being done in
the field of modern lexicography, not enough had been said about future
prospects. New technology had to be used to a greater extent in lexicography, particularly at the lexicon creation stage - e.g. for the
automatic identification of the syntactical and contextual behaviour of
a lexical unit. The age in which machines served only to relieve man
of tiresome and repetitive tasks was over; technical problems were
practically resolved (e.g. the treatment of different sets of characters,
o.g. roman and non-roman, was now being mastered) and lexicography could
profit from the many modelling and simulation techniques developed in
research into artificial intelligence.

Account should be taken of new possibilities in the very structure of
lexica and their presentation: orthographic consultation of a dictionary
was no longer the only means of access to information: access to key words
would be or already was possible on the basis of pronunciation, approximate spelling, constituent elements from a definition or even from an
image. The significance of this technological progress became more apparent
when it was seen in the context of the distribution of information and

265

knowledge by telecommunications networks. From this point of view it was
important for publishers of lexical works to realize that the dictionaries
of tomorrow would no longer be simply available on paper and that a market
already existed for teledictionaries. A number of problems remained to be
solved before the telematics revolution in lexicography was complete.
What attitude should be taken to the question of copyright? It would seem
reasonable to say that words belonged to everybody, but that results of
the use of these words were the author's own property; that servile
copying of a dictionary was therefore not permissible but an intelligent
compilation from multiple sources, implying serious verification and correction and significant rearrangement of the material and involving the
exercise of choice in the words selected and in the formulation of
definitions as a function of the target group, should be considered as an
original and enjoy the same rights as the dictionaries upon which it was
based.

The problem of protecting author's rights was all the more acute because
modern lexicography could hardly be considered in isolation from the
commercial activities of publishing houses, and publishers who had already
opted for automation in their work were unwilling to divulge their secrets
to potential competitors? It was therefore essential to make suitable
arrangements for discussion between all interested parties, and devise
that means of collaboration aimed at avoiding duplicated efforts while
maintaning legitimate rights of all concerned.

A number of participants said that encouragement should be given to the
work being done by university research centres in a number of countries
(particularly France and Italy) on producing inventories of language. Such
virtually exhaustive lexicological banks, constantly updated, could well
serve as a common corpus for lexicographers who could extract the material
for their own dictionaries by dividing, recasting and shaping the material
to suit requirements. This would in no way be an abandonment of his role
by the lexicographer, for lexicography had already achieved recognition
just as lexicology had done, but allowed the lexicographer express his
own creative genius fully by using data of real quality. Publishers would
reap the reward of their participation with government in the finance and
development of lexicology centres by being authorized to draw from them

the material for their own dictionaries.

A number of participants warned attempting to run before being able to
walk: people wanted to computers to translate but it was not yet known
how man managed to read; the raw material of lexicography, the lexical unit
had not yet been defined. There was therefore an urgent need for lexicographers to reach agreement on lexical cataloguing, or at least that they
should work to standardized editorial rules. For some a meta-language
describing dictionary elements was the most realistic approach; for others,
the standards drawn up by experts after examining the various problems for
a number of years resolved most of the difficulties, their only weak point
being that they were not well enough known. Technical Committee 37 dealt with
terminology, TC 46 with documentation and TC 97 with computer problems,
including character sets and keyboards. A list of relevant standards could
be annexed to the report of the symposium, and those who were actually
involved could give opinions which would help in drawing up recommendations
acceptable to the majority.

One last essential question was raised by a number of speakers: how and in
what form to boing about broad-based, candid and effective cooperation
between lexicologists, lexicographers, terminologists, data processing
specialists and publishers. It was suggested that use could be made of
the European Publishers Association but the association would have to
widen its interests and responsibilities. It was also suggested that this
task fell to the Commission, and the organizers of the symposium proposed
that as a first stage seminars should be organized to examine the commercial problems and make a start on practical cooperation. Opinions were
divided on the advisability of calling early meetings of large groups of
specialists, a number of participants held the view that cooperation on
too large a scale generally remained fruitless whilst others felt that
it was not unreasonable for the same research to be undertaken by a
number of teams. A compromise solution could naturally be found during
such seminars, with results or part results of new research being passed
on to interested parties before work had been completed. Other disciplines
had been faced with similar problems and lexicographers could take inspi-
ration from the arrangements made in a number of countries by documentalists,
for example. The essential point was the need for general recognition of
the interdisciplinary nature of modern lexicographical work and for a
genuine will to cooperate.

LIST OF PARTICIPANTS

ADAMO, G.
Ricercatore
C.N.R.-Roma
Lessico Intellettuale Europeo
c/o Istituto di Filosofia
Villa Mirafiori
Via Nomentana, 118
I - 00121 ROMA

AL, B.P.F.
Professeur
Regentesselaan 31
NL - 2341 KN OEGSTRGEEST

ALLAIN, J.-F.
Translator
Council of Europe
F - 67006 STRASBOURG-Cedex

AREND, P.
Dipl.-Uebersetzer
Verband der chemischen Industrie
Karlstrasse 21
D - 6000 FRANKFURT 1

ATKINS, B.T., Mrs.
Lexicographer
Collins Publishers
P.O. Box
UK - GLASGOW

AYTO, J.R.
Lexicographer
Longman Group Ltd.
Burnt Mill
UK - HARLOW, Essex CM20 2JE

BACHRACH, J.A.
Chef de la division de la
traduction
Commission des Communautés
européennes
Bâtiment Jean Monnet
L - 2920 LUXEMBOURG

BOOT, M.
Dept. Computational Linguistics
University of Utrecht
Wilhelminapark 11
NL - UTRECHT

BOS, W., Mrs.
Redaktrice
Uitgeverij Het Spectrum b.v.
Cronenburg 2
NL - 1081 GN AMSTERDAM

BOURDIER, J.-M.
Conseil Marketing
Cabinet J.-M. Bourdier
24, rue de l'Arcade
F - 75008 PARIS

BROUSSE, J.-P.
Terminologiste
O.C.D.E.
2, rue André Pascal
F - 75775 PARIS Cedex 16

BRULE', M.
Chargé de Mission
Franterm
1o, boulevard Raspail
F - 75007 PARIS

BRUSTKERN, J.
Dipl. Informatiker
Institut für Kommunikations
Forschung und Phonetik
Poppelsdorfes Allee 47
D - 5300 BONN 1

CLEAR, J.
Department of English language
Research
Birmingham University
Edgbaston
UK - BIRMINGHAM B15 2TT

COHEN-MAYORCAS, P.
  Traductrice
  Commission des Communautés
  européennes
  D.G. IX/C/7 - ASTR 8/23
  200, rue de la Loi
  B - 1049 BRUXELLES

CONVENTS, J.
  Terminologue/documentaliste
  Conseil des Communautés européennes
  170, rue de la Loi
  B - 1048 BRUXELLES

COPINE, W.
  Fonctionnaire
  Office des Publications officielles
  des Communautés européennes
  5, rue du Commerce
  L - LUXEMBOURG

CUBY, L.
  Chef de Service
  Terminologie
  Conseil
  170, rue de la Loi
  B - 1048 BRUXELLES

DANET, M., Mme
  Chargée d'études
  Cabinet J. Michel Bourdier
  24, rue de l'Arcade
  F - 75000 PARIS

DECOURBE, B.
  SCERGIE
  Directeur des études
  13, rue de Castellane
  F - 75008 PARIS

DE HEER, T.
  Head Informatics Dept.
  IWIS-TNO
  P.O. Box 297
  NL - 2501 BD DEN HAAG

DELAHAYE, M., Mme
  Bibliothécaire-traductrice
  Institut océanographique
  195, rue St. Jacques
  F - 75005 PARIS

DE LUZE, G.
  Directeur littéraire
  Libraire Larousse
  17, rue du Montparnasse
  F - 75298 PARIS, Cedex 06

DEPECKER, L.
  Coordonnateur scientifique
  Franterm
  10, boulevard Raspail
  F - 75007 PARIS

DE ZALESKI, Ch.
  Traductrice
  P.E.
  56, Avenue Pasteur
  L - 2310 LUXEMBOURG

DIAMESSIS, E.
  Educational Counsellor
  Ministry of Education (K.E.M.E.)
  396 Messoycon Street
  GR - ATHENES

EHLERS, H.J.
  Referat Unternehmensaufgaben
  Ernst Klett Stuttgart
  Rotebühlstrasse 77
  D - 7000 STUTTGART

EHRLICH, K.
  Beamte
  KEG
  34, Avenue A. Jonnost
  B - 1040 BRUSSEL

ENDRES-NIGGEMEYER, B., Frau
  Wissenschaftliche Referentin
  G.I.D.
  Lyoner Strasse 44-48
  D - 6000 FRANKFURT 71

ENGEL, G.
  Handelshoejskolen i Kobenhavn
  Fabriksvej 7
  DK - 2000 COPENHAGEN

ENNIS, M.
  Elsevier Int. Bulletins
  256 Banbury Road
  UK - OXFORD OX2 7DH

ENRIQUES, L.
  Vice Presidente
  Nicola Zanichelli Editore
  Via Irnerio 34
  I - BOLOGNA

FANTAPIE', A.
  Somiologue
  Cabinet B. Michel Bourdier
  24, rue de l'Arcade
  F - 75007 PARIS

FLEURY, P.
Somiologue
Cabinet B. Michel Bourdier
24, rue de l'Arcade
F - 75008 PARIS

FRACKENPOHL, G.
Dipl.-Inform.
IdS - Institut für deutsche Sprache
Postfach 5409
D - 6800 MANNHEIM 1

FRANCOIS, P.
Fonctionnaire
Commission des Communautés euro-
péennes - Direction générale
"Marché de l'information et
innovation"
Bâtiment Jean Monnet
L - 2920 LUXEMBOURG

FRANK, H.P.
Sprachdienst
Schweizerische Bundeskanzlei
CH - 3003 BERN

FROIDCOEUR, J.M.
Banque de Données bibliques
Abbaye de Maredsous
B - 5642 DENEE

GALINSKI, C.
Inforterm
Postfach 130
A - 1021 WIEN

GALLAIS-HAMMONO, J., Mme
Université de Metz
Faculté des lettres et sciences
humaines - Département d'Anglais
Ile du Saulcy
F - 57000 METZ

GAUHD, G.
Fonctionnaire
Bureau des Traductions Canada
Secrétariat d'Etat
CANADA - OTTAWA KIA OM5

GIBB, J.M.
Chef de service spécialisé
Commission des Communautés euro-
péennes Direction générale "Marché
de l'information et innovation"
Bâtiment Jean Monnet
L - 2920 LUXEMBOURG

GOETSCHALCKX, J.
Conseiller
Service de traduction à long et à
moyen terme - Commission des
Communautés européennes
Bâtiment Jean Monnet
L - 2920 LUXEMBOURG

GOFFIN, R.
Fonctionnaire (Bureau de
Terminologie)
Commission des Communautés
européennes - Direction générale
"Personnel et administration"
(Bureau de Terminologie)
200, rue de la Loi
B - 1049 BRUXELLES

GRYPDONCK, A.
Secrétaire permanent
Limburg Universitair Centrum
Universitaire Campus
B - 3610 DIEPENBEEK

GUTMACHER, R., Frau
Terminologin
Kommission der Europäischen
Gemeinschaften
Jean-Monnet-Gebäude
L - 2920 LUXEMBURG

HAAS, R.
Fontionnaire
Commission des Communautés
européennes - Direction générale
"Marché de l'information et
innovation"
Bâtiment Jean Monnet
L - 2920 LUXEMBOURG

HAON, H., Mme
Traductrice-Interprète de Japonais
S.F.T.
20, rue Paul Albert
F - 75018 PARIS

HARTMANN, R.R.K.
Director
Language Centre
University of Exeter
Queen's Building
The Queen's Drive
UK - EXETER EX4 4QH Devon

HELLWIG, P.
 Privatdozent
 Universität Heidelberg
 Germanistisches Seminar
 Hauptstrasse 207-209
 D - 6900 HEIDELBERG

HENNING, J.
 Enseignant
 Université Clermont-Ferrand II
 CUST
 B.P. 48
 Rue des Meuniers
 F - 63000 AMBIERE

HESS, K.-D.
 Dipl. Informatiker
 Institut für Kommunikations
 Forschung und Phonetik
 Poppelsdorfes Allee 47
 D - 5300 BONN

HØJER-PEDERSEN, N.
 Consultant
 I/S Datacentralen
 Retortvej 6-8
 DK - 2500 VALBY COPENHAGEN

HUBAC, J.P.
 Chargé de mission DGT
 D G T
 320, avenue de Ségur
 F - 75700 PARIS

INMAN, C.R.H.
 University of Leicester
 Primary Communications
 Research Centre
 University RD
 UK - LEICESTER LE1 7RH

KAMPMANN, M.
 Leiter des Sprachendienstes
 Bayer AG
 D - 5090 LEVERKUSEN 12

KOCH, H.
 Dipl. libersetzer
 Kommission
 12, rue J. Lamort
 L - LUXEMBOURG

KOPELENT, W., Frau
 Wissenschaftliche Angestellte
 Universität des Saarlandes
 Informationswissenschaften FB 5.5
 D - 6600 SAARBRUECKEN

KROLLMANN, F.
 Bundessprachenamt
 Horbeller Strasse
 D - 5030 HURTH BEI KOELN

KROUPA, E., Frau
 Informationswissenschaftlerin
 Universität des Saarlandes
 Informationswissenschaften FB 5.5.
 D - 6600 SAARBRUECKEN

KUCERA, A.
 Lektor
 Oscar Brandstetter Verlag GmbH & Co K(
 Wilhemstrasse 16
 D - 6200 WIESBADEN

LANGMEIER, I.
 KEG Beamte
 21, avenue Renaissance
 B - 1040 BRUXELLES

LANNOY, J.
 Directeur
 Commission des Communautés euro-
 péennes - Direction générale
 "Marché de l'information et
 innovation"
 Bâtiment Jean Monnet
 L - 2920 LUXEMBOURG

LAZZERI, V.
 Correctrice CE
 O.P.O.C.E.
 72, Bd. Napoléon
 L - LUXEMBOURG

LENDERS, W.
 Institut für Kommunikations-
 forschung und Phonetik
 Universität Bonn
 Poppelsdorfer Allee 47
 D - 5300 BONN

LE TELLIER, J.
 Chef service Terminologie
 Cour de Justice des C.E.
 B.P. 1406
 L - LUXEMBOURG

LINDER, J.
 Civilekonom
 Nova Media AB
 Fack
 Storgatan 59
 S - 104 40 STOCKHOLM

LOMAN, J.B.
Systeemvoorbereider
Kluwer n.v.
Singel 5
P.B. 23
NL - 7400 GA DEVENTER

LUNTER, S.
Ernst Klett Druckerei
Abt. Fachberatung Satz
Rotebühlstrasse 77
D - 7000 STUTTGART 1

LURQUIN, G.
Président du CTB
Institut Libre Marie Haps
11, rue d'Arlon
B - 1040 BRUXELLES

LUTTERKORT, E., Frau
Direktor
Europäisches Patentamt
Erhardtstrasse 27
D - 8000 MUENCHEN 2

MARTEL, G.
Chef Service (Traduction)
Bureau des Traduction
15, rue Eddy
CANADA - HULL KIA OM5

MARTIN, P.A.
Project Manager
Term Data
Hansengelstrasse 30
D - 7891 HOHENTENGEN

MARTIN, W.
Associate Professor
University of Leuven & Antwerp
Losbergenlaan 4
B - KESSEL Lo

McNAUGHT, J.
Research Fellow
UMIST - University of
Manchester - Inst. of
Science and Technology
P.O. Box 88
UK - MANCHESTER M60 1QD

MENDES DE LEON, C.
Terminoloque
C.E.
Jean Monnet A2/122
L - LUXEMBOURG

MICHIELS, A.
Assistant
Université de Liège
37, rue du Parc
B - 4020 LIEGE

MOENCH, D.
Internationales Büro
G.I.D.
Ahrstrasse 45
D - 5300 BONN 2

MULLENDER, J.
Ingénieur
Université de Liège
11, bois des chevreuils
B - 4040 TILFF

MURPHY, D.
Civil engineer/editor
CITIS (Dublin) & Inst. CIVIL
ENGRS (London)
12, Fairlawns, Saval Purd.
Ireland - DALKEY, Co:DUBLIN

NAGAO, M.
Professor
Kyoto University
Department of Electrical Engineering
Kyoto University
Japan - SAKYO, KYOTO 606

NEGUS, A.E.
15 Bittern Drive
Biggleswade
UK - BEDFORSHIRE SG16 8DU

NEUMANN, P.
Geschäftsführer
SDV - Saarbrücker Druckerei und
Verlag
Halbergstrasse 3
D - 6600 SAARBRUECKEN

NIES, G.
Linguiste
Informalux
Case Postale 39
L - RODANGE

NISTRUP MADSEN, B.
Lecturer
The Copenhagen School of Economics
and Business Administration
Fabrikvej 7
DK - 2000 COPENHAGEN F

NOEL, J.
  Professeur ordinaire
  Université de Liège
  Allée Cense Rouge 50
  B - 4200 OUGREE

NORDBACK LINDER, H., Mrs.
  Byradirektör
  Utrikesdepartementet
  Rättsavdelningen
  S - 103 23 STOCKHOLM 16

NORLING-CHRISTENSEN, O.
  Managing Editor
  Dictionairies and Encyclopaedias
  Gyldendal Publishers
  Klareboderne 3
  DK - 1001 COPENHAGEN K

OITANA, C.
  Direttore Gruppo DIMA
  Via G. Baretti 36
  I - 10125 TORINO

OLSSON, A.H.
  Hovrättassessor
  Ministry of Justice
  Kanslihuset
  S - 10333 STOCKHOLM

PENNINGS, J.
  Staff Member
  NOBIN
  Burg van Karnebeeklaan 19
  NL - 2585 BA DEN HAAG

PICKEN, C., Mrs.
  Head of Foreign Language Services
  Shell U.K. Administrative Services
  Shell Centre
  UK - LONDON SE1 7NA

POSWICK, R.F.
  Banque de données bibliques
  Abbaye de Maredsous
  B - 5642 DENEE

QUICHERON, J.B.
  Interprete
  Commission
  Documentation Interpretes
  200 Rue de la Loi
  B - 1049 BRUXELLES

QVISTGAARD, B., Mme
  Fonctionnaire (réviseur)
  Commission des Communautés
  européennes - BTB
  200, rue de la Loi (Cort. 1/126)
  B - 1049 BRUXELLES

RAPPARINI, R.
  Fonctionnaire
  Commission des Communautés
  européennes - Direction
  générale "Marché de l'informa-
  tion et innovation"
  Bâtiment Jean Monnet
  L - 2920 LUXEMBOURG

REDA, A.
  Terminologe
  Auswärtiges Amt
  Adenauerallee 139-41
  D - 5300 BONN 1

REICHLING, A.
  Terminologue
  Commission des Communautés
  européennes
  Bâtiment Jean Monnet
  L - 2920 LUXEMBOURG

REINSMA, R.
  Projektleiter
  Uitgeverij Het Spectrum b.v.
  Cronenburg 2
  NL - 1081 GN AMSTERDAM

ROHAERT, A.
  Chef du Bureau de Terminologie
  Parlement européen
  L - LUXEMBOURG/Kirchberg

ROLLING, L.
  Chef de service
  Commission des Communautés
  européennes - Direction générale
  "Marché de l'information et
  innovation"
  Bâtiment Jean Monnet
  L - 2920 LUXEMBOURG

ROSSI-PETTENER, P.
  Scuola Superiore di Lingue Moderne
  Università di Trieste
  I - TRIESTE

ROTONDO, P.P.
Fonctionnaire
Commission des Communautés
européennes - Direction générale
"Marché de l'information et
innovation"
Bâtiment Jean Monnet
L - 2920 LUXEMBOURG

SANE, S.
Lexicographe
BIBLOGRAF S.A.
C. Bruch 151
E - BARCELONE 37

SAROLEA, R., Mme
Terminologue
Commission des Communautés
européennes
200, rue de la Loi
B - 1049 BRUXELLES

SCHAAP, P.J.Ph.
System Designer
NV I.C.U.
Burg van Royensingel 19
NL - 8001 BC ZWOLLE

SCHMITZ, K.-D.
Wissenschaftlicher Mitarbeiter
SFB 100/Proj. K
Liesbet-Dill-Strasse 17
D - 6602 DUDWEILER

SCHMUCK, A.
Abteilungsleiter
Langenscheid-Verlag
Neusser Strasse 3
D - 8000 MUENCHEN 40

SCHOLZE-STUBENRECHT, W.
Redakteur
Bibliographisches Institut AG
Augustaanlage 51
D - 6800 MANNHEIM 1

SCHNORR, V.
Lexikographin
ERNST KLETT
Rotebühlstrasse 57
D - 7000 STUTTGART 1

SEGARICH, G.
Istituto Lessico Commerciale
Carli
I - TRIESTE

SIMONCSICS, E.
Technische Universität Wien
Lascygasse 15/6
A - 1170 WIEN

SMAL, J.
Publisher
Kluwer Technische Boeken
Brink 25
NL - 7411 BS DEVENTER

STAHL, G.
Professeur
Université de Metz
B.P. 222.06
F - 75264 PARIS, Cedex 06

STAS, M.C., Mme
Chargée de Recherches
INIEX.- Institut National
des Industries Extractives
200, rue du Chéra
B - 4000 LIEGE

THOMIERES, D.
Enseignant- chercheur
8, Impasse Barbes
F - 93100 MONTREUIL

TOOD, A.
TEA Coal Research
14, Lower Grosvenor Place
GB - LONDON SW1

TOMBEUR, P.
Directeur CETEDOC
Université Catholique de Louvain
Collège Erasme
Plan Blaise Pascal 1
B - 1348 LOUVAIN-la-NEUVE

TONHOFER, F.
Fonctionnaire
Office des Publications officielles
des Communautés européennes
5, rue du Commerce
L - 2985 LUXEMBOURG

TROJANUS, K.-H.
Dipl.-Uebersetzer
HQ AAFCE (NATO)
Beim Weisenstein 11
D - 6602 SAARBRUECKEN-DUDWEILER

VAN DEN OEVER, D.C.
Publisher
Wolters-Noordhoff BV
P.O.Box 58
NL - 9700 MB GRONINGEN

VAN LOON, J.
Publisher
Van Dale
Mariaplaats 3 II
NL - 3511LH UTRECHT

VIET, L.
Professeur
DRET - Direction Recherches
Etudes et Techniques
26, Bvd Victor
F . 75996 PARIS ARMEES

VOLLMER, J.
Service de traduction
à moyen et à long terme
Bâtiment Jean Monnet
L - KIRCHBERG

VOLLNHALS
Language Department
SIEMENS AG
D - MUENCHEN

WALDORFF, A.
EDB-Planlaeger
Gyldendal Publishers
Klareboderne 3
DK - 1001 COPENHAGEN K

WEINSTOCK, K.
Diplom-Kaufmann
Verlagsgruppe Bertelsmann GmbH
Neumarkter Strasse 18
D - 8000 MUENCHEN 80

WEIS, E.
Professor
Wirtschaftsuniversität Wien
A - WIEN 19

WERNER, H.
Diplominformatiker
Universität des Saarlandes
Projekt J400-D5; 5.5
Informationswissenschaft
D - 6600 SAARBRUECKEN

WHGELER, P.
Fonctionnaire
C.E.E. Bt. JMO.
L - LUXEMBOURG

WIELAND, U.
Fonctionnaire
C.E.E.
15, Rue Gibraltar
L - LUXEMBOURG

YAGIL, S.
I.B.M. - Israel
P.O. Box 33666
Israel - TEL-AVIV 61330

ZAMPOLLI, A.
Professore
Università di Pisa
Via Cuppari 27
I - 56100 PISA